SAY WHAT I AM CALLED
The Old English Riddles of the Exeter Book and the Anglo-Latin Riddle Tradition

Perhaps the most enigmatic cultural artefacts that survive from the Anglo-Saxon period are the Old English riddle poems that were preserved in the tenth-century Exeter Book manuscript. Clever, challenging, and notoriously obscure, the riddles have fascinated readers for centuries and provided crucial insight into the period. In *Say What I Am Called*, Dieter Bitterli takes a fresh look at the riddles by examining them in the context of earlier Anglo-Latin riddles.

Bitterli argues that there is a vigorous common tradition between Anglo-Latin and Old English riddles and details how the contents of the Exeter Book emulate and reassess their Latin predecessors while also expanding their literary and formal conventions. The book also considers the ways in which convention and content relate to writing in a vernacular language. A rich and illuminating work that is as intriguing as the riddles themselves, *Say What I Am Called* is a rewarding study of some of the most interesting works from the Anglo-Saxon period.

(Toronto Anglo-Saxon Series)

DIETER BITTERLI is an associate professor in the Department of English at the University of Zurich.

DIETER BITTERLI

Say What I Am Called:

The Old English Riddles of the Exeter Book and the Anglo-Latin Riddle Tradition

UNIVERSITY OF TORONTO PRESS
Toronto Buffalo London

© University of Toronto Press 2009
Toronto Buffalo London
utorontopress.com

Reprinted in paperback 2019

ISBN 978-0-8020-9352-3 (cloth)   ISBN 978-1-4426-9202-2 (ePUB)
ISBN 978-1-4875-2548-4 (paper)   ISBN 978-1-4426-8907-7 (PDF)

Toronto Anglo-Saxon Series

Library and Archives Canada Cataloguing in Publication

Title: Say what I am called : the Old English riddles of the Exeter Book and the Anglo-Latin riddle tradition / Dieter Bitterli.
Names: Bitterli, Dieter, author.
Series: Toronto Anglo-Saxon series ; 2.
Description: Series statement: Toronto Anglo-Saxon series ; 2 | Paperback reprint. Originally published 2009. | Includes bibliographical references and index.
Identifiers: Canadiana 20190191082 | ISBN 9781487525484 (softcover)
Subjects: LCSH: Riddles, English (Old)—History and criticism. | LCSH: English poetry—Old English, ca. 450–1100—History and criticism. | LCSH: Riddles, Latin—History and criticism. | LCSH: Riddles in literature. | LCSH: Exeter book.
Classification: LCC PR1490 .B48 2019 | DDC 829/.1009—dc23

Published with the support of the Swiss National Science Foundation.

University of Toronto Press acknowledges the financial assistance to its publishing program of the Canada Council for the Arts and the Ontario Arts Council, an agency of the Government of Ontario.

  Canada Council   Conseil des Arts
for the Arts   du Canada

swæsum ond gesibbum

Contents

Acknowledgments ix
Abbreviations and Symbols xi

Introduction 3

PART I: CONTEXTS

1 Latin Riddling and the Vernacular 13
  The House and the Guest (*Riddle* 85) 14
  Animal Worlds 18
  Beasts of Burden (*Riddles* 12, 38, and 72) 26

2 Tell-Tale Birds: The Etymological Principle 35
  Singing Feathers (*Riddle* 7) 38
  Words and Things 44
  Speaking in Tongues (*Riddle* 8) 46

3 Crossings: Combinatorial and Numerical Riddles 57
  The Warriors Embark (*Riddle* 22) 59
  Numerical Monsters (*Riddles* 86 and 36) 68
  Dead Ends (*Riddle* 90) 74

PART II: CODES

4 Runic Strategies 83
  Logographic versus Alphabetic 83
  Sea Horses (*Riddles* 19 and 64) 86
  The Barking Bird (*Riddle* 24) 91

viii   Contents

5   **Bits and Pieces**   98
      Head, Shoulders, Knees, and Toes (*Riddle* 58)   98
      Covered Tracks (*Riddle* 75)   105
      Loose Ends   110

6   **Letter Games**   114
      Ten in All (*Riddle* 13)   115
      Fowl Play (*Riddle* 42)   121
      Men at Wine   124

PART III: TOOLS

7   **Silent Speech**   135
      Scribal Riddles   135
      The Mouthless Messenger (*Riddle* 60)   137
      The Struggling Warrior (*Riddle* 51)   145

8   **Beasts of Battle**   151
      The Missing Brother (*Riddle* 88)   152
      The Lost Lord (*Riddle* 93)   157
      Modes   163

9   **The Flesh Made Word**   170
      Famous, Useful, and Holy (*Riddle* 26)   171
      Under My Skin (*Riddle* 28)   178
      Excarnation   188

10   **Coda**   191
      The Thievish Guest (*Riddle* 47)   191

Bibliography   195
Index   213

Acknowledgments

The Anglo-Saxon riddles about the business of writing and book-making tell us that the painstaking labour of producing a book is ultimately rewarded both in heaven and on earth. In the figurative language of the riddle-poets, the scribe's pen irrigates the furrows on the page, which will yield a rich harvest for the benefit of the readers. In the years it took to complete this book – from its once dry furrows to its present crop – I have been fortunate to receive the expert guidance and help of several colleagues and friends. A great part of my research was conducted at the English Department of the University of Zurich, where Udo Fries taught me the mysteries of Old English language and literature, and where Andreas Fischer encouraged me to develop an early paper on the Exeter Book *Riddles* into a book-length study. I am deeply grateful to both of them for their continuing support and friendship.

Of those who have contributed to this book in various ways and gave generously of their time, I would like to single out for special thanks Hans Sauer, Peter Stotz, Andy Torr, Hildegard L.C. Tristram, Margaret Tudeau-Clayton, and the two anonymous reviewers for the University of Toronto Press; they all read sections of this book in draft and helped to improve it by their perceptive criticisms and suggestions.

I am greatly indebted to Andy Orchard, the editor of the Toronto Anglo-Saxon series, and to Suzanne Rancourt, of the University of Toronto Press, for the trust and confidence that they have had in my project, and for their encouragement and patience. To Barb Porter and Catherine Frost of the Press I extend particular thanks for their skill in correcting and copy-editing my manuscript in its various stages; they heroically ploughed hundreds of acres of archaic language and runic ciphers with unfailing expertise and endurance. The printing was supported by generous grants from the Swiss National Science Foundation and the Dr Josef Schmid-Stiftung.

This book is dedicated to my family, Barbara, Eleonora, Valentina, and Frederic – *swæsum ond gesibbum* – you made me feel less lonely while I was sitting at my desk, typing with three fingers, not unlike a monk in his scriptorium: 'Three fingers write, and the whole body labours.' Even the medieval authors knew that writing a book is a labour of love.

Abbreviations and Symbols

ASE	*Anglo-Saxon England*
ASPR	*The Anglo-Saxon Poetic Records.* Ed. G.P. Krapp and E.V.K. Dobbie. 6 vols. New York: Columbia University Press, 1931–42
BT	*An Anglo-Saxon Dictionary.* Ed. J. Bosworth and T.N. Toller. Oxford: Clarendon Press, 1882–98; and *An Anglo-Saxon Dictionary: Supplement.* Ed. T.N. Toller. Oxford: Clarendon Press, 1908–21
CCCM	Corpus Christianorum: Continuatio Mediaevalis. Vols 1– . Turnhout: Brepols, 1966–
CCSL	Corpus Christianorum: Series Latina. Vols 1– . Turnhout: Brepols, 1953–
CSASE	Cambridge Studies in Anglo-Saxon England
CSEL	Corpus scriptorum ecclesiasticorum Latinorum. Vols 1– . Vienna, 1866–
DML	*Dictionary of Medieval Latin from British Sources.* ed. R.E. Latham, D.R. Howlett, et al. Vols 1– . Oxford: Oxford University Press, 1997–
DOE	*Dictionary of Old English.* Ed. A. Cameron et al. Toronto: Pontifical Institute of Mediaeval Studies, 1986–
EETS OS	Early English Text Society. Original Series. Vols 1– . London: Kegan Paul, Trench, Trübner, 1864–
Gmc	Germanic
IE	Indo-European
Lat.	Latin
MCOE	Venezky, Richard L., and Antonette di Paulo Healey. *A Microfiche Concordance to Old English.* Newark and Toronto: University of Delaware Press, 1980

ME   Middle English
MED   *Middle English Dictionary.* Ed. Hans Kurat, Sherman M. Kuhn, and Robert E. Lewis. Vols 1– . Ann Arbor: University of Michigan Press, 1954–
MGH   Monumenta Germaniae historica. Hanover and Berlin: Weidmann, 1826–
MGH AA   Monumenta Germaniae historica: Auctores antiquissimi. 15 vols
MGH EPP   Monumenta Germaniae historica: Epistolae
MGH PP   Monumenta Germaniae historica: Poetae Latini medii aevi. 6 vols
MLat.   Medieval Latin
MLW   *Mittellateinisches Wörterbuch bis zum ausgehenden 13. Jahrhundert.* Ed. O. Prinz, J. Schneider, et al. Vols 1– . Munich: C.H. Beck, 1967–
ModE   Modern English
ModG   Modern German
NGML   *Novum Glossarium Mediae Latinitatis.* Ed. F. Blatt et al. Vol. L– . Copenhagen: Ejnar Munksgaard, 1957–
OE   Old English
OED   *The Oxford English Dictionary.* 2nd ed. Ed. J.A. Simpson and E.S.C. Weiner. 20 vols. Oxford: Oxford University Press, 1989
OF   Old French
OHG   Old High German
OLD   *Oxford Latin Dictionary.* Ed. P.G.W. Glare. Oxford: Clarendon Press, 1982
PL   Patrologiae cursus completus: Series Latina. Ed. J.-P. Migne. 217 vols. 4 vols index. 5 vols supplement. Paris, 1844–1974
pl.   plural
pret.   preterite
RS   Rerum Britannicarum medii aevi scriptores. Rolls Series
stv   strong verb
WS   West Saxon
wv   weak verb
*   a reconstructed form
>   becomes
<   derives from

SAY WHAT I AM CALLED:
THE OLD ENGLISH RIDDLES OF THE EXETER BOOK
AND THE ANGLO-LATIN RIDDLE TRADITION

Introduction

As the oldest extant collection of vernacular riddles in western Europe, the ninety-five Old English *Riddles* of the Exeter Book (Exeter, Cathedral Library, MS 3501) occupy a unique place within both the history of the genre and the literary heritage of Anglo-Saxon England. Copied in the south of England towards the end of the tenth century, they appear to be a compilation of poetic riddles by perhaps more than one author, inserted in three uneven batches into an anthology of religious and secular poetry in Old English. The codex is defective, especially at the beginning and towards the end, and several leaves are missing, which may account for the fact that there are no solutions to the *Riddles* in the manuscript. In the 150 years since their first appearance in print, the Exeter Book *Riddles* have therefore challenged generations of scholars, whose curiosity and scrutiny have yielded a vast number of scholarly publications, including several critical editions of the text, numerous translations into modern languages, as well as countless articles on various linguistic and literary aspects of the collection.[1]

Much of this scholarly work has been devoted to finding new solutions to the *Riddles* or to supporting earlier proposals, many of which go back to the pioneering studies of Franz Dietrich, Moritz Trautmann, and Frederick Tupper, published more than a century ago. Tupper was also one of the first scholars to take into account the long-standing tradition of riddle-making in Latin, in both verse and prose, which was particularly favoured in the Anglo-Saxon world of monastic reading and teaching. Manuscript

---

1 See the annotated bibliography by Poole, *Old English Wisdom Poetry*, 244–332. All subsequent references to the Exeter Book *Riddles* follow the numbering of Krapp and Dobbie, *The Exeter Book* (=ASPR 3). Unless otherwise indicated, all translations in this book are my own.

collections of Latin riddles circulated in early England, notably those by the late Roman poet Symphosius (4th/5th c. AD) and the Anglo-Saxon churchmen Aldhelm of Malmesbury (d. 709/10), Tatwine (d. 734), and Eusebius (8th c.), whose elegant and learned verse *enigmata* informed the vernacular *Riddles* of the Exeter Book.

The present study proposes a new reading of the Exeter Book *Riddles* in the context of these earlier Anglo-Latin collections and argues for a vigorous, common tradition of Old English and Anglo-Latin enigmatography. In the following chapters, it will be demonstrated how the *Riddles* both emulate and reassess their Latin models by expanding their generic boundaries and rhetorical conventions and how they recreate received topics and themes in a vernacular whose distinctive poetic language and archaic imagery provide a powerful response to this authoritative legacy. In assessing a common Anglo-Saxon tradition of Latin and English riddle literature, however, my readings will not be confined to the obvious earlier verse *enigmata* of Symphosius and his English followers. It is intriguing to note that many of the subjects and themes of the hexametrical *enigmata* and the Old English *Riddles* also occur in lesser-known contexts such as the prose puzzles of the *Collectanea* of pseudo-Bede (8th c.) or the didactical writings of Alcuin of York (d. 804). In his *Disputatio Pippini cum Albino*, a witty riddle-dialogue composed for one of Charlemagne's sons, and in the related *Propositiones ad acuendos iuvenes*, a collection of mathematical problems 'to Sharpen the Young.' Alcuin indeed deploys the same literary strategies that characterize the more elaborate verse riddles of his compatriots. Both texts are crucial to our understanding of the Exeter Book *Riddles* as an original and powerful contribution to the genre. Similarly illuminating parallels to both the Anglo-Latin and the Old English verse riddles can also be found among the sixty-two anonymous *Berne Riddles* (7th c.) and the Carolingian *Lorsch Riddles* (9th c.) as well as in the tenth-century *Reichenau Riddles* and the *Jocoseria* of pseudo-Bede through their playful use of logogriphs and cryptographic writing.

The Old English *Riddles* not only share with these various Latin collections a number of subjects and themes as well as many structural features,[2] but also display the same scholastic interest in natural history, etymology, and wordplay that already marks the earlier *enigmata*. Like their Latin models, the *Riddles* were not produced in a cultural vacuum,

---

2 See Orchard, 'Enigma Variations.'

but emerged from an intellectual milieu of monastic literature and Latin book-learning. Yet they also participate in the indigenous tradition of vernacular poetry, exemplified in the very heroic and 'elegiac' pieces that are preserved alongside the *Riddles* in the Exeter Book. This dialogue between vernacular and the Latin riddles, and between enigmatography and heroic poetry, is many voiced and multilayered and is by no means one-sided.

In the pages that follow, I shall examine these interconnections while focusing on three major thematic groups of *Riddles* and their Latin counterparts: animal and numerical riddles, which include both domestic beasts and the monstrous creatures that inhabited early medieval imagination (chapters 1–3); runic and logographic riddles, which bring into play runes and ciphers as additional clues for the reader to decode (chapter 4–6); and scribal riddles, that is, riddles whose subjects are the tools and activities of the medieval scriptorium (chapters 7–9).

Part I: Contexts

I shall begin in the first chapter ('Latin Riddling and the Vernacular') with some introductory remarks on the collections of Latin *enigmata* that were known or written in early England. The complex nature and extent of the influence of these Latin *enigmata* on the Old English collection will be illustrated by four vernacular animal riddles: the 'fish in the river' (*Riddle* 85), an ingenious rewriting of a three-line poem by Symphosius, and the three 'ox' riddles (nos 12, 38, and 72), which develop a number of themes first addressed in the Anglo-Latin verse *enigmata* of Aldhelm and Eusebius. Reading these exemplary Old English texts against their Latin counterparts will not only help to establish the position of the *Riddles* within the Anglo-Saxon riddling tradition, but also alert us to the inventive ways in which the Old English poets respond to an authoritative Latin canon and how they succeed in redeploying and redefining received rhetorical strategies and themes in the autochthonous context of their vernacular poetry.

From the fish and the ox, I move to enigmatic birds in chapter 2 ('Tell-Tale Birds: The Etymological Principle'), which reviews two of the unique group of four bird riddles on fols 103a–103b of the Exeter Book: the 'swan' (*Riddle* 7) and the 'nightingale' (*Riddle* 8). At the core of both texts is the phenomenon of sound: the resonant wing-beats of the otherwise silent Mute Swan (*Riddle* 7) and the joyful song of the eloquent nightingale (*Riddle* 8). But in addition to the usual vague descriptions and anthropomorphisms, the author now exploits a poetic device already used by the earlier

Anglo-Latin riddle-makers, by applying the principles of medieval etymology. The traditional method, in which the origin of a name (or signifier) was believed to disclose the true meaning of the thing (or signified), was familiar to the Anglo-Saxons from their readings of the Church Fathers, and above all from the *Etymologies* of Isidore of Seville. In the swan and the nightingale riddles, however, this etymological principle is, as it were, inverted, since the reader's starting point here is not the signifier (i.e., the subject's name) but the signified, that is, the etymological 'meaning' of the name to be guessed.

While the fish, the ox, and the nightingale can be identified on the basis of their Latin counterparts, the bizarre and monstrous creatures that are among the subjects of the riddles discussed in my third chapter ('Crossings: Combinatorial and Numerical Riddles'), often leave us baffled as to their true identity. All the texts considered in this chapter employ numbers; yet whenever numbers occur in the *Riddles*, they rarely serve as clues to the solution of the riddle, but rather they engage the reader in their unfathomable arithmetic, which defies any solution. Numbers, animal, and man meet to such a perplexing effect in *Riddle* 22, which – like the 'kinship' riddle, no. 46 ('Lot and his offspring') – shows an affinity with the combinatorial problems of early medieval recreational mathematics; the riddle tells how a band of sixty warriors, together with their fifteen horses, manage to get across a river or inlet with the help of a mysterious 'wagon' (most likely the stars of Charles's Wain, whose movement in the northern sky the riddle describes). Often the author's play with numbers makes his subjects look like grotesque monsters: with 'twelve hundred heads' but only a single eye, the poor 'one-eyed garlic-seller' (*Riddle* 86) does not seem human at all; nor does the bizarre creature of *Riddle* 36, with its twelve feet and eyes, six heads, and two wings, conform to any normative kind of living being. Finally, numbers also pervade the insoluble *Riddle* 90, the only Latin item in the Exeter Book; here, the author depicts an apocalyptical scene of animal violence, which perverts the very laws of nature and logic, while the text nevertheless seems to follow a numerical scheme, whose sense, however, eludes the reader.

Part II: Codes

The riddlers' use of esoteric ciphers and numbers is further examined in chapters 4–6, which focus on the six runic riddles of the Exeter Book. In them Anglo-Saxon futhorc runes are used as linguistic clues alongside the normal roman alphabet in order to encrypt the solution to the riddle. Not surprisingly, three of these runic riddles deal with animals – the 'jay' (no. 24), the 'cock and hen' (no. 42), and the 'hunting dog' (no. 75) – while in the other three, an inanimate object is described in terms of an animal: once we decode the strings of runic letters in the text, the metaphorical 'sea-horse' in *Riddles* 19 and 64 transforms into a ship at sea, just as the toiling, one-footed creature in *Riddle* 58 eventually turns out to be a common well-sweep used for drawing water from a well. In each case, the reader has to follow a different strategy of decoding: the clusters of futhorc letters in *Riddle* 19 have to be transliterated into their roman alphabetic equivalents and read in reverse, while the runic pairs in *Riddle* 64 indicate the first two letters of the words that must be completed and syntactically linked with the surrounding text. Similarly, in *Riddles* 24 and 75, the rune-graphs spell the Old English names for the garrulous jay (*higoræ*) and the hunting dog (*hund*), respectively, but the letters are jumbled and must be rearranged or read backwards in order to make sense. In the remaining two instances, the runes are enumerated and spelled by their rune-names: in *Riddle* 42, they yield the double answer *hana* 'cock' and *hæn* 'hen'; in *Riddle* 58, the rune *rad* indicates the first letter of the Old English word for the well-sweep.

Chapter 4 ('Runic Strategies') opens with some preliminary remarks about manuscript runes in the Exeter Book and elsewhere in the surviving corpus of Old English, before turning to the two runic 'ship' riddles (nos 19 and 64) and the 'jay' (no. 24), which I read in the context of classical and medieval ornithology and bird poetry. Chapter 5 ('Bits and Pieces') deals with the lesser-known *Riddle* 58 and the brief *Riddles* 75 and 76, and it argues for a new understanding of them as complete texts (rather than fragments), whose runic content can be shown to make sense even without editorial emendation. Finally, chapter 6 ('Letter Games') examines the runic 'cock and hen' riddle (no. 42) together with the non-runic *Riddle* 13, whose solution, 'ten chickens,' is believed to be linguistically encoded in the riddle's mysterious six 'brothers' and four 'sisters.' Similar logogriphic puzzles, acrostics, and cryptograms already occur in the Latin *enigmata*, which seem to have inspired the Old English riddle-makers to create their own esoteric letter games, using an archaic and obsolete writing system that harks back to the pre-Christian past. The antiquarian use of rune lore in the *Riddles* evokes this heroic past and its oral literary forms performed by the Germanic *scop*, whose runic skills are exhibited in *Riddle* 42. The runes in the *Riddles*, therefore, not only participate in the author's playful rhetoric, but also exemplify the epistemological transformation implied in the transition from pre-Conversion forms of communication to the Christian scribal culture of later Anglo-Saxon England.

Part III: Tools

The conditions and concepts of Anglo-Saxon literacy and poetry are further explored in the third part of my study (chapters 7–10). Here, I approach the so-called scribal riddles of the Exeter Book, whose subjects are the writing implements and artefacts of the medieval scriptorium, such as the pen, the inkhorn, parchment, and the decorated codex. As I shall demonstrate, these Old English poems develop some of the typical scribal topics of Latin medieval riddling (stylus, wax tablets, reed and quill pen, ink, parchment, letters, etc.) into powerful narratives of hardship, exile, loss, and death, which challenge received poetic conventions and oscillate between the generic boundaries established by modern scholarship. These riddles are self-reflexive in that they allude to the making of poetry and its reproduction in a monastic scribal culture, whose main enterprise was the propagation of literacy through the dissemination of religious texts.

Riddle 51, for instance, describes the movements of the quill pen (OE *feþer*) in the nimble hands of the monastic scribe, who is represented as a 'struggling warrior' and Christian soldier engaged in a campaign to spread the Word of God. In chapter 7 ('Silent Speech'), I discuss this riddle in tandem with its companion piece, the 'reed pen' (*Riddle* 60), which expands upon a three-line *enigma* by Symphosius. Each of the two riddles epitomizes a stage in the history of the technology of writing: in the tenth century, when the Exeter Book was compiled, reed pens were obsolete and associated with Roman scribal practices, while the contemporary quill pen made from the feathers of water fowl was the principal tool of the Anglo-Saxon scribe.

Another characteristic object of the early medieval scriptorium is the inkhorn (OE *blæchorn*), which is the common topic of the two long riddles, nos 88 and 93, explored in chapter 8 ('Beasts of Battle'). The inkhorns in these riddles are made from the antlers of a stag, whose free life in the wilderness of the woods the author contrasts with the confinement of the inkhorn stuck into the scribe's desk. The riddles describe this metamorphosis in terms of a dramatic separation and displacement, reflecting the Germanic ethos of kinship and companionship. Hence, the solitary subject of *Riddle* 88 suffers from the loss of its 'brother' (i.e., the neighbouring horn on the antlers), with whom it shared its glorious youth before it was carried off into the exile and slavery of the scriptorium.

Similarly, the inkhorn in *Riddle* 93 nostalgically recalls its heroic past in the company of its 'lord' (i.e., the stag), while it bravely suffers the tortures of the pointed quill pen that keeps dipping into it. Forced into civilization and domesticated by man, these wretched speakers deploy the formulaic language of Old English verse, to the extent that their moving accounts are reminiscent of the moods and modes of the Old English elegies and the heroic poetry of *Beowulf*. Moreover, their transformation from animal horn to inkhorn connotes the controlling dichotomy of nature versus culture and negotiates the role of archaic, pagan forms of literature within the lettered world of Christian monasticism.

The 'shift from oral performance to chirographic control of writing space,' which marks early medieval culture,[3] is at the heart of my argument in chapter 9 ('The Flesh Made Word'). The riddles discussed in this concluding chapter deal with the manufacture of a medieval codex and its role within the community of the literate. In the first of these, the well-known 'Bible' riddle (no. 26), the complex process of parchment-making, writing, and bookbinding is described at length; yet the turning of beast into book is represented as a cruel murder and a mutilation of the dead body, which, however, is reborn in the form of a richly decorated codex. The same principle also governs the shorter *Riddle* 28, to which I propose the solution, 'codex.' By setting the 'almost obsessive physicality'[4] of these riddles against contemporary accounts of Christian martyrdom and torture, I seek to establish a connection between the bodiliness of the sacred text and the writtenness of the sacred body. Refiguring the transformation of flesh into word as a form of martyrdom and resurrection, the Old English 'book' riddles also suggest the inversion of this figure, namely, that within the Christian community the sacred book functions as a symbol of the Word made flesh.

The concluding coda ('The Thievish Guest') briefly returns to the beginning of my study, giving the last word to the subversive 'bookworm' (no. 47), another riddle of the Exeter Book based upon an *enigma* by Symphosius. It will be shown once more how the Old English *Riddles* playfully expand upon their Latin models in order to create their own verbal universe, which in more than a thousand years of its existence has lost nothing of its haunting mystery and fascination for the reader.

---

3 Kelber, 'Language, Memory, and Sense Perception,' 432.
4 DiNapoli, 'Kingdom of the Blind,' 437.

PART I

Contexts

1 Latin Riddling and the Vernacular

Among the didactic writings of the Anglo-Saxon scholar and poet Alcuin of York (d. 804), the short *Disputatio regalis et nobilissimi iuvenis Pippini cum Albino scholastico* ('Debate between the Princely and Noble Youth Pippin and Alcuin the Teacher') strikes us as a unique blend of rhetorical wit, verbal playfulness, and condensed poetry. The work was written for Charlemagne's son, Pippin, most probably when Alcuin served as an adviser and teacher at the Carolingian court in Aachen between 781 and 794.[1] It is a prose dialogue between the youthful and quick-witted Pippin and his erudite instructor, and it consists of a series of brief puzzles and laconic responses, covering typical school subjects such as the body and its parts, the four elements, and the movements of the heavens. The *Disputatio Pippini cum Albino* follows the structure and content of earlier monastic wisdom literature, but it also includes a genuine series of prose-riddles in conversational form, some of which rephrase older verse-riddles that would have been familiar to Alcuin and his contemporaries. One of these is the well-known 'river and fish' *enigma*, in which the animal and its habitat are described in terms of a silent guest and a noisy house, respectively; the enigmatic guest occupies the house, yet strangely enough, both are moving together:

> ALBINUS: Vidi hospitem currentem cum domu sua, et ille tacebat et domus sonabat.
> PIPPINUS: Para mihi rete, et pandam tibi.[2]

---

1 See Jullien and Perelman, *Clavis des auteurs latins du moyen âge*, 164–5 (listing eleven extant MSS); Bayless, 'Alcuin's *Disputatio Pippini*.'
2 *Disputatio* 98 (ed. Suchier, 'Disputatio Pippini cum Albino,' 142).

ALCUIN: I saw a guest running along with his house, and he was silent while the house was making noise.
PIPPIN: Get me a net, and I'll show him to you.

Rather than actually naming the solution to the riddle, Pippin's response only metonymically alludes to it and thereby wittily matches the accomplished rhetoric and brevity of Alcuin's prose.

The House and the Guest (*Riddle* 85)

The 'river and fish' is one of the most widely told riddles in the long history of the genre, surviving as it does in numerous versions and languages from all over Europe and throughout the centuries.[3] Its first appearance, however, is not in Alcuin's *Disputatio Pippini*, but among the one hundred three-line riddles in Latin hexameters written by the late Roman poet Symphosius (or Symposius). The otherwise unknown Symphosius is 'himself an enigmatic figure'; he probably lived in the fourth or fifth century AD, and he purportedly composed his stylish yet light-hearted riddles extempore as amusements during the boisterous festival of the Roman Saturnalia.[4] Symphosius's *Aenigmata* survive in more than twenty early medieval manuscripts – including the *Codex Salmasianus* of the sixth-century *Anthologia Latina* and four Anglo-Saxon manuscripts – and provided the model for most later collections of metrical riddles, notably those of the Anglo-Latin writers Aldhelm, Tatwine, and Eusebius.[5] Symphosius's elegant century of riddles encompasses a wide range of subjects, both animate and inanimate, including the swimming fish:

---

3 See Tupper, 'Comparative Study of Riddles,' 3, and *Riddles of the Exeter Book*, 225–6; Petsch, 'Rätselstudien,' 2–8.
4 Lapidge and Rosier, *Aldhelm: The Poetic Works*, 243. For the text and numbering of Symphosius's *Aenigmata*, I generally follow Glorie, *Collectiones Aenigmatum Merovingicae Aetatis*, 621–721, with occasional readings from Ohl, *Enigmas of Symphosius*, and Shackleton Bailey's edition of the *Anthologia Latina*.
5 See Glorie, *Collectiones Aenigmatum Merovingicae Aetatis*, 612–15; Finch, 'Symphosius'; Reynolds, *Texts and Transmission*, 12–13; McGowan, 'Corpus of Anglo-Latin Literature,' 22–3; Gneuss, *Handlist*, nos 12, 252, 478, 493. For a useful overview of the early Latin riddle tradition, see Pavlovskis, 'Riddler's Microcosm.'

Est domus in terris clara quae voce resultat.
Ipsa domus resonat, tacitus sed non sonat hospes.
Ambo tamen currunt, hospes simul et domus una.

There is a house on earth, which echoes with a clear voice. The house itself resounds, but the silent guest makes no sound. Yet both the guest and the house run on together.[6]

Its controlled use of metaphor, personification, antithesis, and paradox has made this little riddle a classic example of its genre. Like Alcuin, Symphosius describes the river in terms of a house that, paradoxically, is endowed with a 'voice' and the capacity to run like an animate being, while the fish is represented as the personified 'guest' and occupant of the house, with whom it moves along. The middle line chiastically points up the riddle's central contrast: the noisy house 'resounds' and speaks loudly, whereas its silent guest 'makes no sound.' Only the third and concluding line, however, provides the clinching clue: no real house can run, nor does a living being echo or resound; yet Latin *currere* can mean both 'run' and 'flow,' and thus may apply to either an animate entity or a body of water such as a river; if the house is a river, then its silent guest must be a fish.

Long before Alcuin paraphrased it in his *Disputatio*, the 'river and fish' – together with nine other verse riddles by Symphosius – was incorporated verbatim into the Latin redactions of the once immensely popular *Historia Apollonii regis Tyri* (ca. 500), from where it was subsequently adopted into the late-medieval *Gesta Romanorum* and further spread into the folk literatures of early-modern Europe.[7] In the Middle Ages, the Apollonius romance also circulated in various vernacular translations and adaptations. The earliest of these is the Old English *Apollonius of Tyre* (ca. 1000), which has survived incomplete, however, and unfortunately lacks the section containing the Symphosian riddles.[8] Yet in early England the riddle of the river and the fish not only was known from Symphosius's collection and the Apollonius romance, but was also transmitted in anthologies of monastic school texts. One such miscellany is

---

6 *Aenigma* 12 (ed. Glorie, *Collectiones Aenigmatum Merovingicae Aetatis*, 633; trans. adapted from Ohl, *Enigmas of Symphosius*, 45, and Allen and Calder, *Sources and Analogues*, 173–4).
7 *Historia Apollonii regis Tyri*, 42 (ed. Schmeling, 34, 74, 123). See Archibald, *Apollonius of Tyre*, 25–6, 181.
8 See Goolden, *Old English 'Apollonius of Tyre,'* 59–60.

the *Collectanea* of pseudo-Bede, an anonymous compilation from predominantly Irish and Anglo-Saxon materials of the eighth century.[9] Its loosely arranged entries consist of witty puzzles and riddle-questions drawn from biblical and monastic sources, which are conflated with excerpts from Aldhelm's *Enigmata* and five of Symphosius's verse-riddles, including the 'river and fish.'[10]

Given this rich textual history, it is safe to say that by the end of the tenth century, when the Exeter Book was compiled, the riddle of the swimming fish existed in Anglo-Saxon England in various forms and contexts. When exactly it first appeared in Old English we do not know; the single extant version in the Exeter Book may well be older than the one that must have occurred in the now lost chapters of the Old English *Apollonius of Tyre*. It would be interesting to compare the two versions, since there is a lacuna in the text of the Exeter Book on which the alternative version might shed some light. On the other hand, we know that the anonymous translator of the Apollonius romance was generally faithful to the Latin original, and his version may therefore have looked quite unlike the one in the Exeter Book, which is remarkable for its liberties and its different narrative point of view. The text in the critical edition by Krapp and Dobbie reads:

Nis min sele swige,   ne ic sylfa hlud
ymb [...] unc dryhten scop
siþ ætsomne.   Ic eom swiftre þonne he,
þragum strengra,   he þreohtigra.
Hwilum ic me reste;   he sceal yrnan forð.   5
Ic him in wunige   a þenden ic lifge;
gif wit unc gedælað,   me bið dead witod.[11]

My hall is not silent, nor am I myself loud; about [...]; the Lord created for the two of us a journey together. I am swifter than he, at times stronger, he [is] more enduring. [5] Sometimes I rest; he must run forth. I dwell in him forever, as long as I live; if we two separate, I am doomed to death.

---

9 Dekkers and Gaar, *Clavis Patrum Latinorum*, 367–8 (no. 1129); Lapidge and Sharpe, *Celtic-Latin Literature*, 333 (no. 1257). The new edition with translation and commentary by Bayless and Lapidge, *Collectanea Pseudo-Bedae*, now supplants the text in PL 94:539–60.

10 *Collectanea Pseudo-Bedae*, 101–2, 239–41 (ed. and trans. Bayless and Lapidge, 132–5, 150–3) = Symphosius, *Aenigmata* 1, 7, 4, 12, 10. Of these riddles, only the 'fish in the river' also occurs in both the Apollonius romance and Alcuin's *Disputatio*.

11 *Riddle* 85 (ASPR 3:238); there is a lacuna in line 2.

All the basic elements are there: the metaphorical framework (the house and its occupant), the antithesis of the silent fish in the noisy river, and their travelling together. Yet the Old English author not merely translates his source, but explores its imagery more extensively by adding a vivid description of the common journey (3–5) and by making the dumb fish the speaker of the riddle – a paradox in itself.[12] The subject of *Riddle* 85 is, in fact, more properly 'the fish in the river' rather than the 'river and fish' (which is the title of its Latin source in most manuscripts). This notable shift of focus is no doubt deliberate. Presenting the fish as both the subject and the speaker of the riddle conforms to the rhetorical principle employed in a number of the Exeter Book *Riddles*, many of which use the so-called 'I am' pattern in order to introduce their enigmatic subject and represent it in terms of an animate being that is able to speak. As Andy Orchard notes, the riddle has thus been transformed from a 'third-person descriptive *enigma*' (Symphosius) into a 'third-person observation riddle' beginning with 'I saw' (Alcuin), and into an 'I am' riddle that employs the rhetorical device of *prosopopoeia*, characterizing its personified subject as a speaking, sentient being.[13] Typically in the *Riddles*, this power of speech creates an 'invented persona' and constructs an 'enigmatic narrative or monologue,' so that even inanimate objects are presented as if they were 'endowed with volition, emotion and capacity of action'; this enables the author 'to disguise the identity of his subject,' while remaining true to its nature and characteristics.[14]

Furthermore, the Old English 'fish in the river' is also considerably longer than its Latin source. Lines 3–5 compare the fish's swimming movements and the continual flow of the water: although the river is 'more enduring' (*þreohtigra*, 4), the nimble fish takes pride in being 'swifter' (*swiftre*, 3) and even 'stronger' (*strengra*, 4) than the element that surrounds it. The string of comparatives sets up a dynamic contrast, and informs the poem with a sense of discovery and heroic pride. Another addition not found in any of the

---

12 See Nelson, 'Paradox of Silent Speech,' esp. 610–11.
13 Orchard, 'Enigma Variations,' 295. Among the ninety-five *Riddles*, Ann Stewart ('Old English Riddle 47,' 230–1) has counted forty-eight 'first-person narratives' of the *Ic seah* type, against twenty-one 'third-person eyewitness accounts' (*Ic seah*) and eight 'third-person hearsay accounts' (*Ic wat* or *Ic gefrægn*). For a list of the different opening formulas in the *Riddles*, see Bartlett, *Larger Rhetorical Patterns*, 94–5.
14 Orton, 'Technique of Object-Personification,' 5.

Latin versions is the riddle's almost gnomic conclusion. Like the speakers in Old English wisdom poetry, the fish meditates upon the nature of its existence and the inevitability of loss and death. Fish and water were created together by God (2–3) and are therefore inseparable until their common 'journey' comes to an end.[15] Yet their symbiosis is more than just an amusing irony, as in Symphosius's riddle, since it exemplifies the divine order of God's Creation.

Read as a Christian rewriting of an older pagan text, the Old English *Riddle* 85 invites further considerations about the Exeter Book *Riddles* as a whole and about their position within the predominantly Latin tradition of riddle-making in the early Middle Ages. The marked shift from the external narrator of the Latin riddle to the talkative yet silent speaker in the vernacular version may reflect no more than a rhetorical convention prevalent in vernacular riddling. Yet the fish that proudly and freely moves in its element may also be understood as a trope for the Anglo-Saxon riddle-author, who himself operates from within an authoritative and continuing 'stream' of chiefly Latin riddle-making, on which he draws and depends. Just as the travelling fish delights in its freedom, so the Old English author self-confidently explores the literary space of a long-established genre and negotiates its rhetorical strategies while using his own idiom with almost subversive liberty, vivacity, and panache. A silent guest in a noisy house, he nevertheless leaves an audible mark.

Animal Worlds

The dependence of the Old English *Riddles* upon their Latin models is not always as obvious as in the case of the 'fish in the river.' As for the influence of Symphosius's collection on the *Riddles*, it is noteworthy that of the ninety-five *Riddles* in the Exeter Book, no more than a handful can actually be said to rephrase Symphosian tristichs, and even if they do, they always expand upon their Latin source. Apart from *Riddle* 85, this is true for the Old English 'anchor' (no. 16), the 'bookworm' (no. 47), the 'reed pen' (no. 60), the grotesque 'one-eyed garlic-seller' (no. 86), and perhaps the 'bellows' (no. 37).[16] Two of these – the 'fish in the river' and the 'bookworm'

---

15 Cf. Genesis 1.20–1, and *Order of the World*, 82–5 (ASPR 3:166): in the Creation, God 'joined together ... the fish with the water' (*teofenede ... fisc wið yþum*).
16 Cf. Symphosius, *Aenigma* 2 (*Harundo*) and *Riddle* 60 ('reed pen'); *Aenigma* 16 (*Tinea*) and *Riddle* 47 ('bookworm'); *Aenigma* 61 (*Ancora*) and *Riddle* 16 ('anchor'); *Aenigma* 73 (*Uter*) and *Riddle* 37 ('bellows'); *Aenigma* 95 (*Luscus alium vendens*) and *Riddle* 86 ('one-eyed garlic-seller'). See Whitman, *Old English Riddles*, 111–22.

– are animal riddles, and since animals, in particular, are a perennially popular and ubiquitous topic of enigmatography, it is no surprise that the animal world is featured prominently in both the Latin *enigmata* collections and the Old English *Riddles*. Among the ninety-five *Riddles*, there are at least fifteen poems about animals. This number, however, includes only those items whose solutions have met with universal approval or that are considered very likely to deal with some animal: *Riddle 7*, the 'swan'; *Riddle 8*, the 'nightingale'; *Riddle 9*, the 'cuckoo'; *Riddle 10*, the 'barnacle goose'; *Riddles* 12, 38, and 72, all describing an ox; *Riddle 13*, the 'ten chickens'; *Riddle 15*, the 'porcupine'; *Riddle 24*, the 'jay'; *Riddle 42*, 'cock and hen'; *Riddle 47*, the 'bookworm'; *Riddle 57*, probably swallows or similar birds; *Riddle 75*, the 'hunting dog'; *Riddle 77*, the 'oyster'; and *Riddle 85*, the 'fish in the river.' More uncertain are nos 20 (a falcon or hawk?), 74 (a water bird?), 76 (a hen?), 78 (a water animal?), and 82 (a crab?).[17] Individual animals also occur in *Riddle 22*, which uses seven different terms for 'horse'; in the long rendering of Aldhelm's 'Creation' (*Riddle 40*); in the obscure Latin *Riddle 90*; or in *Riddles* 19 and 64, both of which describe a ship in terms of a horse carrying a man and a hawk. In addition, allusions to animals are made in some riddles whose solutions are mostly everyday objects, such as no. 17, the 'beehive,' referring to the bees that are kept in it, or the two 'inkhorn' riddles (nos 88 and 93), which contains descriptions of the stag and its antlers, from which the inkhorns are made.

Even if some of the Old English animal riddles such as the 'swan,' the 'barnacle goose,' or the 'porcupine' have no immediate source or analogue in the extant Latin riddle collections, a closer look reveals many connections and parallels, especially in the tendency to present the enigmatic subject by means of Plinian natural history or Isidorian etymology, a principle first introduced by Aldhelm. The vernacular poets of the Exeter collection followed the earlier Anglo-Latin enigmatists by exploiting Latin school texts and bestiaries in search of the extraordinary and marvellous, which they, too, would make the subject of their riddles. Indeed, there is a similar range from the domestic and familiar to the exotic and rare in the many Latin *enigmata* about animals that circulated in late Anglo-Saxon England, including the classic three-liners by Symphosius.

As one critic has observed, Symphosius's collection displays a predilection for the real and tangible, rather than the abstract and mythological; his

---

17 For a list of solutions proposed until 1980, see Fry, 'Exeter Book Riddle Solutions.' For 'porcupine' as the most likely solution to *Riddle 15*, see Bitterli 'Exeter Book Riddle 15'; for *Riddles* 77 and 82, see Salvador [Bello], 'Oyster and the Crab.'

Aenigmata are concerned with the 'concrete material world,' which includes inanimate objects and man-made contrivances as well as plants and a large number of animals.[18] Apart from the fish (no. 12: *Flumen et piscis*), Symphosius treats the chick (no. 14: *Pullus in ovo*), the viper (no. 15: *Vipera*), the bookworm (no. 16: *Tinea*), the spider (no. 17: *Aranea*), the snail (no. 18: *Coclea*), the frog (no. 19: *Rana*), the tortoise (no. 20: *Testudo*), the mole (no. 21: *Talpa*), the ant (no. 22: *Formica*), the fly (no. 23: *Musca*), the weevil (no. 24: *Curculio*), the mouse (no. 25: *Mus*), the crane (no. 26: *Grus*), the crow (no. 27: *Cornix*), the bat (no. 28: *Vespertilio*), the hedgehog (no. 29: *Ericius*), the louse (no. 30: *Peduculus*), the fabulous phoenix (no. 31: *Phoenix*), the bull (no. 32: *Taurus*), the wolf (no. 33: *Lupus*), the fox (no. 34: *Vulpes*), the goat (no. 35: *Capra*), the hog (no. 36: *Porcus*), the mule (no. 37: *Mula*), the tigress (no. 38: *Tigris*), the mythical centaur (no. 39: *Centaurus*), and the sponge (no. 63: *Spongia*).[19] In nearly all of these *enigmata*, the humanlike beast, bird, fish, or insect is the speaker who jovially describes itself, usually revealing its identifying characteristic, its habitat, or some aspect of its relation to man.

It was the verbal dexterity of Symphosius's verse, however, that earned him the admiration of his early medieval readers. One of them was the Anglo-Saxon scholar, abbot, and bishop Aldhelm of Malmesbury (d. 709/10), 'the riddling saint'[20] and author of 100 Latin verse riddles. Aldhelm's *Enigmata* provide a virtuoso display of the author's command of hexametrical verse, which is why Aldhelm incorporated them in his massive *Epistola ad Acircium*, a composite work on Latin metrics and biblical numerology.[21] The riddles were inserted to illustrate the principles and patterns discussed in the two metrical treatises of the same work, *De metris* and *De pedum regulis*. In these, Aldhelm quotes excerpts from several of Symphosius's riddles – including those about

---

18 Pavlovskis, 'Riddler's Microcosm,' 220–2.
19 The titles are those given in Shackleton Bailey, *Anthologia Latina*, 202–34; cf. Glorie, *Collectiones Aenigmatum Merovingicae Aetatis*, 622–721.
20 Bryant, *Dictionary of Riddles*, 21. The story of Aldhelm's saintly life and miracles at his shrine is told at length by William of Malmesbury in *De Gesta pontificium Anglorum libri quinque*, 5 (ed. Hamilton, 330–443). For Aldhelm's life and the chronology of his works, see Lapidge, 'Career of Aldhelm.'
21 See Lapidge and Herren, *Aldhelm: The Prose Works*, 12–13, 31–3; Lapidge and Rosier, *Aldhelm: The Poetic Works*, 61–9; Orchard, *Poetic Art of Aldhelm*, 6; Lapidge, 'Aldhelm,' 26. Aldhelm's *Enigmata* have been critically edited by Ehwald, *Aldhelmi Opera*, 97–149, and Glorie, *Collectiones Aenigmatum Merovingicae Aetatis*, 359–540.

the spider, the ant, the weevil, and the hog[22] – and praises the late Roman enigmatist for his metrical skill and playful language:

> Nam Simfosius poeta, versificus metricae artis peritia praeditus, occultas enigmatum propositiones exili materia sumpta ludibundis apicibus legitur cecinisse et singulas quasque propositionum formulas tribus versiculis terminasse.
>
> For the poet Symphosius, a versifier endowed with the skill of metrical art, is said to have sung the hidden representations of *enigmata* with meagre material composed in playful language, and to have ended every single arrangement of the representations in three short verses.[23]

Although Aldhelm was inspired by Symphosius, he did not simply copy him. It is true that both authors offer a sizable and well-rounded collection of exactly 100 hexameter verse riddles; yet significantly, Aldhelm altogether avoids the tristich, the three-line verse pattern employed by Symphosius, and instead experiments with varying lengths, from the four-line tetrastich to the eighty-three-line *polystichon* of his final riddle (no. 100: *Creatura*). As a consequence, Aldhelm's *Enigmata* are not only longer, but also generally less poignant and light-hearted than those of his model. Moreover, as Andy Orchard notes, in Aldhelm's collection, the 'riddling element has all but disappeared,' and instead a 'heavily didactic element' prevails.[24] The reason for this is that Aldhelm's concern was radically different from that of Symphosius, whose pragmatic pagan world Aldhelm challenged with his mystical contemplations of the Creation. As Michael Lapidge observes, Aldhelm attempted 'to evoke the life-forces of gestation, birth and death which animate the universe' in order to 'lead the reader to contemplate God's Creation afresh.'[25] In this, Aldhelm's Christian universe is comparable to that of the anonymous author of the so-called *Berne Riddles*, which frequently refer to kinship, progeny, parturition, and death.[26] This earliest medieval

---

22 Aldhelm, *De metris* 10 and *De pedum regulis* 113, 121 (ed. Ehwald, 95, 154, 167).
23 *De metris* 6 (ed. Ehwald, *Aldhelmi Opera*, 75–6; trans. Orchard, *Poetic Art of Aldhelm*, 157). For Aldhelm's indebtedness to Symphosius, see Orchard, ibid., 155–61, and Manitius, 'Zu Aldhelm und Baeda,' 610–14.
24 Orchard, *Poetic Art of Aldhelm*, 158.
25 Lapidge, 'Aldhelm,' 26, and *Anglo-Latin Literature*, 9.
26 Pavlovskis, 'Riddler's Microcosm,' 230–1.

riddle collection perhaps dates from the seventh century and comprises sixty-two Latin verse riddles, each consisting of six rhythmical hexameters, covering a variety of subjects from household tools, foods, and plants, to the sun, the moon, and the stars. Aldhelm may have studied the collection, which has come down to us in nine medieval manuscripts, including the eighth-century Codex Bernensis 611 (hence the name). In some of these, the author is referred to as *Tullius*, but nothing is known about this least studied of all medieval riddle-poets, who was perhaps a Lombard familiar with Mediterranean flora and food.[27] As to their subject matter, the *Berne Riddles* are clearly indebted to Symphosius, although there are noticeably few riddles dealing with animals: only the bee, sheep, silkworm, fish, sponge, and sea-snail are treated in separate riddles, while a few others are alluded to elsewhere, as in the riddles about the egg, parchment, and the mousetrap.[28]

Aldhelm, on the other hand, shares with Symphosius a notable fondness for the animal world. More than a third of Aldhelm's *Enigmata* deals with beasts, both real and mythical, indigenous and exotic. Yet it appears that Aldhelm carefully avoided writing about those animals that had already been dealt with by late Roman riddle-maker. In Aldhelm's menagerie, we now find the leech, the silkworm, the water spider or pond-skater (as if to complement Symphosius's bookworm and spider); the crab, the ant-lion,[29] and the locust (not the equally voracious weevil); the midge, the hornet, and the bee (Symphosius has only the fly); the mussel, the cuttlefish, and the sea fish (not the freshwater fish); the salamander and the devilish serpent (instead of the frog and viper); and the cock, the peacock, and the stork (cf. Symphosius's chicken and crane). In addition, Aldhelm includes the dove, the owl, the nightingale, the raven, the swallow, the ostrich, and the eagle (to Symphosius's crow), the sow (to the hog), the young ox (to the bull), the ram (to the goat), the beaver, the dog, the cat, and the weasel, as well as the camel, the

---

27 Archer Taylor (*Literary Riddle before 1600*, 59) calls him the 'first medieval riddle-master in Italy.' The *Berne Riddles* are edited by Glorie, in *Collectiones Aenigmatum Merovingicae Aetatis*, 541–610.
28 *Berne Riddles* 21 (*De ape*), 22 (*De ove*), 28 (*De serico*), 30 (*De pisce*, a variation of the 'river and fish' riddle), 32 (*De spongia*), 43 (a variation of the 'silkworm'), and 47 ('sea snail').
29 *Myrmicoleon* (*Enigma* 18), an ant-like insect described by Gregory the Great and Isidore of Seville; see Lapidge and Rosier, *Aldhelm: The Poetic Works*, 249n16.

elephant, and the lion (to the tigress); and since Symphosius had already included the centaur from Greek mythology and the legendary phoenix, Aldhelm took the Minotaur and the unicorn.[30]

Judging by the large number of extant manuscripts, Aldhelm's *Enigmata* were widely disseminated both in early England and on the continent, often circulating independently of his metrical treatise.[31] In Anglo-Saxon England, they triggered a vogue of riddle-making. Following Aldhelm, the Mercian grammarian and archbishop Tatwine (d. 734) composed forty short verse-riddles in Latin hexameters, to which a certain Eusebius (perhaps Hwætberht, an eighth-century Northumbrian abbot) added another sixty to complete the traditional one hundred.[32] Tatwine's forty *Enigmata* are clearly modelled on Aldhelm's collection, whose spiritual concern and earnestness they share. The Christian character of Tatwine's collection and its didactic purpose are apparent from his choice of subject matter, which includes ecclesiastical objects (bell, altar, cross, lectern, and paten) and the classroom (letters and writing implements), as well as a number of abstract topics connected with Christian doctrine and teaching such as 'faith, hope and charity,' the seven liberal arts, and the four scriptural senses. There is only one animal riddle among Tatwine's *Enigmata* – the 'squirrel' – but his follower, Eusebius, added many more, again quite unsystematically, covering quadrupeds and other land animals (the ox, the cow, the bull calf, the tiger, the panther, the chameleon, the leopard, the hippopotamus, the lizard, the scorpion, and various kinds of serpent), birds (the chicken, the stork, the ostrich, the owl, and the parrot), and water animals (the fish, the remora or sucking-fish, the torpedo fish, and

---

30 Aldhelm, Enigmata 10 (*Molosus*), 12 (*Bombix*), 14 (*Pavo*), 15 (*Salamandra*), 16 (*Luligo*), 17 (*Perna*), 18 (*Myrmicoleon*), 20 (*Apis*), 22 (*Acalantida*), 26 (*Gallus*), 28 (*Minotaurus*), 31 (*Ciconia*), 34 (*Locusta*), 35 (*Nycticorax*), 36 (*Scinifes*), 37 (*Cancer*), 38 (*Tippula*), 39 (*Leo*), 42 (*Strutio*), 43 (*Sanguisuga*), 47 (*Hirundo*), 56 (*Castor*), 57 (*Aquila*), 60 (*Monoceros*), 63 (*Corbus*), 64 (*Columba*), 65 (*Muriceps*), 71 (*Piscis*), 75 (*Crabro*), 82 (*Mustela*), 83 (*Iuvencus*), 84 (*Scrofa praegnans*), 86 (*Aries*), 88 (*Basiliscus*), 96 (*Elefans*), 99 (*Camellus*).
31 Lapidge and Herren, *Aldhelm: The Prose Works*, 13, 31, 187n1. Glorie (*Collectiones Aenigmatum Merovingicae Aetatis*, 360–4) and Stork (*Through a Gloss Darkly*, 11–12) list thirty-one surviving manuscripts and fragments of Aldhelm's *Enigmata*.
32 Tatwine's and Eusebius's riddles are edited by Glorie, in *Collectiones Aenigmatum Merovingicae Aetatis*, 165–208, 209–71, respectively.

the water-serpent) as well as the fabulous dragon and the chimera.[33] Eusebius's sixty hexametrical *Enigmata* are generally less demanding than those of his predecessors. For the most part they are tetrastichs, often describing their subject with a set of contrasting or paradoxical statements in a way similar to that of the rather straightforward riddles of Symphosius.

Another Anglo-Saxon riddler was Boniface (d. 754), the famous missionary to Germany and author of a cycle of twenty *Enigmata*, each in the form of an acrostic, whose subjects are the Christian virtues and vices.[34] There are no beasts in Boniface's theological riddles, yet the animal world briefly resurfaces in the treatment of the chicken and the ox in the anonymous *Lorsch Riddles*. This group of only twelve hexametrical riddles is strongly influenced by Aldhelm, and perhaps is of English origin. They uniquely survive in a ninth-century manuscript from the Carolingian scriptorium of Lorsch Abbey, which also contains the *enigmata* of Symphosius and Aldhelm as well as other Anglo-Latin works.[35]

In the early Middle Ages, Latin riddles were frequently transmitted in groups and anthologies. An interesting case in point is the ninth-century Codex Vaticanus, Reg. lat. 1553. Following the *Enigmata* of Boniface, this Carolingian manuscript contains fifty-two riddles culled from the *Berne* collection, together with forty-five by Symphosius and five by Aldhelm, all inserted according to their subject matter, so that those riddles dealing with the same topic appear together.[36] In Anglo-Saxon England, even larger numbers of *enigmata* were compiled for school use and monastic reading. This is evident from two codices copied at Canterbury before the Conquest, each of which assembles the

---

33 Tatwine, *Enigma* 17 (*De scyrra*); Eusebius, *Enigmata* 12 (*De bove*), 13 (*De vacca*), 37 (*De vitulo*), 38 (*De pullo*), 40 (*De pisce*), 41 (*De chelidro serpente*), 42 (*De dracone*), 43 (*De tigri bestia*), 44 (*De panthera*), 45 (*De caneleone*, a conflated description of the giraffe and the chameleon), 46 (*De leopardo*), 47 (*De scitali serpente*), 49 (*De anfibina serpente*), 50 (*De sauro lacerto*), 51 (*De scorpione*), 52 (*De cymera*), 53 (*De y[ppo]potamo pisce*), 54 (*De oceano pisce*), 55 (*De tuspedo*, i.e., the torpedo fish), 56 (*De ciconia avi*), 57 (*De strutione*), 58 (*De noctua*), 59 (*De psitaco*), 60 (*De bubalo*, recte: *De bubone*). The titles are those in the manuscript Cambridge, University Library, Gg.5.35.
34 Glorie, *Collectiones Aenigmatum Merovingicae Aetatis*, 273–343.
35 Codex Vaticanus, Pal. lat. 1753. The *Lorsch Riddles* are edited by Glorie, in *Collectiones Aenigmatum Merovingicae Aetatis*, 345–58; the 'chicken' and the 'ox' are numbers 8 and 11, respectively.
36 See Finch, 'Bern Riddles.'

riddles of Symphosius alongside those by Aldhelm, Tatwine, and Eusebius.[37] One of these anthologies is the famous 'Cambridge Songs' manuscript (Cambridge, University Library, Gg. 5.35), which – apart from the three complete centuries of *enigmata* – also comprises nineteen logogriphic puzzles attributed in the manuscript to Bede as well as a dozen verse riddles on various school subjects such as *De Arithmetica, De Grammatica, De Rheorica*, and so on. Moreover, both manuscripts contain Old English and Latin glosses for the riddles of Aldhelm, whose flamboyant style and arcane vocabulary occasionally baffled even his medieval readers.

There is no doubt that the anonymous author(s) who wrote the Exeter Book *Riddles* was (or were) familiar with the earlier Latin *enigmata*, especially those of Aldhelm and his Anglo-Latin imitators. The influence of Latin riddle-making on the Old English collection is arguably most evident in the fact that two of its items are close translations from Aldhelm: *Riddle* 35 (the 'mail-coat'), which also survives in an early Northumbrian version, and the incomplete *Riddle* 40 (the 'Creation'), by far the longest riddle in the Exeter Book, running to 108 lines.[38] Moreover, towards the end of the collection and for no apparent reason, the compiler incorporated a poem (*Riddle* 90) that is written entirely in Latin. Its five lines are composed in the vein of the Latin *enigmata*, but – as I shall argue in chapter 3 – since there is no analogue in any of the extant collections and its lines are partly corrupt and their meaning obscure, the riddle is insoluble.

However, there are many riddles in the Exeter Book that do have counterparts and parallels both in the earlier Latin verse *enigmata* as well as in the prose puzzles of Alcuin and pseudo-Bede. While it is often impossible to identify a single concrete source, it seems rather that the Old English author(s) drew on a common stock of themes and

---

37 Cambridge, University Library, Gg.5.35, and London, British Library, Royal 12.C.xxiii, are the only extant manuscripts containing the riddles of Tatwine and Eusebius. See Ker, *Manuscripts Containing Anglo-Saxon*, nos 16, 263; Rigg and Wieland, 'Canterbury Classbook'; O'Brien O'Keeffe, 'Aldhelm's Enigma no. C,' 64–6; Stork, *Through a Gloss Darkly*; Gneuss, *Handlist*, nos 12, 478 (cf. also nos 252, 489, 493, 661, 845, 850).
38 Cf. Aldhelm, *Enigmata* 33 (*Lorica*) and 100 (*Creatura*). The Northumbrian version is the so-called *Leiden Riddle*, which in its unique manuscript (Leiden University Library, Cod. Vossinus Lat. 4° 106) was added to a Carolingian copy of the riddles of Symphosius and Aldhelm; see Smith, *Three Northumbrian Poems*; Wilcox, 'Transmission of Literature and Learning,' 57–60. For *Riddle* 40 and its Latin original, see O'Brien O'Keeffe, 'Aldhelm's Enigma no. C.'

phrases, and that sometimes only a line or two of a Latin *enigma* provided the starting point for the poet's own examination of a subject or argument. This is true not only for those *Riddles* that rewrite a familiar *enigma* such as the 'fish in the river' (no. 85), but also for the many lesser-known items that expand upon concepts and strategies first explored by Aldhelm and his followers, as will become apparent from the following discussion of the three Old English 'ox' riddles and their Anglo-Latin analogues.

Beasts of Burden (*Riddles* 12, 38, and 72)

Even in the total number of riddles the compiler of the Exeter Book appears to have followed the scheme of the Latin collections with their canonical centuries. There are ninety-five items in the Exeter Book that are generally considered to constitute separate riddles, but since the manuscript is partly defective and some of its final leaves are missing, it is most likely that the Old English *Riddles* once also totalled 100.[39] The unfinished character of the collection, as well as the fragmentary text of some of the *Riddles*, indeed suggest that they were arbitrarily selected and – at least towards the end of the book – rather hastily copied by the scribe who single-handedly produced the whole manuscript. This impression tallies with the prevailing sense of experimentalism and almost pioneering spirit, which seems to haunt the entire collection. This becomes further apparent in the fact that some of the topics are dealt with in more than one riddle. Not only does the first section of *Riddles* (nos 1–59, fols 101r–115r) open with three items on the storm (nos 1–3), but also more trivial subjects such as the horn (nos 14 and 80), the bellows (nos 37 and 87), and the key (nos 44 and 91) are doubled, as are 'ship' (nos 19 and 64), 'book' (nos 26 and 28), 'chalice' (nos 48 and 59), 'water' (nos 66 and 84), 'inkhorn' (nos 88 and 93), and perhaps 'flail' (nos 4 and 52), 'onion' (nos 25 and 65), and 'spear' (nos 73 and 92).

---

39 Since the scribe did not consistently indicate the beginning and end of an item, there is no critical consensus about the total number of *Riddles*; most widely accepted is the number given by Krapp and Dobbie (ASPR 3), who count ninety-three *Riddles*, whereas Williamson (*Old English Riddles*) has ninety-one and Muir (*Exeter Anthology*) ninety-four. For the palaeography and codicology of the Exeter Book, see Chambers, Förster, and Flower, *Exeter Book*, 55–67; ASPR 3:ix–xxv; Conner, 'Exeter Book Codex' and *Anglo-Saxon Exeter*, 48–147.

The three Old English 'ox' *Riddles* (nos 12, 38, and 72) illustrate this significant point. Read together, each manifests a different intertextual access to the Latin *enigmata* and exemplifies the manner in which the Old English poet(s) succeeded in rewriting their Latin sources. Their common subject is an ox: more precisely, *Riddle* 12 only cursorily describes the animal and instead focuses on the various uses of oxhide when made into leather; in *Riddle* 38, a young ox is nourished by its mother before it enters the service of man; whereas in *Riddle* 72, the ox's story of how it grew up to become a plough animal is turned into a moving narrative of affection, exile, and hardship. Here, as elsewhere in the Exeter Book *Riddles*, the subject itself is nothing new, but its treatment is a dramatic departure from the received generic parameters of early medieval riddling.

The subject of the ox occurs in the *Enigmata* of Aldhelm and Eusebius (twice), as well as in the anonymous *Lorsch Riddles* and the *Collectanea* of pseudo-Bede.[40] Each author approaches the subject differently, offering his own variation of what was a common theme. Aldhelm's hexastich first focuses on the young ox or bull calf – hence its title in most manuscripts, *Iuvencus* or *De iuvenco*:

Arida spumosis dissolvens faucibus ora
Bis binis bibulus potum de fontibus hausi.
Vivens nam terrae glebas cum stirpibus imis
Nisu virtutis validae disrumpo feraces;
At vero linquit dum spiritus algida membra,   5
Nexibus horrendis homines constringere possum.

Easing my parched mouth with foaming jaws, I thirstily drank up liquid from four fountains. While alive I break up the fertile sods of earth with its deep roots through the efforts of my mighty strength. [5] But when the breath leaves my cold limbs, I am able to bind men with fearsome fetters.[41]

The opening two lines describe how the mother cow is suckling her young: the four fountains (literally 'twice two fountains') are the four teats of the udder, from which the thirsty calf drinks. Once grown, the ox is strong enough to be used for ploughing (3–4), until it is slaughtered and its hide made into leather thongs (5–6). Aldhelm was the first

---

40 See Erhardt-Siebold, *Die lateinischen Rätsel*, 170–3.
41 *Enigma* 83 (ed. Glorie, *Collectiones Aenigmatum Merovingicae Aetatis*, 503; trans. Lapidge and Rosier, *Aldhelm: The Poetic Works*, 88).

riddle-poet to combine the motif of the four nourishing fountains with the 'living-dead' antithesis and the witty paradox of the leather as the 'dead binder.' All these elements reoccur in the ox riddles of Eusebius, the *Lorsch* collection, and the pseudo-Bedan *Collectanea*. While the *Lorsch* riddle is essentially a rather uninspired rendering of Aldhelm's *enigma*,[42] Eusebius's version packs all three themes into a succinct tetrastich, which nonetheless lacks the metrical elegance and verbal aplomb of its convoluted source. Eusebius's riddle is entitled *De vitulo*, 'On the calf':

> Post genitrix me quam peperit mea, sepe solesco
> Inter ab uno fonte rivos bis bibere binos
> Progredientes; et si vixero, rumpere colles
> Incipiam; vivos moriens aut alligo multos.

> After my mother has given me birth, I often use to drink of twice two streams coming from one source. And if I live, I shall begin to break up hills; or if I die, I bind many living.[43]

As Peter Clemoes observes, Eusebius establishes a 'time sequence' of events, moving from past (*peperit*, 1) to present (*solesco*, 1) and future tense (*vixero ... incipiam*, 3–4).[44] Within this scheme, the author typically operates with perplexing numbers, antithesis, and paradox: the calf seems to drink simultaneously from one, two, and four sources (*uno ... bis ... binos*, 2); and the adult ox retains its strength even when dead, ironically binding the 'living' (*vivos ... alligo*, 4). Unlike Aldhelm, who merely speaks of 'men' (*homines*, 6) bound by fetters, Eusebius's *vivos moriens* (4) points up a much sharper contrast. Eusebius's poem finds a remarkably close parallel among the prose puzzles of the *Collectanea* of pseudo-Bede (no. 194); here, the riddle is boiled down to a laconic statement:

> Vidi filium inter quatuor fontes nutritum: si vivus fuit, disrupit montes; si mortuus fuit, alligavit vivos.

---

42 *Lorsch Riddle* 11 (ed. Glorie, *Collectiones Aenigmatum Merovingicae Aetatis*, 357); the parallels to Aldhelm are listed by Glorie, ibid.
43 *Enigma* 37 (ed. Glorie, *Collectiones Aenigmatum Merovingicae Aetatis*, 247; trans. adapted from Allen and Calder, *Sources and Analogues*, 164).
44 Clemoes, *Interactions of Thought and Language*, 104.

I saw a son reared among four springs: if he was alive, he broke up mountains; if he was dead, he bound the living.[45]

The *vivus/mortuus* antithesis almost literally corresponds to Eusebius's concluding conundrum, which again appears in the Old English *Riddle* 38:

> Ic þa wiht geseah   wæpnedcynnes,
> geoguðmyrþe grædig;   him on gafol forlet
> ferðfriþende   feower wellan
> scire sceotan,   on gesceap þeotan.
> Mon maþelade,   se þe me gesægde: 5
> "Seo wiht, gif hio gedygeð,   duna briceð;
> gif he tobirsteð,   bindeð cwice."[46]

I saw that creature of the male sex, greedy for the joy of youth; as a gift to himself he let four bright life-sustaining fountains shoot forth, resound naturally. [5] A man spoke, who said to me: 'This creature, if he survives, breaks up the hills; if he is rent asunder, he binds the living.'

The riddle's greedy *wiht* (1) is, of course, the thirsty young ox: it belongs to 'the male sex' (*wæpnedcynnes*, 1), both biologically and grammatically, since the Old English word for ox, *oxa*, is a masculine noun, so the line provides an additional clue to the riddle's solution.[47] As in the Latin analogues, the four 'life-sustaining fountains' (*ferð-friþende feower wellan*, 3) metaphorically refer to the mother cow's teats; yet in an image of sheer exuberance and youthful vigour, the author adds that the white milk is 'bright' (*scire*, 4) and that it noisily gushes into the suckling's mouth.[48] The riddle's conclusion reads almost like a translation from Eusebius, but here, the double contrast of living/dead and breaking/binding is reinforced by the verb *toberstan*, 'to burst

---

45 *Collectanea Pseudo-Bedae*, 194 (ed. and trans. Bayless and Lapidge, 144–5 [trans. adapted]); see ibid., 243; Tupper, *Riddles of the Exeter Book*, 99.
46 ASPR 3:199.
47 See BT, s.v.; Jordan, *Die altenglischen Säugetiernamen*, 164–7.
48 The half-line *on gesceap þeotan* (4b) is difficult, but most likely refers to the sound made by the milk gushing from the teat; see Williamson, *Old English Riddles*, 157; BT Supplement, s.v. 'gesceap.'

asunder, to be rent asunder':[49] alive and yoked to the plough, the ox rends the earth, but when rent itself, it paradoxically binds the living.

Perhaps the most striking departure from the Latin analogues, however, is the riddle's unusual narrative structure. Not only is there a first-person narrator describing the enigmatic subject, but confusion is caused by the introduction of a second narrator, whose account is embedded in the first narrative. Acting as the riddle's riddler, this subordinated narrator has puzzled generations of critics and commentators. For some he is a 'prescient country bystander' (Williamson), 'a second observer chipping in' (Clemoes), or simply 'a wise stranger' (Pinsker and Ziegler), while several early scholars believed that the enigmatic *Mon* refers to either Aldhelm or Eusebius, who act as the poet's informants.[50] Critics agree, though, that the presence of this second speaker sets up 'a dramatic situation,' and that his unexpected 'speech act' lends 'emphasis to the concluding paradox,' which constitutes a 'miniature riddle' within the riddle.[51] Even if we should not identify the second speaker with any of the Anglo-Latin riddle-masters, it is clear from what has been said that the Old English author is, as it were, engaged in an intertextual dialogue with its Latin predecessors, whose accomplished *enigmata* haunt and inform their vernacular counterparts.

Another Old English variation on the theme of the 'ox turned into leather' is *Riddle* 12. This time, the motif of the binding fetters is developed with the figure of the Welsh serf:

Fotum ic fere,   foldan slite,
grene wongas,   þenden ic gæst bere.
Gif me feorh losað,   fæste binde
swearte Wealas,   hwilum sellan men.
Hwilum ic deorum   drincan selle   5
beorne of bosme,   hwilum mec bryd triedeð

---

49 BT, s.v.; see also Clemoes, *Interactions of Thought and Language*, 105. As a number of commentators have observed, the line is metrically irregular or corrupt; see Williamson, *Old English Riddles*, 257–8.
50 Williamson, *Feast of Creatures*, 186; Clemoes, *Interactions of Thought and Language*, 183; Pinsker and Ziegler, *Die altenglischen Rätsel*, 240. See also Dietrich, 'Die Räthsel des Exeterbuchs,' 455; Ebert, 'Über die Räthselpoesie der Angelsachsen,' 50; Prehn, *Komposition und Quellen der Rätsel des Exeterbuches*, 71.
51 Williamson, *Old English Riddles*, 255; Clemoes, *Interactions of Thought and Language*, 105.

felawlonc fotum, hwilum feorran broht
wonfeax Wale wegeð ond þyð,
dol druncmennen deorcum nihtum,
wæteð in wætre, wyrmeð hwilum   10
fægre to fyre; me on fæðme sticaþ
hygegalan hond, hwyrfeð geneahhe,
swifeð me geond sweartne. Saga hwæt ic hatte,
þe ic lifgende lond reafige
ond æfter deaþe dryhtum þeowige.[52]   15

I move on feet, slit the earth, the green fields, as long as I carry a spirit. If I lose my life, I bind fast the dark Welshmen, sometimes better men. [5] Sometimes I give a brave man drink from my bosom; sometimes a very proud bride treads on me with [her] feet, sometimes a dark-haired Welshwoman, brought from afar, carries and presses me, a foolish drunken maidservant, on dark nights, [10] wets [me] in water, sometimes warms [me] gently by the fire; her wanton hand sticks into my bosom, turns [me] frequently, sweeps across me who is black. Say what I am called, who, while alive, ravage the land, and after death serve men.

As elsewhere in the Exeter Book *Riddles*, the 'dark Welshmen' (*swearte Wealas*, 4) represent the enslaved labourers and underdogs of Anglo-Saxon society. They are stereotypically called 'dark' because of their dark hair – as opposed to the 'fair-haired' members of the aristocracy. Hence, the female servants, too, are said to have dark hair, as in *Riddle* 52, where the 'dark-haired Welshwoman' (*wonfah Wale*) is holding two fettered captives (!), probably a flail.[53] Here, the *wonfeax Wale* (8) is ridiculed as the 'foolish drunken maidservant' (*dol druncmennen*, 9): her 'wanton hand' (*hygegalan hond*, 12) is suggestively fingering the enigmatic speaker, while the text obliquely refers to various objects made of oxhide: a leather cloth, wetted in water and dried by the fire; a leather bottle, pressed and turned in the hands of the thirsty; and shoe soles, which, however, protect not the feet of the poor maidservant, but only those of a 'very proud bride' (*bryd ... felawlonc*, 6–7).[54] That the compliant speaker, who himself moves on feet (*Fotum*

---

52 *Riddle* 12 (ASPR 3:186).
53 *Riddle* 52.6 (ASPR 3:207).
54 Cf. the shoemaker's leather products in Ælfric's *Colloquy*, 170–4 (ed. Garmonsway, 34–5), including slippers, shoes, various bottles, and so forth. For an overview of Anglo-Saxon leather production, see Cameron, 'Leather-work.'

ic fere, 1), should be trampled upon by the haughty, is part of the riddle's humour, as is the catalogue of suggestive movements performed by the shameless maid, which places this riddle among the so-called obscene or sexual riddles of the collection.[55] None of this is contained within the Latin ox riddles. The only distant parallel is Symphosius's tristich about the leather boot made from the skin of cattle:

> Maior eram longe quondam, dum vita manebat;
> At nunc exanimis, lacerata, ligata, revulsa;
> Dedita sum terrae, tumulo sed condita non sum.
>
> Once, while there was still life in me, I was much larger. But I am lifeless now; I have been lacerated, bound and torn. I have been consigned to the ground, but I haven't been hidden away in a tomb.[56]

Symphosius already uses the same 'alive/dead' contrast that both opens and closes *Riddle* 12. Furthermore, the pretended speaker in the Latin riddle is similarly humiliated, living a dull life as footwear (which is nevertheless preferable to death). More than Symphosius's 'lifeless' boot, however, the transformed subject of the Old English riddle gains new life in the restless hands of the maidservant. Having himself once laboured, the speaker ends up with those who labour; yet he seems to enjoy his posthumous service in the company of the lowly, whose frequent caresses and nightly advances make him one of theirs, that is, a 'dark one' (*sweartne*, 13).

In the third and longest of the Old English ox riddles (no. 72), the Welsh serf is again presented as the 'dark herdsman' (*sweartum hyrde*, 11), who now rears the young ox. The riddle occurs on one of the damaged leaves towards the end of the manuscript, where there is a large hole across the page, so that the beginning of its text is partly lost:

> Ic wæs lytel [................................]
> fo[..
> ....]te geaf [........................

---

55 See Gleißner, *Die 'zweideutigen' altenglischen Rätsel*, 340–2; Tanke, 'Ideology and Figuration'; Higley, 'Wanton Hand'; Rulon-Miller, 'Sexual Humour and Fettered Desire.'
56 *Aenigma* 56 (ed. Glorie, *Collectiones Aenigmatum Merovingicae Aetatis*, 677; trans. adapted from Allen and Calder, *Sources and Analogues*, 163). Cf. *Lorsch Riddle* 11.6–7 (ed. Glorie, ibid., 357): 'Necnon humanis praebens munimina plantis / Frigoris a rigidis inlaesas reddo pruinis.'

................]pe þe unc gemæne [....
.........................] sweostor min   5
fedde mec [..........]   oft ic feower teah
swæse broþor,   þara onsundran gehwylc
dægtidum me   drincan sealde
þurh þyrel þearle. Ic þæh on lust,
oþþæt ic wæs yldra   ond þæt anforlet   10
sweartum hyrde. Siþade widdor,
mearcpaþas Walas træd,   moras pæðde,
bunden under beame,   beag hæfde on healse;
wean on laste   weorc þrowade,
earfoða dæl. Oft mec isern scod   15
sare on sidan;   ic swigade,
næfre meldade   monna ængum
gif me ordstæpe   egle wæron.⁵⁷

I was small [...] gave [...] that [was] common to both of us [...] [5] my sister fed me; often I pulled at four dear brothers, each of whom separately at times gave me to drink abundantly through a hole. I took [it] gladly [10] until I was older and gave it up to the dark herdsman. I travelled farther, trod the paths in the Welsh borderland, traversed the moors, bound under a beam, I had a ring on my neck; on my trail of misery I endured labour, [15] a great deal of hardship. Often the iron hurt me sorely on [my] side; [but] I was silent, never complained to any man, even if the pricks of the pointed [iron] were painful to me.

This is, yet again, a completely different approach to some of the themes originally found in the Latin *enigmata*. What is legible of the poem's opening lines suggests that there is a puzzling play with terms for various family members, whose referents are not actually related. The speaker's 'sister' (*sweostor*, 5) is the mother cow, who is briefly mentioned as the *genitrix* 'mother' in Eusebius's calf riddle quoted above and now nourishes her young; while the 'four dear brothers' (*feower ... swæse broþor*, 6–7) are the Aldhelmian 'fountains' of the mother's teats, which also occur in *Riddle* 38 and from which the young animal drinks abundantly and gladly.⁵⁸ Together with its mother, the young ox is kept and reared by the 'dark herdsman,'

---

57 *Riddle* 72 (ASPR 3:232–3, except line 10: *an forlet*; my punctuation).
58 I follow Trautmann (*Die altenglischen Rätsel*, 126–7, 191) and Pinsker and Ziegler (*Die altenglischen Rätsel*, 303) and take *þæh* (9) as the past tense of *þicgan* 'to take food, to eat or drink' (BT, s.v.); cf. *Beowulf*, 618b (ed. Klaeber, 24): *he on lust geþeah*.

until it is made to till the fields and to walk across the moors 'in the Welsh borderland,' or literally: to tread the 'Welsh borderpaths' (*mearcpaþas Walas*, 12). Yet fate has changed: yoked to the plough with beam and ring, the ox now experiences nothing but 'misery' (*wean*), 'labour' (*weorc*), and 'hardship' (*earfoða*), driven by the iron point of the ploughman's goad (13–8).

There is no life/death dichotomy in this riddle; instead, there is a dramatic contrast between the speaker's carefree youth and his troubled present, which divides the text into two distinct halves. A remote analogue for the second half can be found in Eusebius's riddle on the ox:

Nunc aro, nunc operor, consumor in omnibus annis;
Multae sunt cereres, semper desunt mihi panes;
Et segetes colui, nec potus ebrius hausi.

Now I plough, now I toil, jaded throughout the years; many harvests come, but no bread I get; many acres I cultivated, but never tasted malty drinks.[59]

It is obvious that the Latin example is a far cry from the mournful soliloquy in the vernacular riddle, whose language and mood is reminiscent of the so-called Old English elegies, with their melancholy accounts of personal misfortune, separation, and exile, and their nostalgic recollections of a happier past. Like his Latin predecessors, the Old English author employs the rhetorical principle of personification: in an enigmatic monologue, the invented persona both conceals and reveals its true identity; yet here, this monologue is developed into a moving narrative, which boldly expands and ultimately obliterates traditional generic boundaries.

In conclusion, we may say that the three ox poems of the Exeter Book demonstrate how the Old English *Riddles* develop their themes and imagery from the authoritative body of the Latin *enigmata* and how they transform these themes and images into something genuine and new. As we have seen, each of the three riddles enacts this transformation in its own way: *Riddle* 38 engages in an intertextual dialogue with its Latin sources; in *Riddle* 12, the reborn oxhide in the hands of the permissive maid embodies, as it were, the poetic potential and subversive power of the vernacular; while in *Riddle* 72, the toiling ox of the borderlands becomes a trope for the Old English poets' oscillation between adopted and autochthonous forms of literary expression.

---

59 *Enigma* 12.1–3 (ed. Glorie, *Collectiones Aenigmatum Merovingicae Aetatis*, 222; trans. Erhardt-Siebold, ibid.).

2 Tell-Tale Birds: The Etymological Principle

It has been argued that, as a collection, the Exeter Book *Riddles* lack an ordering scheme, and that the arrangement in which the three uneven sets of riddles were copied into the manuscript is rather haphazard.¹ At least for two groups of poems at the beginning of the collection, this is not quite true. The *Riddles* open on fols 101a–102b of the Exeter Book with three poems – the two short *Riddles* 1 and 2 and the long *Riddle* 3 – whose common subject is the storm in its various manifestations (wind, rain, thunder, lightning) and with its destructive power on land and at sea.² This first batch is followed by three short items generally solved as 'flail,' 'bell,' or 'bucket' (no. 4); 'shield' or 'chopping block' (no. 5); and 'sun' (no. 6). Then, on fols 103a–103b, the scribe copied a second thematic group, this time consisting of four bird riddles: no. 7, the 'swan' (OE *swan ~ swon*); no. 8, the 'nightingale' (OE *nihtegale*); no. 9, the 'cuckoo' (OE *geac*); and no. 10, the 'barnacle goose' (MLat. *bernaca ~ bernekke ~ bernecta*).³

Such signs of an ordering hand come as no surprise if we consider that the earlier Anglo-Latin riddle collections already show similar thematic links in

---

1 For example, Tupper, *Riddles of the Exeter Book*, lxiii–lxxix.
2 ASPR 3:180–3. Since the beginnings of *Riddles* 2 and 3 are not marked by initials in the MS, some editors and commentators have taken *Riddles* 1–3 as one long riddle, thus numbering it *Riddle* 1. See Lapidge, 'Stoic Cosmology,' 5–9.
3 No OE name for the barnacle goose (*Branta leucopsis*) survives. It is called *bernaca* in Gerald of Wales, *Topographia Hibernica* I.15 (ed. Dimock, 47–8), *bernekke* in Alexander Neckam, *De naturis rerum* 1.48 (ed. Wright, 99–100), and *bernecta* in Gervase of Tilbury, *Otia imperialia* 3.123 (ed. Banks and Binns, 818–21). See *OED*, s.v. *barnacle* n2; Kitson, 'Old English Bird-Names,' 16.

their opening items. For example, Aldhelm begins his magisterial series of riddles with four tetrastichs about the related subjects 'earth' (*Terra*), 'wind' (*Ventus*), 'cloud' (*Nubes*), and 'nature' (*Natura*) before he branches out into sundry subjects that follow each other without any discernible order.[4] In formal terms, the ordering principle of Aldhelm's one hundred *Enigmata* lies in the increasing length of the poems (moving from four to five hexameters and so on). Thematically, however, the four cosmological riddles open a theological bracket that is triumphantly closed by the lengthy and climactic Creation riddle at the end (no. 100: 'Creatura'). Thus, not only did Aldhelm's four opening poems inform the three Old English storm riddles (*Riddles* 1–3) in terms of their subject matter and their style, but the scheme also explains the position of the storm riddles within the vernacular collection, which open, as it were, with an Aldhelmian gesture.

This sense of thematic arrangement also becomes apparent in the Latin collections of Tatwine and Eusebius. Here, the opening items cover matters of theology, the medieval school, and the scriptorium. From 'philosophy' and the seven liberal arts, 'faith, hope, and charity,' and the four scriptural senses, Tatwine moves to the letters of the alphabet and from there to 'parchment' and 'pen,' the latter a subject that Symphosius already had put at the beginning of his collection.[5] Accordingly, Eusebius starts out with God, the angels, and the devil, and descends from 'man,' 'heaven,' and 'earth' to the letters of the alphabet.[6] As one critic has observed, such an order is 'occasioned by a Christian conception of the universe' and follows the traditional medieval 'chain of being.'[7] The principle is almost encyclopedic, especially in the case of Eusebius, who often exploits book knowledge derived from Isidore's *Etymologies* and concludes his collection with little clusters of riddles about exotic beasts, fishes, and birds. The groupings of the three storm poems (nos 1–3) and the four bird riddles (nos 7–10) within the Exeter Book may thus be explained as an attempt to follow a pattern that was established by the Latin riddle-makers or their copyists and anthologists.

---

4 Aldhelm, *Enigmata* 1–4 (ed. Glorie, *Collectiones Aenigmatum Merovingicae Aetatis*, 383–7).
5 Tatwine, *Enigmata* 1–6 (ed. Glorie, *ibid.*, 168–73); cf. Symphosius, *Aenigmata* 1 (*Graphium*) and 2 (*Harundo*).
6 Eusebius, *Enigmata* 1–7 (ed. Glorie, *Collectiones Aenigmatum Merovingicae Aetatis*, 211–17). Note that the *Lorsch Riddles* collection also opens with the subjects 'man,' 'soul,' and 'water' (ed. Glorie, ibid., 347–9).
7 Whitman, 'Aenigmata Tatwini,' 15–16.

These solutions of *Riddles* 7–10 – 'swan,' 'nightingale,' 'cuckoo,' and 'barnacle goose' – are supported, on the one hand, by external evidence from classical and medieval natural history and poetry, or by analogues and parallels from the Latin *enigmata*. On the other hand, there are a number of structural, stylistic, and lexical parallels and interconnections among the four riddles as well as between this group and the other bird riddles of the collection, notably numbers 13 (the 'ten chickens'), 24 (the 'jay'), 42 ('cock and hen'), 57 (probably 'swallows'), and 74 (a water bird?). In each of the four poems, the subject to be guessed, viz., the bird, is speaking, and the descriptions typically centre on the identifying characteristic that, according to medieval bird lore, distinguishes the animal from other species and serves as the crucial clue for the informed reader to solve the riddle. Thus, *Riddle* 7 revolves around the swan's feathers, which make a singing sound when in flight; *Riddle* 8 highlights the varied voice of the indefatigable nightingale; in *Riddle* 9, the parasitic cuckoo miraculously survives at the expense of its fellow nestlings; and in *Riddle* 10, the barnacle goose relates the story of its extraordinary generation in the sea.

To what extent the author(s) of these four bird riddles made use of traditional knowledge from classical or medieval literature and natural history is more difficult to assess. Accounts of the nightingale's melodious song were numerous, especially in Latin poetry, from classical authors to the more immediate models of the early Christian period and Carolingian age. The cuckoo's nesting behaviour also was well known. Several classical authorities had described it, and since the cuckoo – like the nightingale – has always been a regular summer visitor to England, its nest-parasitism would have been observed in Anglo-Saxon times.[8] However, it is a different case with the two water birds, the swan and the barnacle goose (*Riddles* 7 and 10). We know that accounts of the swan's singing feathers circulated early in Greek animal lore and fable literature. Yet apart from *Riddle* 7 and a brief allusion in the Old English *Phoenix*, there is no evidence that the belief gained currency in western medieval thought and literature, whether Latin or vernacular. Finally, the legend of the barnacle goose (*Riddle* 10) – unlike the bird lore of the other three riddles of this group – cannot be traced back further than the Exeter Book. The first accounts of the bird's fabulous

---

8 For detailed discussion of the Exeter 'cuckoo,' see Bitterli, 'Survival of the Dead Cuckoo.'

generation from shells adhering to driftwood or from trees date from only the late twelfth or early thirteenth centuries.[9] It does seem most likely that the myth originated in Britain, where the arctic barnacle geese spend the winter and where the story must have been handed down for several generations before entering post-Conquest encyclopedias and bestiaries.

Nevertheless, despite the potentially 'popular' origin of the legend itself, the barnacle goose of *Riddle* 10 is treated as a learned and bookish subject – as are the swan, the nightingale, and the cuckoo. Not only do the riddles about the swan and the nightingale, in particular, exploit the received knowledge of natural history and bird lore but, more important, both employ the principles of Isidorian etymology in order to provide a clue to the name of their subject – a repeated feature in the Anglo-Latin *enigmata*. As I shall attempt to demonstrate in the following pages, each of these two riddles is built upon a string of etymological clues that suggest the vernacular name of the subject to be guessed, that is, OE *swan ~ swon* for the singing yet silent creature of *Riddle* 7 and OE *nihtegale* for the nightly crooner of *Riddle* 8.

Singing Feathers (*Riddle 7*)

In *Beowulf*, the compound *swanrad*, the 'swan's road,' is used as a kenning for the sea. The young hero decides to journey with his men from Geatland to Denmark in order to help the Danish king in his struggle against Grendel:

> Het him yðlidan
> godne gegyrwan;   cwæð, he guðcyning
> ofer swanrade   secean wolde,
> mærne þeoden,   þa him wæs manna þearf.

[Beowulf] ordered a good seagoing vessel to be made ready for him; he said that he wished to seek out over the swan's road the war-king, the famous prince, since he had need of men.[10]

---

9 See Heron-Allen, *Barnacles in Nature and Myth*; Donoghue, '*Anser* for Exeter Book Riddle 74.'
10 *Beowulf*, 198b–201 (ed. Klaeber, 8; trans. Swanton, 43). See Metcalf, 'Ten Natural Animals,' 387.

There are three European species of swans.[11] Of these, the wild and migrant Whooper Swan (*Cygnus cygnus*) and Bewick's Swan (*Cygnus columbianus*) are only winter visitors to northern Britain and Ireland; they breed on the arctic tundra of northernmost Eurasia and migrate southwest to the lakes, marshes, and sheltered bays around the southern North Sea, and – like the swans in *Beowulf* – flocks cross the Kattegat, the strait between Sweden and Denmark. The third and best-known species is the Mute Swan (*Cygnus olor*), the typical swan of many freshwater lakes and ponds. Like the others, it is large and entirely white, but it has a gracefully curved neck, and its bill is orange with a black knob. It is the most numerous and widespread of the European swans, and it has the most southerly breeding range, which includes the British Isles and parts of northern and central Europe, where its distribution is more patchy and where many stocks were introduced in the sixteenth and seventeenth centuries. In England, the Mute Swan has probably always been indigenous, at least in the eastern parts of the country, where its bones have been recovered on several Romano-British sites.[12] Today, the species is mainly resident and semi-feral, but in medieval Britain, there were both wild and domesticated stocks, for Mute Swans were a source of food and often were owned by the local nobility and protected by the Crown. Even in Anglo-Saxon England, the privilege of keeping swans on open waters was already granted by the king. A charter dating from 966 states that King Edgar (r. 959–75) gave the abbots of Crowland in Lincolnshire the right to take possession of stray swans in their area – obviously wild Mute Swans.

Until the nineteenth century, however, no distinction was made between the three species, and in Old English they appear to have been indiscriminately referred to as *swan* ~ *swon* or *ilfetu* ~ *ylfetu* ~ *ylfet(t)e*.[13] Yet one of the distinctive characteristics of the Mute Swan, namely, the

---

11 The following is based on Cramp et al., *Birds of Europe*, 1:372–91.
12 Parker, 'Birds of Roman Britain,' 210. For the early history, see Ticehurst, *Mute Swan in England*, 1–17; Birkhead and Perrins, *Mute Swan*, 7–22; Harrison, *Birds of Britain*, 48; Meaney, 'Birds on the Stream of Consciousness,' 123.
13 See BT and *MCOE*, s.v.; Whitman, 'Birds of Old English Literature,' 173–4. Peter Kitson ('Swans and Geese,' 79–82, and 'Old English Bird-Names,' 16) argues that *swan* was the word for the Mute Swan and *ylfetu* for the Whooper Swan, on the grounds that some Anglo-Saxon glossaries make a distinction between *swan*, for Latin *olor*, 'swan,' and *ylfetu*, for Latin *cygnus* 'swan'; but this distinction is not consistently maintained.

musical sound of its wingbeats, was already known in Anglo-Saxon England. The noisy Whooper Swan and Bewick's Swan utter loud bugling and whooping calls, especially when in flight, while their wingbeats are not generally audible. By contrast, the Mute Swan is almost always silent – hence its modern name – but when it is flying, its broad wings produce a strong, throbbing noise, described by ornithologists as a 'loud, penetrating, rhythmic singing sound resembling *vaou-vaou-vaou*' that is audible for one to two kilometres and is peculiar to this species.[14] This very musical throb is the theme of the 'swan' in the Exeter Book:

> Hrægl min swigað   þonne ic hrusan trede,
> oþþe þa wic buge   oþþe wado drefe.
> Hwilum mec ahebbað   ofer hæleþa byht
> hyrste mine   ond þeos hea lyft,
> ond mec þonne wide   wolcna strengu   5
> ofer folc byreð.   Frætwe mine
> swogað hlude   ond swinsiað,
> torhte singað,   þonne ic getenge ne beom
> flode ond foldan,   ferende gæst.[15]

My clothing is silent when I tread the ground or inhabit the dwellings or stir the waters. Sometimes my trappings and this high air lift me up over the abodes of the heroes, [5] and the strength of the clouds then bears me far over the people. My adornments sound loudly and make melody, sing clearly, when I am not resting on water and land, a travelling spirit.

The only other surviving reference to the swan's singing feathers in Old English is made in *The Phoenix*, which also is preserved only in the Exeter Book. In the first half of this poem, which is based on Lactantius's *De ave Phoenice* (early 4th c.), the song of the phoenix is said to be sweeter and more beautiful than any music, including that of the *swanes feðre*:

> Ne magon þam breahtme   byman ne hornas,
> ne hearpan hlyn,   ne hæleþa stefn
> ænges on eorþan,   ne organan,

---

14 Cramp et al., *Birds of Europe*, 1:372, 377.
15 *Riddle* 7 (ASPR 3:184–5; my punctuation).

sweghleoþres geswin,   ne swanes feðre,
ne ænig þara dreama   þe dryhten gescop
gumum to gliwe   in þas geomran woruld.[16]

Neither trumpets, nor horns, nor the sound of the harp, nor the voice of any man on earth, nor organs, nor the strain of melody, nor the swan's feathers, nor any of the sounds which the Lord created for men's joy in this sorrowful world may equal that song.

Interestingly, the feathers are not mentioned by Lactantius, who speaks instead of the 'dying swan' (*olor moriens*) and thus refers to the old myth that the swan sings most beautifully when it is about to die.[17] The parallel within the Exeter Book was discovered in 1859 by Franz Dietrich, who was also the first to propose 'swan' as the solution to *Riddle 7*.[18] To support this view, Dietrich quotes a passage from a Greek letter written by the patristic theologian and bishop Gregory of Nazianzus (d. 389). In this letter, Gregory relates the fable of the swallows and the swans, whose wings are said to produce a musical noise. The story tells how the chatty and gregarious swallows once reproach the swans for being taciturn and reclusive; they will never sing in public, the swallows say, as if they were ashamed of their voices. Indeed, the swans reply, few are privileged to hear their singing, but their song is all the more pleasing and more beautiful, 'when we spread our wings to Zephyr, so that he inhales something sweet and harmonious.'[19] This fable probably originated in ancient Greece; references to the sound of the swan's wings can be found in the anonymous *Homeric Hymns* and in Aristophanes' *The Birds*.[20] Unlike the latter, the writings of

---

16 *The Phoenix*, 134–9 (ASPR 3:97–8).
17 Lactantius, *De ave Phoenice*, 49 (ed. Brandt, 138): 'Sed neque olor moriens imitari posse putetur.'
18 Dietrich, 'Die Räthsel des Exeterbuchs,' 462. This solution has been universally accepted (see Fry, 'Exeter Book Riddle Solutions,' 22), though only Wells ('Old English Riddles,' 61–3), Kitson ('Swans and Geese,' 79–82), and Meaney ('Birds on the Stream of Consciousness,' 122–3) correctly identify the species as the Mute Swan.
19 Gregory of Nazianzus, *ep.* 114 (PG 37: 212), quoted by Dietrich, 'Die Räthsel des Exeterbuchs,' 462, and Williamson, *Old English Riddles*, 152. It is no. 416b in Halm's *Fabulae Aesopicae collectae* 200–1, but it is not included in the more recent editions of Aesopian fables by Hausrath, Perry, and Chambry.
20 *Homeric Hymns* 21, 1–2 (ed. and trans. Evelyn-White, 446–7): 'the swan sings with clear voice to the beating of his wings'; Aristophanes, *The Birds*, 769–72 (ed. and trans. Rogers, 207): 'the swans ... with clatter of wings Apollo praising.'

Gregory of Nazianzus, including some of his letters, were once widely read and even translated into Latin in the early Middle Ages; Aldhelm, Bede, and Alcuin knew some of Gregory's writings, probably from the Latin translation by Rufinus of Aquileia (d. 411/2).[21] Although, no Latin version of Gregory's fable survives, it nevertheless provides some evidence that the story of the swan's musical wings was part of early Christian animal lore, even if such a tradition did not find its way into the classical and medieval encyclopedias and zoological writings. The latter may comment on the swan's voice and its supposed death-song but they make no mention of the musical throb of its wings.[22] In his *Etymologies*, Isidore of Seville, for example, holds that the swan's Latin name, *cygnus*, derives from *canere* 'to sing,' and that the swan's long, curved neck makes its voice sweet and melodious:

> Cignus autem a canendo est apellatus, eo quod carminis dulcedinem modulatis vocibus fundit. Ideo autem suaviter eum canere, quia collum longum et inflexum habet, et necesse est eluctantem vocem per longum et flexosum iter varias reddere modulationes. Ferunt in Hyperboreis partibus praecinentibus citharedis olores plurimos advolare, apteque ad modum concinere.[23]

> *Cygnus* ['swan'] comes from *canere* ['to sing'], because the swan pours out sweet song with melodious sounds. It sings so pleasantly because it has a long and bent neck, and so the voice, winding through the long and curved way, necessarily produces varied modulations. They say that in the northern regions of the world, flocks of swans fly to the music of the lyrists, singing together harmoniously and in time.

Unlike Isidore's swan, the creature in the Old English riddle does not sing at all. Even its wings are silent at first: 'My clothing is silent (*Hrægl min swigað*) when I tread the ground' (1). From its opening line, the riddle focuses on the bird's plumage, which is metaphorically referred to as 'clothing' or 'garment' (*hrægl*). In the course of the poem, two additional nouns

---

21 See Geerard, *Clavis Patrum Graecorum*, 2:187–8; Ogilvy, *Books Known to the English*, 153–4.
22 See Keller, *Die antike Tierwelt*, 2:213–20; Thompson, *Glossary of Greek Birds*, 179–86; Toynbee, *Animals in Roman Life*, 259–61; Rowland, *Birds with Human Souls*, 169–74.
23 Isidore, *Etym.* 12.7.18–19 (ed. André, 237). This belief was adopted by Hrabanus Maurus, *De rer. nat.* 8.6 (PL 111:245) and became part of the bestiary tradition; see André, *Les noms d'oiseaux en latin*, 64; Capponi, *Ornitologia latina*, 215–16; White, *Book of Beasts*, 118–19; George and Yapp, *Naming of the Beasts*, 131.

are used for the feathers, and again they are accompanied by the possessive adjective: *hyrste mine* (4) and *frætwe mine* (6), that is, the 'trappings' and 'adornments' that cover the swan's body. Not surprisingly, these words also occur together elsewhere in the collection, and in two instances they also refer to the plumage of a bird: *hrægle* and *hyrste* (with *mine*) are the feathers of the barnacle goose in *Riddle* 10, and *hrægl* and *frætwe* are those of the chicken in *Riddle* 13.[24] Only in the swan riddle, however, are all three terms combined in what Peter Kitson has called a 'triple patterning of words,' in which the riddler progresses from the prosaic *hrægl* to the more poetic *hyrste* and *frætwe*.[25]

The narrative of *Riddle 7* follows the bird's journey from the 'ground' or surface of the earth to the ethereal regions of the sky. The poem opens with a brief description of the creature's habitat (1–2); here, the language is deliberately oblique, and what is said in these two lines would fit any species of waterfowl. Then, the focus shifts to the bird's flight (3–6a): the swan spreads its wings and is lifted up into the sky. Finally, we are given the clinching clue: the wings produce their musical sound and 'sing clearly' (6b–9). With each line, the riddler reveals more about the swan's characteristics and its relationship to man. Its habitat embraces land, water and air: like all waterfowl, it walks on the ground (*hrusan trede*, 1), where it builds its nest (*wic buge*, 2) and breeds;[26] in search of food, it swims or dives and thereby stirs the waters (*wado drefe*, 2); when it flies, its wings and the 'high air' (*hea lyft*, 4) raise it, so that 'the strength of the clouds' (*wolcna strengu*, 5), that is, the wind, bears it far and wide over the people (*ofer folc*, 6) and their homes (*byht*, 3). All three natural elements – water, land, and air – are referred to once again in the concluding line: when not resting on water or land (*flode ond foldan*), the swan flies in the air like a 'travelling spirit' (*ferende gæst*, 9). The latter expression has posed an additional puzzle to many commentators, since *gæst* can mean both 'spirit' (with a long *æ*) and 'guest' or 'stranger' (with a short *æ*). But this ambiguity could well be deliberate. If we bear in mind that, even in

---

24 Additionally, in *Riddles* 11 and 14, *hrægl* and *hyrste* and *frætwum* and *hyrstum* refer to the decorations on a wine cup and a horn, respectively; and in *Riddle* 31, the birdlike musical instrument is 'adorned with trappings' (*frætwed hyrstum*). *Frætwe* is also used for the bird's plumage in *The Phoenix* (lines 71 and 192); cf. *DOE*, s.v.
25 Kitson, 'Swans and Geese,' 79. Analogously, in *Riddle* 9, the 'clothes' (*wedum*), the 'protecting garment' (*hleosceorpe*) and the 'covering' (*sceate*) stand for the plumage of the bird hatching the cuckoo's egg.
26 Cf. *Riddle* 15.8 (of the porcupine in its burrow): *ic wic buge* 'I inhabit [my] dwelling.'

Anglo-Saxon England, some of the populations of wild Mute Swans may have migrated within the country (as they occasionally do today), then the expression 'travelling guest' or 'travelling stranger' seems appropriate, especially since no distinction was made between the mostly sedentary Mute Swan and the two migrating species from the far north. On the other hand, *gæst* may refer to the creature's living spirit, as in the animal riddles numbers 9 ('cuckoo') and 12 ('ox'), where the same word provides an important clue, namely, the information that the subject to be guessed is an animate being[27] – which also appears to be implied here.

Words and Things

The key element in the structure of the Exeter 'swan' is the striking antithesis of silence and sound. From the opening statement – *Hrægl min swigað* (1) – the poem almost audibly progresses to the climactic tripling of *s*-words, when the bird's flight-feathers start to resonate (6b–8a):

> Frætwe mine
> swogað hlude   ond swinsiað,
> torhte singað.

My adornments sound loudly and make melody, sing clearly.

The rhythmic repetition, reinforced by the alliterative verse pattern, mirrors the threefold verbal variation that is used for the bird's plumage (*hrægl, hyrste,* and *frætwe*), while the three verbs – *swogað, swinsiað,* and *singað* – echo the initial *swigað* (1) and resolve it in their resounding triad. Such clustering exploits the rhetorical devices of *onomatopoeia* (the words imitate the musical sound of the feathers), *paronomasia* (the words sound similar but differ in meaning), and *homoeoptoton* or grammatical rhyme (the words share the same inflexional ending and create a rhyme).[28]

In addition to these more obvious stylistic effects, all three *sw-*words together provide an ingenious – and hitherto unnoticed – pun with their unisonous suggestion of the riddle's solution, OE *swan ~ swon*. Such wordplay is akin to the etymologizing technique employed in the nightingale riddle

---

27 Cf. *Riddle* 9.8: *wearð eacen gæste* 'I was endowed with a spirit'; *Riddle* 12.2: *þenden ic gæst bere* 'as long as I am alive.'
28 Greenfield, *Old English Poems*, 87; Nelson, 'Rhetoric of the Exeter Book Riddles,' 434–5.

(no. 8, discussed below) and in a number of Anglo-Latin *enigmata*, many of which draw upon Isidore's *Etymologies*.²⁹ Just as Isidore relates the meaning of Latin *cygnus* 'swan' to the verb *canere* 'to sing,' so the Old English author exhibits what may be called the latent etymology of the bird's vernacular name, which is likewise based on the relation between noun and verb. In other words: the *swan* is so named because it is silent (*swigað*) when it rests or swims, yet loudly sings with its feathers (*swogað ... swinsiað*) when it flies. At least for OE *swinsian* 'make melody' and *swan ~ swon* (and its Germanic cognates) this etymological connection is indeed linguistically plausible and even very likely.³⁰ For Isidore of Seville – as for generations of his readers – such an awareness of language is instrumental to any deeper understanding of God's Creation, in which there is 'a necessary and primordial relation between words and things' and a universal harmony that is echoed in the phonetic correspondences between words.³¹ Isidorian etymology, therefore, is more than simply a linguistic process; it is a 'category of thought.'³² As Isidore says in the first book of his *Etymologies*:

> Etymologia est origo vocabulorum, cum vis verbi vel nominis per interpretationem colligitur ... Cuius cognitio saepe usum necessarium habet in interpretatione sua. Nam dum videris unde ortum est nomen, citius vim eius intellegis. Omnis enim rei inspectio etymologia cognita planior est.
>
> Etymology is the origin of words, when the meaning [lit. 'force'] of a verb or a noun is inferred through interpretation ... The knowledge of a word's etymology often has an indispensable usefulness for interpreting the word, for when you have seen whence a word has originated, you understand its meaning more quickly. Indeed, one's insight into anything is clearer when its etymology is known.³³

In the same passage, Isidore goes on to classify possible types of etymologies (*Etym.* 1.29.3–5): those furnished from their rationale (*ex causa* – such as *reges* 'kings,' from *recte agendo* 'acting correctly'), those from their origin (*ex*

---

29 See Howe, 'Aldhelm's *Enigmata*'; Lendinara, 'World of Anglo-Saxon Learning,' 277; Ziolkowski, *Talking Animals*, 44–5. See also Hill, 'Ælfric's Use of Etymologies.'
30 Cf. OHG *swan ~ swon* < Gmc **swana-* < IE **swen-* 'to sound' (Lat. *sonare*). The name may originally have been applied only to the singing Whooper and Bewick's Swans. See *OED* and Holthausen, *Altenglisches etymologisches Wörterbuch*, s.v. *swan*.
31 Tilliette, 'Etymology,' 503.
32 Curtius, *European Literature*, 495–500.
33 Isidore, *Etym.* 1.29.1–2 (ed. Lindsay; trans. adapted from Barney et al., 54–5).

origine – such as *homo* 'man,' from *humus* 'earth'), and those from the contrary (*ex contrariis* – such as *lutum* 'mud,' from *lavare* 'to wash'). In addition to these etymologies, there are also purely grammatical derivations and loan words and words based on sounds (*ex vocibus* – such as *garrulus* 'jackdaw,' from *garrulitas* 'garrulity'). Examples of all these types are given throughout the twenty books of the *Etymologies*. In each instance, the etymological principle serves as 'the preferred tool of the knowledge of beings' and 'the method, by which the correspondence in sound between two or more signifiers enlightens us as to the reality of the signified.'[34] As a name formed *ex causa*, Isidore's explanation of *cygnus* < *canere* precisely establishes such a phonetic correspondence in order to explain the swan's characteristics through the etymological meaning or 'force' (*vis*) of its name. Isidore thereby chooses 'the road from designation to essence, from *verba* to *res*.'[35]

Accordingly, the Old English poet's suggestive wordplay from *swigian* 'to be silent' (1) to *swogan* 'to sound' and *swinsian* 'to make melody' (7) implies an etymology of the word *swan*, 'swan,' which is based on both *causa* and *vox*. In the riddle, the name *swan* becomes the hidden 'force' and the driving principle within an intrinsic web of descriptive and etymological clues. For the reader, then, solving the riddle and finding the creature's name implies grasping the linguistic 'force' and meaning of this name by laying bare its covert etymology. Yet, in a process that is almost a reversal of the Isidorian method, we have to start from the 'essence' in order to arrive at the 'designation' and move from the descriptive *res* of the riddle to the *verbum* of its solution.

Speaking in Tongues (*Riddle* 8)

Etymology, wordplay, and lexical variation similarly govern the rhetoric of *Riddle* 8, which is arguably the earliest English nightingale poem. Again, the bird itself is speaking:

Ic þurh muþ sprece   mongum reordum,
wrencum singe,   wrixle geneahhe
heafodwoþe,   hlude cirme,
healde mine wisan,   hleoþre ne miþe.

---

34 Tilliette, 'Etymology,' 503.
35 Curtius, *European Literature*, 496.

Eald æfensceop,   eorlum bringe 5
blisse in burgum,   þonne ic bugendre
stefne styrme;   stille on wicum
sittað swigende.   Saga hwæt ic hatte,
þe swa scirenige   sceawendwisan
hlude onhyrge,   hæleþum bodige 10
wilcumena fela   woþe minre.³⁶

I speak through [my] mouth in many languages, sing with modulations, frequently change [my] head-voice, cry out loudly, hold my tune, do not refrain from singing. [5] An old evening poet, I bring joy to the noblemen in the towns, when I shout with varying sound; quiet in [their] dwellings they sit in silence. Say what I am called, who, like an actress, [10] loudly imitate a jester's tunes, announce to the heroes many welcome things with my voice.

The contrast could hardly be greater: following the majestic Mute Swan, which nature has endowed with music-making feathers but which does not sing (*Riddle* 7), the small and notoriously ugly nightingale here indulges in a virtuoso recital of its melodious and blissful singing, equalled only by the garrulous jay of *Riddle* 24 (discussed in chapter 4). The poem is all music, uttered by the soliloquacious bird, which is portrayed as a welcome herald of daylight and springtime – a role traditionally assigned to the nightingale in pre-modern literature and natural history.

The solution 'nightingale,' however, has not been unanimously accepted. It was first suggested in 1859 by Franz Dietrich, who also considered the alternative 'pipe,' though he later preferred 'woodpigeon' (OE *cuscote*); the latter – like Trautmann's 'bell' (OE *clucge*) and Mackie's 'chough' or 'jackdaw' (OE *ceo*) – tries to account for the indistinct mark that precedes the riddle in the manuscript and has been misinterpreted as a 'c'-rune.³⁷ The mark was added much later by a different hand, however, and rather resembles the letter *n*, which might, in fact, stand for OE *nihtegale*, ME *niʒtingale*, or ModE *nightingale*.³⁸ Apart from Pinsker and Ziegler, who propose the

---

36 *Riddle* 8 (ASPR 3:185, except line 8: *nigende* (MS); my punctuation).
37 Dietrich, 'Die Räthsel des Exeterbuchs,' 462–3, 239–40; Trautmann, 'Die Auflösungen der altenglischen Rätsel,' 48; Mackie, 'Text of the Exeter Book,' 76; Swaen, 'Riddle 9 (6, 8).' For the supposed 'c'-rune, see Williamson, *Old English Riddles*, 53 (pl. IV), 154–6; Muir, *Exeter Anthology*, 656.
38 See *OED*, s.v. *nightingale*, 1; Whitman, 'Birds of Old English Literature,' 158–9; Kitson, 'Old English Bird-Names,' 489.

unlikely answer 'flute,' most critics agree that the riddle refers to a songbird: Tupper, pointing out the similarities between this poem and *Riddle* 24, favours 'jay,' as do Krapp and Dobbie; others argue for 'thrush' or 'starling,' while most other commentators – including Trautmann and Williamson in their editions – suggest 'nightingale.'[39]

The stylistic and lexical parallels to the 'jay' (*Riddle* 24) are obvious. In both poems, the bird elaborately describes the variety and mimicry of its song, the difference being that the nightingale imitates the musical performance of man, whereas the jay copies the barking, bleating, and yelling of its fellow animals. Compare:

Ic þurh *muþ* sprece mongum *reordum* (*Riddle* 8.1)
glidan *reorde muþe* gemæne (*Riddle* 24.5–6)

healde mine wisan, *hleoþre* ne miþe (*Riddle* 8.4)
ic onhyrge ... guðfugles *hleoþor* (*Riddle* 24.4–5)

þonne ic bugendre *stefne* styrme (*Riddle* 8.6–7)
Ic ... wræsne mine *stefne* (*Riddle* 24.1)

swa scirenige (*Riddle* 8.9)
swa hund ... *swa* gat ... *swa* gos ... *swa* hafoc (*Riddle* 24.2–3)

sceawendwisan hlude *onhyrge* (*Riddle* 8.9–10)
ic *onhyrge* þone haswan earn (*Riddle* 24.4).

Unlike all the other birds that have been put forward as the solution to *Riddle* 8, both the nightingale and the jay have always been known as particularly musical and loquacious songsters. Only the nightingale (*Luscinia megarhynchos*), however, is the old (that is, traditional) 'evening poet' (*eald æfensceop*, 5), since it delivers its harmonious song not only late in the evening and early in the morning, but often through the night[40] – or, in the words of the Old English riddler (8.4):

healde mine wisan, hleoþre ne miþe.

I hold my tune, do not refrain from singing.

---

39 See Fry, 'Exeter Book Riddle Solutions,' 22; Poole, *Old English Wisdom Poetry*, 401; Muir, *Exeter Anthology*, 656. Two recent supporters of the solution 'nightingale' are Salvador Bello, 'Evening Singer of Riddle 8,' and Meaney, 'Birds on the Stream of Consciousness,' 124–30.
40 Cramp et al., *Birds of Europe*, 5:627, 632.

The nightingale is, indeed, the sleepless 'singer of the night,' as its name suggests: the Latin *luscinia* probably derives from **lusci-cinia* 'singing in the twilight'; analogically, the Old English *nihtegale* and its cognates are compounds from the Germanic **naht-* 'night,' and **gal-a* 'sing, yell.'[41] Another well-known fact is that nightingales are migratory birds: they spend the winter in Africa and return to the thickets and woodlands of southern and eastern England in April, leaving again at the end of summer.[42] Hence, the 'many welcome things' (*wilcumena fela*, 11) that the songbird in the riddle announces, together with the 'joy' it brings (*bringe blisse*, 5–6), refer to the old notion that the nightingale signals the rising of the sun and the long-awaited arrival of spring.

It is well documented that in western literature and natural history, from classical antiquity to modern times, the nightingale habitually appears as a nightly singer and a 'deare, good Angell of the Spring.'[43] In medieval poetry, references to the nightingale as a symbol of spring and love abound. In the Middle English *Harley Lyrics*, the bird returns in April, when 'the woods grow green' and the 'leaf and grass and blossom springs':

When þe nyhtegale singes þe wodes waxen grene;
lef ant gras ant blosme springes in Aueryl, y wene.[44]

In the early Middle English debate poem *The Owl and the Nightingale* (ca. 1200), the nightingale argues that, in springtime, she sings *alle longe niȝt* to make everybody happy:

Ac ich alle blisse mid me bringe,
Ech wiȝt is glad for mine þinge
An blisseþ hit wanne ich cume,
An hiȝteþ aȝen mine kume.[45]

---

41 *OLD* and Walde and Hofmann, *Lateinisches etymologisches Wörterbuch*, s.v. *luscinia*; André, *Les noms d'oiseaux en latin*, 98; Skeat, *Etymological Dictionary*, s.v. *nightingale*; Holthausen, *Altenglisches etymologisches Wörterbuch*, s.v. *galan* and *nihtegale*.
42 Cramp et al., *Birds of Europe*, 5:629–30.
43 Ben Jonson, *The Sad Shepherd* II.vi.85 (ed. Herford/Simpson, 37). For the classical and medieval tradition, see Thompson, *Glossary of Greek Birds*, 16–22; Capponi, *Ornitologia latina*, 314–18; Pfeffer, *Change of Philomel*, 26–37; Rowland, *Birds with Human Souls*, 105–11; Gellinek-Schellekens, *Voice of the Nightingale*; George and Yapp, *Naming of the Beasts*, 175–7.
44 *Harley Lyrics* 25.1–2 (ed. Brook, 63).
45 *Owl and the Nightingale*, 331, 433–6 (ed. Stanley, 59, 62).

But I bring all joy with me, every creature is glad because of me and rejoices when I come and looks forward to my coming.

To 'bring joy' (*bringe blisse*), the nightingale insists later in the poem (707ff.), also means to remind the faithful of the heavenly bliss of Paradise and to move the clerics and monks to offer their prayers at night. Again, the Middle English poet exploits the topos of the nightingale as the joyful harbinger of spring, which can be best heard at night – exactly as in the Exeter Book riddle, where the same words are used (5–6a):

Eald æfensceop,   eorlum *bringe*
blisse in burgum.

The bird's extraordinary power of song, of course, had already aroused the interest of the early natural historians and encyclopedists. The first detailed account of the nightingale's tuneful singing comes from Pliny the Elder: in his *Natural History*, he says that in early spring the bird chants incessantly 'for fifteen days and nights':

> ... in una perfecta musicae scientia: modulatus editur sonus et nunc continuo spiritu trahitur in longum, nunc variatur inflexo, nunc distinguitur conciso, copulatur intorto, promittitur revocato, infuscatur ex inopinato, interdum et secum ipse murmurat, plenus, gravis, acutus, creber, extentus, ubi visum est, vibrans, summus, medius, imus. breviterque omnia tam parvulis in faucibus, quae tot exquisitis tibiarum tormentis ars hominum excogitavit.
>
> ... there is the consummate knowledge of music in a single bird: the sound is given out with modulations, and now is drawn out into a long note with one continuous breath, now varied by managing the breath, now made staccato by checking it, or linked together by prolonging it, or carried on by holding it back; or it is suddenly lowered, and at times sinks into a mere murmur, loud, low, bass, treble, with trills, with long notes, modulated when this seems good – soprano, mezzo, baritone; and briefly all the devices in that tiny throat which human science has devised with all the elaborate mechanism of the flute.[46]

Each bird, Pliny adds, has its individual tunes, while the younger ones 'practise their music, and are even given verses to imitate' (10.83).

---

46 Pliny, *Nat. hist.* 10.81–2 (ed. Mayhoff, 2:243; trans. Rackham, 345).

Whereas Pliny indulges in his minute and musical description of the bird's artistic performance, early Christian theologians, primarily thought of the nightingale as a joyful herald of daylight. In his *Hexaemeron* – a commentary on the six days of Creation, which was known to Aldhelm and Bede – Ambrose of Milan (d. 397) calls the nightingale an 'everwatchful guardian.'[47] At night, Ambrose writes, the bird 'keeps long watch over her nest' and 'solaces with the sweetness of her song the sleepless labours of a long night.' The nightingale thus may 'arouse a sleeper from his slumber,' as it is 'accustomed to signal the dawn of a new day and to spread abroad joy more penetrating than the morning light.'[48] Isidore of Seville uses this feature to account for the bird's Latin name, *luscinia*; in his *Etymologies*, he explains:

> Luscinia avis inde nomen sumpsit quia cantu suo significare solet diei surgentis exortum, quasi lucinia.
>
> The nightingale [*luscinia*] is a bird that took its name because it is accustomed to indicate by its song the onset of the rising sun, like a light-bringer [*lucinia*].[49]

In one way or another, Pliny's, Ambrose's, and Isidore's learned remarks about the nightingale were absorbed into the bestiaries and natural histories of the high and late Middle Ages, but it is the bird's beautifully warbling song that repeatedly made it the subject of early Christian poetry in Latin. For example, Paulinus of Nola (d. 431) compares his own hymns to the 'many tunes' and 'the sweet voice' of the 'bird of spring,' which 'with one tongue pours forth many voices, changing its tune'; and Venantius Fortunatus (d. ca. 600), in an Easter poem, singles out *filomela*, the nightingale, that fills the air with her sweet melody, praising God.[50] In the seventh century, the Spanish bishop and poet, Eugenius of Toledo (d. 657), wrote four short poems about the nightingale (*Carm.* 30–3). One of them is a riddle-like distich, in which the bird calls itself the 'companion of the night' and 'friend of sweet song'; a second distich and a brief dialogue are about the vigilant bird, which sings in its nest through the night,

---

47 See Ogilvy, *Books Known to the English*, 59; Gneuss, *Handlist*, nos 20, 61.5, 194, 778; Anderson Bankert, Wegmann, and Wright, *Ambrose in Anglo-Saxon England*.
48 Ambrose, *Exam.* 5.12.39, 5.24.85 (ed. Schenkl, CSEL 32.1:171, 199; trans. Savage, 193–4, 222).
49 Isidore of Seville, *Etym.* 12.7.37 (ed. André, 253; trans. adapted from Barney et al., 266).
50 Paulinus of Nola, *Carm.* 23.27–32 (ed. Hartel, CSEL 30.2:194–206); trans. Pfeffer, *Change of Philomel*, 26); Venantius Fortunatus, *Carm.* III.9.29–30 (ed. Leo, MGH AA 4.1:59–62).

making us sleep. In the fourth poem, the nightingale's charming song is said to surpass all human music and to cheer up the sad:

vox, philomela, tua curarum semina pellit,
   recreat et blandis anxia corda sonis.

Your voice, nightingale, dispels the seeds of care, it restores the anxious heart by its charming sounds.[51]

Eugenius's poems, whose variety and elegance inspired many imitators, are extant in a large number of manuscripts, including the tenth-century codex Paris, Bibliothèque Nationale, MS lat. 8440. Apart from Eugenius's verse, this anthology of Latin poetry also contains the riddles of Symphosius and Aldhelm and thus bears witness to the close affinity between medieval animal poetry and riddling.[52] One such link is precisely Aldhelm, whose *Enigmata* also include a poem about the nightingale, which not only is rooted in the tradition of Latin nightingale poetry, but actually combines this tradition with that of medieval riddling. In Aldhelm's poem – as in the Old English riddle – the bird is speaking:

Vox mea diversis variatur pulchra figuris,
Raucisonis numquam modulabor carmina rostris;
Spurca colore tamen, sed non sum spreta canendo:
Sic non cesso canens fato terrente futuro;
Nam me bruma fugat, sed mox aestate redibo.

My glorious voice warbles with various melodies: I shall never sing my songs with a harsh-sounding beak. For all that I am dusky in colour, yet I am not to be scorned for my singing; thus I do not cease singing in the face of a frightening future fate: for winter puts me to flight, but I shall return as soon as summer comes.[53]

---

51 Eugenius of Toledo, *Carm.* 33.5–6 (ed. Vollmer, MGH AA 14:254). Cf. *Ecbasis captivi*, 1063 (ed. Zeydel, 84): *Plectris dulcisonis curarum semina pellis*.
52 See *Catalogus codicum manuscriptorum bibliothecae regiae*, 3.2:459; Glorie, *Collectiones Aenigmatum Merovingicae Aetatis*, 159; Codoñer, 'Eugenius of Toledo'; Ziolkowski, *Talking Animals*, 42.
53 *Enigma* 22 (*Acalantida*) (ed. Glorie, *Collectiones Aenigmatum Merovingicae Aetatis*, 405; trans. Lapidge and Rosier, *Aldhelm: The Poetic Works*, 74). See Scott, 'Rhetorical and Symbolic Ambiguity,' 125–6.

Aldhelm's accomplished hexameters, in turn, informed the nightingale poem of another eminent Anglo-Saxon, namely, Alcuin of York (d. 804).[54] In his famous *Carmen* 61, Alcuin laments the loss of his bird, which brought him so much joy:

> Quae te dextra mihi rapuit, luscinia, ruscis,
>   Illa meae fuerat invida laetitiae.
> Tu mea dulcisonis implesti pectora musis,
>   Atque animum moestum carmine mellifluo.

> Nightingale in the broom, the hand which stole you from me was envious of my joy. You filled my heart with sweet-sounding poetry and my unhappy mind with honeyed song.[55]

The bird's 'swelling voice,' Alcuin continues, would produce 'sweet tunes in different melodies,' which were like 'odes to the Creator.' Even 'on gloomy nights,' his little companion would not stop praising God with 'sacred songs,' urging the pious to stay awake and follow her example:

> Hoc natura dedit, naturae et conditor almus,
>   Quem tu laudasti vocibus assiduis:
> Ut nos instrueres vino somnoque sepultos,
>   Somnigeram mentis rumpere segniciem.

> This was the gift of Nature and of Nature's kindly creator whom you praised with unceasing voice, in order to urge us when sodden with wine and slumber to shake off the idleness of our minds, clogged with sleep.[56]

From Alcuin to Fulbert of Chartres (d. 1028) and John Pecham (d. 1292), the tradition of Latin nightingale poetry continues into the late Middle Ages and beyond. There is no doubt that the author of the Exeter Book *Riddle* 8 was familiar with the long-established images and beliefs associated with this bird in natural history and poetry. For a model, the Old English poet could have turned to Aldhelm's *enigma*, but despite their identical subject, the two riddles have surprisingly little in common. While both

---

54 See Erhardt-Siebold, *Die lateinischen Rätsel*, 183; Ziolkowski, *Talking Animals*, 43.
55 Alcuin, *Carm.* 61.1–4 (ed. Dümmler, MGH PP 1:274–5; trans. Godman, *Poetry of the Carolingian Renaissance*, 145).
56 Ibid. (lines 19–22). Note the parallel in *Owl and the Nightingale*, 707–42 (ed. Stanley).

poems open with a reference to the nightingale's modulating voice and end with a clue about its migration, only Aldhelm alludes to the brownish colour of the nightingale's plumage (which does not seem to match the lovely song). The Old English riddle, on the other hand, focuses almost exclusively on the variety and musicality of the bird's song and therefore 'abounds in words for sound-making, speaking, and singing,' as Robert DiNapoli has observed.[57] Within only eleven lines, the author uses a spectacular succession of ten different verbs to echo the richly varied song: *sprece* 'I speak' (1); *singe* 'I sing' (2); *wrixle* 'I change' (2); *cirme* 'I cry out' (3); *healde* 'I hold' (4); *ne miþe* 'I do not refrain' (4); *bringe* 'I bring' (5); *styrme* 'I shout' (7); *onhyrge* 'I imitate' (10); and *bodige* 'I announce' (10). No fewer than eight different nouns refer to the song: the bird's 'languages' or 'speeches' (*reordum*, 1), the 'modulations' (*wrencum*, 2), the 'head-voice' (*heafodwoþe*, 3),[58] the 'tune' (*wisan*, 4), the 'melody' or 'singing' (*hleoþre*, 4), the varying 'sound' or 'voice' (*stefne*, 7), the 'jester's tunes' (*sceawendwisan*, 9), and simply the 'voice' (*woþe*, 11).

Many of these expressions correspond to those used both by Pliny in his section on the nightingale and by the medieval Latin poets quoted above, yet nowhere do we find such a concentration of terms and phrases that are 'associated with the making of poetry' and thereby enact 'the poem's central conceit of the songbird as poet.'[59]

The key to this conceit is again etymology. In a typical form of poetic anthropomorphism, the creature in the riddle is characterized as an 'evening poet' (*æfensceop*, 5) and an 'actress' (*scirenige*, 10), who – like a medieval minstrel – imitates 'a jester's tunes' (*sceawendwisan*, 9). The word *scirenige* has been interpreted as a variant form of *scericge*, meaning 'actress,' 'mime,' or 'female jester.'[60] As a feminine noun referring to a female person, it thus provides an important clue, since both Old English *nihtegale* and Latin *luscinia* (or *philomela*) are feminine, too.[61] Moreover, both terms – *æfensceop* and *scirenige* – are central to the riddle's etymological principle, in which the

---

57 DiNapoli, 'Kingdom of the Blind,' 433.
58 A hapax legomenon meaning the 'voice of/from the head,' that is, the sound uttered 'through the mouth' (1), but not the modern 'headvoice' in the sense of a higher register of the voice (cf. Williamson, *Old English Riddles*, 156–7).
59 DiNapoli, 'Kingdom of the Blind,' 433.
60 BT, s.v. *scericge*; Cosijn, 'Anglosaxonica,' 128; see Tupper, *Riddles of the Exeter Book*, 85–6; Williamson, *Old English Riddles*, 158.
61 However, only the male adult nightingale actually sings; see Cramp et al., *Birds of Europe*, 5:634–5. See also Trautmann, 'Das Geschlecht in den altenglischen Rätseln,' 325.

subject to be guessed names itself through the meaning of its name. The scheme is the same as in the preceding *Riddle 7*, where the name of the enigmatic creature is suggested by the three verbs – *swigian* 'to be silent'; *swogan* 'to sound'; and *swinsian* 'to make melody' – each of which functions as a poetic etymon of *swon* 'swan.' In the same way, here, the loudly singing 'evening poet' and the nightly 'actress' not only are descriptive clues, but are to be understood as etymologizing circumlocutions for the word *nihtegale*, the 'singer of the night.'

Yet what confuses us are the real humans, who are cryptically referred to as 'noblemen' (*eorlum*, 6) and 'heroes' (*hæleþum*, 10). Elsewhere in the *Riddles*, *eorl* and *hæleþ* are no more than synonyms of *mon* or *wer* and may be translated by 'man,' 'human being' or, in the plural, 'people.' Here, the two distinctly poetic terms must be seen as part of the songbird's literary vocabulary, which is deliberately elaborate and polysemous and is meant to mislead us, as if this singing *sceop* and actress were delivering her minstrelsy to a company of princely warriors. On closer inspection, though, the humans in this riddle are members of an urban community, who live in towns (*in burgum*, 6), occupying their houses or 'dwellings' (*wicum*, 7). There is a marked difference between these humans on the one side and the nightingale on the other, for the former remain completely 'quiet' (*stille*), while the latter cries out 'loudly' (*hlude*).[62] The adverb *hlude* is the only content word in the poem that occurs twice – once at the beginning (3) and again towards the end (10) – and it effectively frames the adjective *stille* in line 7, where the townspeople are said to be sitting at home 'in silence' (*swigende*, 8), raptly listening to the scurrilous chat.[63] These noble listeners are quiet and silent in their houses, while the solitary nightingale delivers its loud and exuberant song through the night. Such an antithetical pattern parallels that of the swan riddle (no. 7); yet here, the juxtaposition of animal and man and of sound and

---

62 The nightingale's song is indeed 'extremely vigorous,' with repeated loud sequences and characteristic phrases of crescendo (Cramp et al., *Birds of Europe*, 5:627, 634–5).

63 *Swigende* is an emendation of MS *nigende* (following Ettmüller, *Engla and Seaxna Scôpas and Bôceras*, 292; Cosijn, 'Anglosaxonica,' 128; Tupper, *Riddles of the Exeter Book*, 8, 85; and Trautmann, *Die altenglischen Rätsel*, 6, 71); most other editors retain the MS reading and interpret it as an otherwise unrecorded variant form of *hnigende* 'bending' or 'bowing down' (as first suggested by Grein, *Bibliothek der angelsächsischen Poesie*, 374). The latter might be explained as an echo of Alcuin, *Carm.* 61.21 (*vino somnoque sepultos*), but it is perhaps safer to opt for *swigende*, which fits in perfectly, both metrically – note the additional alliteration – as well as contextually. Cf. *Riddle* 48.2–4, where *swigende* similarly contrasts with the shouting of a 'loud voice' (*hlude stefne*), and *Riddle* 85.1: *swige ... hlud*.

silence creates an oscillating drama of outside and inside, nature and civilization. The author's rhetoric of personification and etymology, however, makes the man-like songbird a figure for the Old English riddle-poet: like the nightingale, the riddle-maker performs his verbal art for the noble and lettered members of Anglo-Saxon society. Hence, the virtuoso *æfensceop* resembles the native English poet, whose powerful song explores the literary registers and voices of vernacular verse in response to the authoritative tradition of Latin poetry, which he seeks to emulate and outdo.

3 Crossings: Combinatorial and Numerical Riddles

The *Disputatio Pippini cum Albino* is not the only didactical work associated with the name of Alcuin of York. The Anglo-Saxon scholar and poet is also believed to be the author – or at least the compiler – of a collection of some fifty mathematical problems in Latin prose, known as *Propositiones ad acuendos iuvenes*. These short 'Problems to Sharpen the Young' belong to the genre of recreational mathematics and were probably written – like Alcuin's *Disputatio* – for the Court of Charlemagne.[1] Many of the *Propositiones* show close affinities to the riddling questions of the early medieval wisdom dialogues as well as to the Latin *enigmata* and the Old English *Riddles*. These interconnections are strikingly illustrated by the fact that in the late tenth-century Codex Augiensis 205, not only are Alcuin's mathematical problems referred to as *enigmata*, but they are also immediately followed by a short series of anonymous riddles in Latin, the so-called *Reichenau Riddles* (discussed below). Moreover, in another continental manuscript from the monastery of Saint-Martial at Limoges, written by Ademar of Chabannes in 1023–5, the *Propositiones* are transmitted, among other texts, together with the riddles of Symphosius.[2]

The structural parallels between problems and riddles proper lie primarily in the question-and-answer pattern of the *Propositiones*, each of which is followed by its solution in most of the thirteen surviving manuscripts. Furthermore, nearly all problems feature a concluding formula

---

1 See Jullien and Perelman, *Clavis des auteurs latins du moyen âge*, 482–5. The critical edition is Folkerts, *Die älteste mathematische Aufgabensammlung*.
2 MS Leiden, Bibliotheek der Rijksuniversiteit, Voss. lat. Oct. 15. See Glorie, *Collectiones Aenigmatum Merovingicae Aetatis*, 614; Folkerts, *Die älteste mathematische Aufgabensammlung*, 19.

similar to those of the Latin and Old English riddles, such as 'Dic, qui potest,' 'Solvat, qui potest,' and 'Dic, rogo, sapiens.'[3] But there are also parallels in terms of subject matter: for instance, Alcuin's three combinatorial problems about people marrying each other's siblings or parents deal with confusing constellations among family members, which are similar to those described in the so-called relationship or kinship riddles. The problem about a father and his son marrying a young woman and her mother, respectively, may serve as an example:

> PROPOSITIO DE PATRE ET FILIO ET VIDUA EIUSQUE FILIA.
> Si relictam vel viduam et filiam illius in coniugium ducant pater et filius, sic tamen, ut filius accipiat matrem et pater filiam, filii, qui ex his fuerint procreati, dic, quaeso, quali cognatione sibi iungantur.
> ABOUT A FATHER AND A SON AND A WIDOW AND HER DAUGHTER.
> If a relict, or widow, and her daughter take a father and son in marriage, so that the son marries the mother and the father the daughter, what, please tell me, is the relationship of their sons?[4]

The answer is that the two sons are both uncle and nephew to one another. In the Latin tradition of the *Ioca monachorum*, such humorous puzzles about paradoxical family constellations often deal with biblical figures, as does the Old English *Riddle* 46. Its domestic setting depicts Lot, the Old Testament patriarch, as a man drinking wine with his two incestuous daughters and their two sons:

> Wer sæt æt wine   mid his wifum twam
> ond his twegen suno   ond his twa dohtor,
> swase gesweostor,   ond hyra suno twegen,
> freolico frumbearn;   fæder wæs þær inne
> þara æþelinga,   æghwæðres mid   5
> eam ond nefa.   Ealra wæron fife
> eorla ond idesa   insittendra.[5]

---

3 See Orchard, 'Enigma Variations,' 289 and n35.
4 *Propositio* 11b (ed. Folkerts, *Die älteste mathematische Aufgabensammlung*, 51; trans. adapted from Hadley and Singmaster, 'Problems to Sharpen the Young,' 109). See Folkerts, 'Die Alkuin zugeschriebenen *Propositiones*,' 279; Singmaster, 'Some of Alcuin's Propositions,' 22.
5 *Riddle* 46 (ASPR 3:205; my punctuation).

A man sat at wine with his two wives and his two sons and his two daughters, dear sisters, and their two sons, noble first-born children. In there was the father of these noble youths, [who were] at the same time each other's uncle and nephew. In all there were five men and women sitting within.

The source for this bizarre muddle is Genesis 19.30–8, where Lot's daughters ply their father with wine and sleep with him so that each becomes pregnant with a son. In the riddler's language, the intoxicating wine is disguised as an innocent drink at the family table; and yet something seems to be wrong in this household: how can a man and two wives with their two sons, two daughters, and two grandsons make a family of only five people? The explanation is that Lot's two daughters are also his 'wives,' so that their two sons (Moab and Ben-Ammi) – like the two sons in Alcuin's problem – are at once each other's uncle and nephew. The numbers seem paradoxical because they do not add up, but rather express the relationships among the five family members involved.[6] Similar riddles about Lot and his offspring also occur in various early modern collections, which suggests that this is a truly universal puzzle with a long history in literature and folklore.[7] Clearly, the Old English Lot riddle and Alcuin's kinship problems ultimately stem from one tradition: they operate with the same rhetorical strategies and require from the reader the same kind of combinatorial wit.

The Warriors Embark (*Riddle* 22)

The *Propositiones ad acuendos iuvenes* were composed to exercise the skills of computation alongside those of logical thinking. As the oldest collection of recreational mathematics in the west, they contain arithmetical, geometrical, and combinatorial problems, many of which occur here for the first time. Among these are the four so-called river-crossing problems.[8] They are typically concerned with a group of people or objects that have to be transported over a river, using a boat that is too small to carry all of them at same time. In one of these 'river-crossing problems,' three jealous friends and their three sisters, who are individually coveted by the three men, need to get across; in another, there is a family with two children, but the boat can

---

6 Barley, 'Structural Aspects,' 164.
7 See the Hebrew, German, Scandinavian, and English analogues listed by Tupper, *Riddles of the Exeter Book*, 178.
8 See Folkerts, 'Die Alkuin zugeschriebenen *Propositiones*,' 279, 281; Singmaster, 'Some of Alcuin's Propositions,' 19–21; Gropp, '*Propositio de lupo et capra et fasciculo cauli.*'

take either one adult or both children. Each time, this can be achieved only through a number of rowings across and back, involving different combinations of passengers (or cargo). Well known from numerous later versions in many languages throughout the world is the problem about a man who has to transport a wolf, a goat, and a load of cabbages, without any of them suffering damage:

PROPOSITIO DE LUPO ET CAPRA ET FASCICULO CAULI.
Homo quidam debebat ultra fluvium transferre lupum et capram et fasciculum cauli, et non potuit aliam navem invenire, nisi quae duos tantum ex ipsis ferre valebat. Praeceptum itaque ei fuerat, ut omnia haec ultra omnino illaesa transferret. Dicat, qui potest, quomodo eos illaesos ultra transferre potuit.

SOLUTIO.
Simili namque tenore ducerem prius capram et dimitterem foris lupum et caulum. Tum deinde venirem lupumque ultra transferrem, lupoque foras misso rursus capram navi receptam ultra reducerem, capraque foras missa caulum transveherem ultra, atque iterum remigassem, capramque assumptam ultra duxissem. Sicque faciente facta erit remigatio salubris absque voragine lacerationis.

ABOUT A WOLF, A GOAT AND A BUNCH OF CABBAGES.
A man had to take a wolf, a goat and a bunch of cabbages across a river. The only boat he could find could only take two of them at a time. But he had been ordered to transfer all of these to the other side in good condition. How could this be done?

SOLUTION.
I would take the goat and leave the wolf and the cabbage. Then I would return and take the wolf across. Having put the wolf on the other side I would take the goat back over. Having left that behind, I would take the cabbage across. I would then row across again, and having picked up the goat take it over once more. By this procedure there would be some healthy rowing, but no lacerating catastrophe.[9]

In a similar fashion, Exeter Book *Riddle* 22 tells a strange story of sixty warriors who want to get across a stretch of water with their horses, yet the water is not shallow enough for them to wade through it. The opening lines read:

---

9 *Propositio* 18 (ed. Folkerts, *Die älteste mathematische Aufgabensammlung*, 54–5; trans. Hadley and Singmaster, 'Problems to Sharpen the Young,' 112).

Crossings: Combinatorial and Numerical Riddles 61

> Ætsomne cwom   LX monna
> to wægstæþe   wicgum ridan;
> hæfdon XI   eoredmæcgas
> fridhengestas,   IIII sceamas.
> Ne meahton magorincas   ofer mere feolan,   5
> swa hi fundedon,   ac wæs flod to deop,
> atol yþa geþræc,   ofras hea,
> streamas stronge.

Sixty men together came to the shore, riding horses; the horsemen had eleven [stately?] stallions, four white horses. [5] The young warriors could not pass over the sea as they aspired, but the flood was too deep, dire [was] the press of the waves, the banks [were] high, the currents strong.

The whole company then mounts a mysterious 'wagon' (*wægn*, 9), which carries both men and horses to the other side, where they disembark in safety:

> Ongunnon stigan þa
> on wægn weras   ond hyra wicg somod
> hlodan under hrunge;   þa þa hors oðbær   10
> eh ond eorlas,   æscum dealle,
> ofer wætres byht   wægn to lande,
> swa hine oxa ne teah   ne esna mægen
> ne fæthengest,   ne on flode swom,
> ne be grunde wod   gestum under,   15
> ne lagu drefde,   ne of lyfte fleag,
> ne under bæc cyrde;   brohte hwæþre
> beornas ofer burnan   ond hyra bloncan mid
> from stæðe heaum,   þæt hy stopan up
> on oþerne,   ellenrofe,   20
> weras of wæge,   ond hyra wicg gesund.[10]

Then the men began to climb on a wagon, and loaded their horses [10] together under the pole; then the wagon bore the horses, steeds and noblemen, proud of their spears, across the abode of the water to the land; yet no ox drew it, nor the strength of servants, nor a draught[?]-horse, nor did it swim on the flood, [15] nor wade on the bottom beneath [its] guests, nor did

---

10 *Riddle* 22, 1–21 (ASPR 3:191–2, except line 16: *on lyfte* for MS *of lyfte*).

it stir up the sea, nor fly from the air, nor turn back. Nevertheless it brought the warriors over the stream from the high shore, and their white horses with them, so that they stepped up [20] on the other side, the brave men from the sea and their horses safe and sound.

Poetic periphrasis and lexical variation are driven to extremes in this riddle. A plethora of words and synonyms used for the men and their horses circumscribe and constantly reinvent the protagonists of this seemingly simple narrative, and yet they are evasive in their persistence, as things become increasingly unclear with each new term the author adds. There are as many as eight distinct words for the men (*monna*, 1; *eoredmæcgas*, 3; *magorincas*, 5; *weras*, 9 and 21; *eorlas*, 11; *gestum*, 15; *beornas*, 18; and *ellenrofe*, 20) and seven for their horses (*wicg*, 2, 9 and 21; *fridhengestas*, 4; *sceamas*, 4; *hors*, 10; *eh*, 11; *fæthengest*, 14; and *bloncan*, 18),[11] and eight different expressions are used for the body of water they cross (*mere*, 5; *flod*, 6 and 14; *yþa geþræc*, 7; *streamas*, 8; *wætres byht*, 12; *lagu*, 16; *burnan*, 18: *wæge*, 21). Even the shore or bank on either side of the water is first called *wægstæþe* (2), then *ofras* (7), *lande* (12), and finally *stæde* (19). For the strange 'wagon' or 'wain,' by contrast, no synonyms are used. Instead, the same word – *wægn* – occurs twice (9 and 12), and the only detail that is furnished is the 'pole' (*hrunge*, 10), which some have taken to refer to the cross-beam supporting the covering over the wagon.[12] This unique *wægn* thus literally moves from one shore to the other, driven, as it were, by the alliterating words and synonyms washing around it. Yet from the long anaphoric string of negatives with *ne* in lines 13–17, it is clear that this 'wagon' is neither an ordinary vehicle, such as a cart drawn by an animal, nor a vessel like the boat in Alcuin's river-crossing problems.

The subject of *Riddle* 22, in fact, is neither the crossing of a river, nor a 'bridge,' nor the 'month of December' (as some early critics suggested). Rather, the riddle describes the movement of stars in the night sky, more precisely, the group of stars in the constellation of the Great Bear (Ursa Major) known in English as 'Charles's Wain' or 'The Plough.' This solution, which was first proposed in 1958 by L. Blakeley,[13] is sustained by an analogue in the

---

11 Cf. *Beowulf*, 856a (ed. Klaeber, 32): *beornas on blancum*.
12 A hapax legomenon; see Tupper, *Riddles of the Exeter Book*, 118; Trautmann, *Die altenglischen Rätsel*, 84; Pinsker and Ziegler, *Die altenglischen Rätsel*, 195.
13 Blakeley, 'Riddles 22 and 58,' 241–7; recently supported by Murphy, 'Riders of the Celestial Wain.' See Fry, 'Exeter Book Riddle Solutions,' 23; Muir, *Exeter Anthology*, 658.

collection of Aldhelm, who knew Charles's Wain under its biblical name, 'Arcturus':

> Sidereis stipor turmis in vertice mundi:
> 'Esseda' famoso gesto cognomina vulgo;
> In giro volvens iugiter non vergo deorsum,
> Cetera ceu properant caelorum lumina ponto.
> Hac gaza ditor, quoniam sum proximus axi,   5
> Qui Ripheis Scithiae praelatus montibus errat,
> Vergilias numeris aequans in arce polorum;
> Pars cuius inferior Stigia Letheaque palude
> Fertur et inferni manibus succumbere nigris.

> At the summit of the universe I stand, hemmed in by starry throngs. I bear the name *esseda* ['war-chariot'] in common parlance. Revolving continually in a circle I never incline downwards, as do the other stars of the heavens (which) hasten to the sea. [5] I am enriched by this endowment, since I am nearest to the pole, which stands out above the Rhipaean mountains of Scythia [i.e., the far north]. I equal in number the Pleiades at the summit of the sky, the lower part of which is said to sink down in the Stygian or Lethean swamp among the black shades of hell.[14]

Aldhelm's hexameters are replete with learned allusions and book knowledge, exhibiting an ornate style that sets it clearly apart from the Old English *Riddle* 22, and yet on closer inspection, there are some striking correspondences between the two texts. For instance, Aldhelm says that the seven stars of Charles's Wain are always visible and 'never incline downwards' like other stars that dip below the horizon and literally sink into the sea; rather, they revolve 'continually in a circle' in the northern sky, the lower part of which was believed to touch the borders of the underworld (3). Similarly, the wagon in *Riddle* 22 does not 'turn back' (17) on its perilous journey across the deep water, while its

---

14 *Enigma* 53 (ed. Glorie, *Collectiones Aenigmatum Merovingicae Aetatis*, 443; trans. Lapidge and Rosier, *Aldhelm: The Poetic Works*, 80–1). The name 'Arcturus' occurs in Job 9.9, 38.31, discussed by Isidore, *De nat. rer.* 26.1. Actually, Arcturus is the name for the very brilliant star in the constellation Bootes in the northern hemisphere, while Charles's Wain or The Plough is the group of the seven prominent stars in the constellation Ursa Major (the Great Bear) near it; see *OED*, s.v. *Arcturus*, *Charles's Wain*, and so forth, and *DML* and *MLW*, s.v. *Arcturus*.

warlike passengers are unscathed by the floods beneath them. Indeed, Aldhelm's image of the celestial 'war-chariot' that keeps revolving above the drowning sea and hell appears to be recreated in the splendid *wægn*, which crosses from one bank to the other and yet, paradoxically, does not swim (*ne on flode swom*, 13) nor 'stir up the sea' (16). This becomes even more evident once we look into Aldhelm's source, namely, Isidore's *De natura rerum* (26.3), where Charles's Wain and its movements are described as follows:

> Arcturus ille est quem Latini Septentrionem dicunt, qui septem stellarum radiis fulgens in se ipso revolutus rotatur, qui ideo Plaustrum vocatur quia in modum vehiculi volvitur et modo tres ad summa elevat, modo quattuor inclinat. Hic autem in caeli axe constitutus semper versatur et numquam mergitur, sed dum in se ipso volvitur, et nox finitur.[15]
>
> Charles's Wain is named *Septentrio* in Latin. Shining brightly with its seven stars, it circles revolving in itself. It is called *Plaustrum* ['Wain'] because it rotates like a vehicle, now lifting three stars towards the zenith, now pulling four down. Placed on the heaven's axis, it always rotates and never sinks [below the horizon], but as it keeps rolling in itself, the night closes.

Isidore states that Arcturus is also known as *Septentrio* or *Plaustrum* in Latin, and that the latter name comes from its likeness to a vehicle or wagon (Lat. *plaustrum*). Aldhelm, too, was well aware that there were several names for this well-known asterism, and in his riddle he alludes to this fact by saying that 'in common parlance' (*vulgo*) the group of stars is called *esseda* 'war-chariot' (2). Ironically, as a Latin word, the poetic *esseda* is far from common and is not an actual name for any star or constellation; rather, it serves as a learned linguistic clue to the more familiar Latin term *Plaustrum* 'Wain,' which, if Aldhelm had used it instead, would give away the solution to the riddle. What is more, the word *esseda* also suggests its equivalent in the vernacular (*vulgo*) – that is, in English – since to the Anglo-Saxons the stars of Charles's Wain were, in fact, known as *wægn ~ wæn* or *Carles wæn*.[16] Of these, the short *wægn* is attested in early Old English verse and occurs in the Alfredian *Boethius*, where it renders the original Latin *Arcturi sidera* from Boethius's poetic description of Arcturus in his 'Consolation of

---

15 Fontaine, *Isidore de Séville*, 267; my capitalization of names; cf. Isidore, *Etym.* 3.71.6.
16 See BT, *DOE*, and *MCOE*, s.v.

Philosophy.'[17] The longer name *Carles wæn*, on the other hand, survives only in Ælfric's *De temporibus anni* (ca. 993), an eclectic work largely based on Isidore's *De natura rerum*, and the earliest astronomical treatise in the English language. Translating Isidore almost verbatim, Ælfric explains:

> Arcton hatte an tungel on norðdæle, se hæfð seofon steorran, and is forði oðrum naman gehaten Septemtrio, þone hatað læwede men Carles wæn, se ne gæð næfre adune under ðissere eorðan, swa swa oðre tunglan doð. Ac he went abutan hwilon up, hwilon adune, ofer dæg and ofer niht.[18]

> 'Arcton' is the name of a star in the northern sky; it has seven stars and is therefore also called 'Septentrio,' which people commonly call 'Charles's Wain.' It never goes down below this earth, as other stars do, but it turns around, sometimes up and sometimes down, throughout the day and throughout the night.

All this evidence strongly suggests that *Riddle 22* describes the asterism invariably identified in Latin and English as Arcturus, Plaustrum, Wain, or Charles's Wain. The majestic wagon that crosses the sea without help, yet neither swims nor wades nor flies 'from the air' (16), must denote the group of stars in the northern sky whose circling movements Isidore and Ælfric describe in their cosmological writings and that Aldhelm had already made the subject of one of his *enigmata*. Within the poem's dense web of metaphors, the central image of the crossing wagon serves as both a hub and an etymological clue to the riddle's solution, OE *wægn* or *Carles wægn*.

As an image for the movement of the heavenly bodies, the wagon was, of course, known from classical mythology. Alcuin, for instance, uses it in his *Disputatio Pippini cum Albino* when he compares the astronomical year to a four-horse chariot that moves through the zodiac. Pippin asks his master about the course of the year, and Alcuin replies in his characteristically poetic fashion:

PIPPINUS: Quid est annus?
ALBINUS: Quadriga mundi.

---

17 Blakeley, 'Riddles 22 and 58,' 243. See Alfred's *Boethius* 39.3 and *Metre* 28.10 (ed. Sedgefield, *King Alfred's Old English Version*, 126, 198); the original passage is Boethius, *Consolatio philosophiae* 4.c.5.
18 Ælfric, *De temporibus anni* 9.6 (ed. Henel, 68; my punctuation).

66   Contexts

PIPPINUS: Quis ducit eam?
ALBINUS: Nox et dies, frigus et calor.
PIPPINUS: Quis est auriga eius?
ALBINUS: Sol et luna.
PIPPINUS: Quot habent palatia?
ALBINUS: Duodecim.
PIPPINUS: Qui sunt praetores palatiorum?
ALBINUS: Aries, Taurus, Gemini, Cancer, Leo, Virgo, Libra, Scorpius, Sagittarus, Capricornus, Aquarius, Pisces.
PIPPINUS: Quot dies habitant in uno quoque palatio?
ALBINUS: Sol XXX dies et decem semis horas; luna duos dies et octo [recte: sex] horas et bisse unius horae.[19]

PIPPIN: What is the year?
ALCUIN: A four-horse chariot of the world.
PIPPIN: Who pulls it?
ALCUIN: Night and day, cold and heat.
PIPPIN: Who is the charioteer?
ALCUIN: The sun and the moon.
PIPPIN: How many palaces do they have?
ALCUIN: Twelve.
PIPPIN: Who are the governors of these palaces?
ALCUIN: Aries, Taurus, Gemini, Cancer, Leo, Virgo, Libra, Scorpio, Sagittarius, Capricorn, Aquarius, and Pisces.
PIPPIN: How many days do they stay in each palace?
ALCUIN: The sun [stays] thirty days and ten half-hours; the moon two days and six hours and two thirds of an hour.

Here, Alcuin playfully summarizes what he more fully expounded in his letters to Charlemagne and what he knew from the computistical and cosmological writings that were in circulation at the time, notably Bede's *De temporum ratione* and *De natura rerum* (which builds upon Isidore of Seville's earlier treatise of the same name).[20] In the early Middle Ages, the

---

19 *Disputatio* 68–73 (ed. Suchier, 'Disputatio Pippini cum Albino,' 140).
20 Alcuin, *Epist.* 148, 155 (ed. Dümmler, MGH EPP 4:238–9, 250); cf. Bede, *De temporum ratione*, 39, and *De natura rerum*, 21. According to all authorities, the duration for the moon is two days, six hours, and two-thirds of an hour; the *octo* in Alcuin's *Disputatio*, therefore, is a mistake for *sex*, as Wilmanns in his edition ('Disputatio regalis et nobilissimi iuvenis Pippini cum Albino scholastico,' 551) correctly observes.

science of *computus* and astronomy was fundamental to the reckoning of Easter and other movable feasts, and in Anglo-Saxon England, in particular, there was a deep interest in ecclesiastical computation, which culminated in the well-known Easter controversy. Bede (*Hist. eccl.* 4.2) reports that *computus* and astronomy were taught in the celebrated school of Theodore and Hadrian at Canterbury, where Aldhelm was trained. In one of his letters, Aldhelm himself talks about his studies of computation and the zodiac; but his profound knowledge of astronomy is arguably best evident in his *Enigmata*, several of which deal with heavenly bodies and stellar constellations.[21]

Riddle 22 should be seen in this typically Anglo-Saxon context of monastic cosmology, riddle-making, and recreational mathematics. But why are there sixty men in the Old English riddle, and why do they have fifteen horses? Or are there only eleven horses, four of them being white ones? The sources agree that Arcturus has seven bright stars, which – according to Isidore – revolve in two groups of three (*tres*) and four (*quattuor*) stars. The latter may account for the 'four white horses' (*IIII sceamas*, 4) in the Old English text, but the remaining numbers simply do not add up. If the number sixty just refers to an indefinitely large amount of stars – as Blakeley holds – then the troop of warriors who embark on the *wægn* perhaps stand for what Aldhelm calls the 'starry throngs' (1) that encompass the seven stars of Arcturus or Charles's Wain.[22] Whatever these numbers exactly mean, *Riddle* 22 evidently describes the moving yet constant stars in the vast northern sky. Much weight is given in the narrative to these mysterious travellers, and it is this strong personification that distinguishes the Old English riddle from its Latin counterparts and creates a typically heroic setting for the natural phenomenon described. With their spears and their stately horses, this troop of brave noblemen (*eorlas*, 11) appear strangely unreal and archaic. In the end, when they all disembark on the other side, their crossing is represented as a heroic act, since the author now refers to them as the 'brave ones' (*ellenrofe*, 20), worthy of being remembered alongside the seafaring heroes of Old English poetry. It is in this shift of focus and mode that we again find the author's attempt to adopt and recreate in the vernacular a subject

---

21 Aldhelm, *Epist.* 1 (trans. Lapidge and Herren, *Aldhelm: The Prose Works*, 153). For the various cosmological subjects in the Latin *enigmata*, see Erhardt-Siebold, *Die lateinischen Rätsel*, 241–9, 258–61, and the 'Index systematicus' in Glorie, *Collectiones Aenigmatum Merovingicae Aetatis*, 913.
22 Blakeley, 'Riddles 22 and 58,' 244–5.

known from the Latin riddling tradition. However, there is nothing of the erudite rhetoric and mythological paraphernalia of Aldhelm's polished verse, nothing of the spirited humour of Alcuin's river-crossing problems and riddle dialogue. Instead, the movement of the heavens and the stars is presented as a ghostly pageant of heroic warriors carrying their arms and leading their horses over the battleground of the elements.

Numerical Monsters (*Riddles* 86 and 36)

From the evidence that can be gleaned from the extant manuscripts, it is safe to say that numerical puzzles in Latin were widely disseminated in the Middle Ages, and that the boundaries between recreational mathematics on the one side and literary riddling on the other must have been fluid. Mathematical problems often employ narrative structures akin to those of descriptive riddles, while numbers and number games have always been occasional elements in riddles, ancient, medieval, and modern.[23] In many of them, numbers enumerate things or parts of what they describe and thus serve as clues to lead the reader to the solution. But often numbers may also simply confuse and mislead the reader. Symphosius's three-liner about the grotesque 'one-eyed garlic-seller' (*Luscus alium vendens*) is a famous example:

> Cernere iam fas est quod vix tibi credere fas est:
> Unus inest oculus, capitum sed milia multa.
> Qui quod habet vendit, quod non habet unde parabit?
>
> Now may you see what you scarcely may believe: one eye within, but many thousand heads. Whence shall he, who sells what he has, procure what he has not?[24]

The 'thousand heads' (2) are the garlic bulbs, while the 'one eye within' (2) belongs to the vendor, who sells thousands of his 'heads' but himself, alas,

---

23 For the use of numbers in the Anglo-Latin riddles, see Erhardt-Siebold, *Die lateinischen Rätsel der Angelsachsen*, 256–61. The frequent appearance of animals in the problems further links them to the tradition of Latin fable literature; not surprisingly, three of the thirteen extant manuscripts of the *Propositiones* also contain the fables of Avian and Aesop-Romulus; see Folkerts, *Die älteste mathematische Aufgabensammlung*, 19–20, 33–4.

24 *Aenigma* 95 (ed. Glorie, *Collectiones Aenigmatum Merovingicae Aetatis*, 716; trans. Ohl, ibid.)

remains one-eyed because he cannot trade a 'head' for an eye. The comical little poem is one of perhaps six riddles by Symphosius that found their way into the Exeter Book. In the Old English version, the one-eyed man is portrayed as a monstrous *wiht* walking among ordinary people:

> Wiht cwom gongan, þær weras sæton
> monige on mæðle, mode snottre;
> hæfde an eage ond earan twa,
> ond II fet, XII hund heafda,
> hrycg ond wombe ond honda twa, 5
> earmas ond eaxle, anne sweoran
> ond sidan twa. Saga hwæt ic hatte.[25]

A creature came walking where men were sitting, many in an assembly, wise in mind. It had one eye and two ears and two feet, twelve hundred heads, [5] a back and a belly and two hands, arms and shoulders, one neck and two sides. Say what I am called.

To Symphosius's eye and heads, the Old English author adds his expanded catalogue of body parts, which he neatly enumerates around the freakish 'twelve hundred heads' (*XII hund heafda*, 4) in the middle of the poem. Nothing is said about the man's activity as a vendor or pedlar of garlic, however, and – as many critics have noted – if there were no Latin source identifying the subject, the Old English riddle would remain utterly obscure and insoluble. Instead, the Old English poet contrasts the outlandish 'creature' with an almost equally strange assembly of wise men. In the *Riddles*, this 'conventional *locus* of the wisdom tradition' is usually employed with reference to the 'wise readers' who are able to solve the riddle.[26] Here, this topos is given an ironic twist: the wise men already know and see what the reader has yet to find out.

Numerical monsters like the one-eyed garlic-seller also haunt the Anglo-Latin riddle collections. Aldhelm's tetrastich about a 'Woman Giving Birth to Twins' is a case in point. The riddle gains its comic effect from its absurd enumeration of body parts:

> Sunt mihi sex oculi, totidem simul auribus hausi,
> Sed digitos decies senos in corpore gesto;

---

25 *Riddle* 86 (ASPR 3:238).
26 DiNapoli, 'Kingdom of the Blind,' 453.

70 Contexts

> Ex quibus ecce quater denis de carne revulsis
> Quinquies at tantum video remanere quaternos.
>
> I have six eyes, I listen at the same time with as many ears, but I have sixty digits on the body; when forty of these have been ripped from my flesh, I seem to retain only twenty.[27]

Outside Aldhelm's 100 *Enigmata*, the same riddle also survives in the eighth-century miscellany of pseudo-Bede, where it was compiled together with the following short prose version:

> Vidi mulierem cum sex oculis, cum sexaginta digitis, cum tribus linguis, cum uno ore loquentem.
>
> I saw a woman with six eyes, with sixty digits, with three tongues, speaking with one mouth.[28]

The subject goes back to Symphosius, who wrote a very similar three-line riddle about 'A Woman Pregnant with Twins' (*Aenigma* 93). Aldhelm was so fond of the theme that he further elaborated upon it in his riddle about a 'Pregnant Sow.' This time, the numbers are grotesquely multiplied to six heads, twelve eyes, twenty-four feet, and no fewer than ninety-six 'nails':

> Nunc mihi sunt oculi bis seni in corpore solo
> Bis ternumque caput, sed cetera membra gubernant.
> Nam gradior pedibus suffultus bis duodenis,
> Sed decies novem sunt et sex corporis ungues.
>
> Now I have twice six eyes in a single body; and twice three heads; but they are controlled by my other limbs. I walk sustained by twice twelve feet, but there are ninety-six nails on my body.[29]

The 'twice three heads' are those of the mother sow and her five piglets; hence, together they have twelve eyes, twenty-four feet, and 'ninety-six nails,' which are the mother's sixteen digits plus those of the young. There

---

27 *Enigma* 90 (ed. Glorie, *Collectiones Aenigmatum Merovingicae Aetatis*, 509; trans. Bayless and Lapidge, *Collectanea Pseudo-Bedae*, 145).
28 *Collectanea* 199 (ed. and trans. Bayless and Lapidge, 144–5).
29 *Enigma* 84.1–4 (ed. Glorie, *Collectiones Aenigmatum Merovingicae Aetatis*, 503; trans. adapted from Lapidge and Rosier, *Aldhelm: The Poetic Works*, 88).

are six perfectly normal pigs in all, yet the subject of the riddle appears to be far from domestic, but rather to belong to the monstrous races that inhabit the initials and marginal zones of medieval manuscripts and maps. In Old English literature, similar representations of otherness occur in texts such as the *Marvels of the East* and the *Letter of Alexander to Aristotle* (both preserved in the *Beowulf* manuscript) in their accounts of outlandish monstrosities and purported wonders of the Orient, including dog-headed men and polycephalous beasts.[30] Against this backdrop of the exotic and fantastic, the innocent garlic-seller, the mother with twins, and the pregnant sow become shape-shifting creatures who mask their true identities behind our cultural concepts of the normal and the abnormal.

The same kind of grotesque humour informs other Exeter Book *Riddles* operating with numbers. For instance, the enigmatic creature of *Riddle* 36 (which most commentators take to be a ship) has twelve feet, two wings, twelve eyes, and six heads. To make things even more abstruse, the poem contains some cryptic writing that does not fit into the surrounding text and appears to be a scribal interpolation. It consists of a sequence of three words in Old English, each of which is followed by its encrypted Latin equivalent. As it stands in the manuscript, the sequence interrupts the two halves of what is actually line 4 of the Old English text:

```
Ic wiht geseah   on wege feran,
seo wæs wrætlice   wundrum gegierwed.
Hæfde feowre   fet under wombe
ond ehtuwe
monn · h · w · M · wiif · m · x · l · kf wf · hors · qxxs ·        5
         ufon on hrycge;
hæfde tu fiþru   ond twelf eagan
ond siex heafdu.   Saga hwæt hio wære.
For flodwegas;   ne wæs þæt na fugul ana,
ac þær wæs æghwylces   anra gelicnes                              10
horses ond monnes,   hundes ond fugles,
ond eac wifes wlite.   Þu wast, gif þu const,
to gesecganne,   þæt we soð witan,
hu þære wihte   wise gonge.³¹
```

---

30 For the *Marvels of the East* and the *Letter of Alexander*, their Latin sources, and their connections to the possibly Anglo-Saxon *Liber monstrorum*, see Orchard, *Pride and Prodigies*.
31 *Riddle* 36 (ASPR 3:198; my italics).

I saw a creature travel on the way; it was splendidly [and] wondrously adorned. It had four feet under the belly and eight above on the back. [5] *Man homo, woman mulier, horse equus.* It had two wings and twelve eyes and six heads. Say what it was. It crossed the watery ways; it was not a bird alone, [10] but there was the likeness of each of these: a horse and a man, a dog and a bird, and also the shape of a woman. You know how to say, if you can, so that we may know the truth, what the nature of this creature is.

Whether the encoded line belongs to the original text or was added by the copyist, we do not know. Perhaps it was taken from a marginal note in the scribe's exemplar and mistakenly copied into the text in an awkward attempt to provide a clue about the riddle's solution. Whatever its original purpose, the cryptographic system behind it was widely known in the early Middle Ages, and is sometimes referred to as *notae sancti Bonifatii*. The code is explained in a short treatise about alphabets and letters (*De inventione linguarum*) that has been printed under the name of Hrabanus Maurus (d. 856), who was a student of Alcuin's at Tours before he became Abbot of Fulda and Archbishop of Mainz.[32] In this treatise, the transmission of secret writing practices is attributed to Saint Boniface (d. 754), the famous Anglo-Saxon missionary to Germany and author of twenty Latin verse riddles. As Bernhard Bischoff writes: 'According to the short tract *De inventione linguarum* ... Boniface transmitted two systems of cipher in which the vowels *a e i o u* were expressed by points or by the immediately following consonants *b f k p x*; the latter system goes back to antiquity. English examples of the use of this cipher make the tradition plausible.'[33] Both in early England and on the continent, the Bonifatian method of vowel substitution was mostly used in scribal subscriptions and short notes, yet interestingly, the same system could also be employed to encode the solutions to riddles. In an eleventh-century Symphosius manuscript (Vatican City, BAV, Barb. lat. 721), for instance, the titles of most riddles are given in ciphers, such as *GRBPHKXM* (for *GRAPHIUM* 'stylus'), *CBTFNB* (for *CATENA* 'chain'), *CXCXRBKTB* (for *CUCURBITA* 'gourd'), and so on.[34] Another, even earlier example

---

32 The text is in PL 112:1579–84. The passage concerning the 'notae sancti Bonifatii' has been edited by Levison, *England and the Continent*, 291–2, and Derolez, *Runica Manuscripta*, 353. For examples in early English and continental manuscripts, see Levison, *England and the Continent*, 292–4, and Tupper, *Riddles of the Exeter Book*, 155.
33 Bischoff, *Latin Palaeography*, 177.
34 See Finch, 'Codex Vat. Barb. Lat. 721, 175; Orchard, 'Enigma Variations,' 285.

is the already mentioned manuscript of Alcuin's *Propositiones*, Codex Augiensis 205, a late tenth-century class-book written at Reichenau Abbey. Here, too, the code is playfully used in one of the titles, which reads: *Propositio de cursu cbnks bc fxgb lfpprks*, that is: *Propositio de cursu canis ac fuga leporis* 'Problem About a Pursuing Dog and a Fleeing Hare.'[35] Moreover, the same manuscript also contains, attached to Alcuin's *Propositiones*, six anonymous, short riddles in Latin, the so-called *Reichenau Riddles*, which are grouped under the heading *Enigmata rkskbklkb*, that is, *Enigmata risibilia* or 'Amusing Riddles.'[36] Here, the encrypted title indicates the technique of Bonifatian vowel substitution used in the riddles, each of which is followed by its solution in secret writing. One of these is the ubiquitous 'ship':

Portat animam et non habet animam:
non ambulat super terram neque in caelo.
Naxks [= Navis].[37]

It carries a soul, yet is has no soul;
it does not travel on the earth or in the sky.
Ship.

As Seth Lerer has shown, a similar cryptographic code was used by the anonymous glossator who annotated Aldhelm's *Enigmata* in the eleventh-century 'Cambridge Songs' manuscript (Cambridge, UL Gg.5.35). Here, the marginal and interlinear glosses such as *ut MFP* (for *ut LEO* 'like a lion') or *ut NPOT ethnae* (for *ut MONS ethnae* 'like Mount Etna') explicate some of the concepts in Aldhelm's 'Creation' riddle. In these examples, both vowels and consonants are substituted by the letters following them in the alphabet, to the effect that these glosses sustain the enigmatic process and 'multiply the puzzles in the poem.'[38]

---

35 Alcuin, *Propositiones ad acuendos iuvenes*, 26 (ed. Folkerts, *Die älteste mathematische Aufgabensammlung*, 59); cf. ibid., 17.
36 The *Reichenau Riddles* are edited by Müllenhoff and Scherer, *Denkmäler deutscher Poesie und Prosa*, 13–14; see Schupp, *Deutsches Rätselbuch*, 30–1, 280, 315; Tomasek, *Das deutsche Rätsel im Mittelalter*, 129–30. For the manuscript (Karlsruhe, Badische Landesbibliothek, Codex Augiensis 205), see Holder, *Die Reichenauer Handschriften*, 1:466–9; Autenrieth, 'Purcharts Gesta Witigowonis im Codex Augiensis CCV.'
37 *Reichenau Riddle* 2 (ed. Müllenhoff and Scherer, *Denkmäler deutscher Poesie und Prosa*, 13).
38 Lerer, *Literacy and Power*, 110.

In the cryptogram of the Exeter *Riddle* 36, only the vowels are transposed. However, the scribe evidently had some trouble with the code, writing an Anglo-Saxon 'wynn' instead of 'p' and 'r' while omitting or jumbling other letters.[39] Correctly deciphered, the three Latin words are *homo, mulier*, and *equus*, translating Old English *monn* 'man,' *wiif* 'woman' and *hors* 'horse.' Together they seem to account for the eight feet on the enigmatic creature's back, as suggested by some critics who argue for the solution 'ship.'[40] The riddle, they point out, describes a ship at sea, carrying a man, a woman, and a horse – and perhaps a dog; but otherwise, interpretations vary. Williamson, for example, disregarding the interpolated line completely, suggests that 'the four feet under the ship's belly are the oars; the eight feet above belong to the four oarsmen. The wings are sails; the twelve eyes and six heads belong to the four oarsmen and two figureheads fore and aft ... The shape of the horse is the ship itself ('sea-horse' is a common kenning for 'ship') with its birdlike sail. The man is a sailor. The likeness of the dog and the face of a woman may describe the figure-heads.'[41] Williamson certainly has a point, especially in comparing this riddle to the runic *Riddles* 19 and 64, which represent the ship as a metaphorical 'sea-horse,' whose sails are likened to a bird. In *Riddle* 36, it seems, neither should what the author describes be taken literally. Rather, the people and animals mentioned in lines 10–12 are only a 'likeness' (*gelicnes*, 10) and a 'shape' (*wlite*, 12) of the creature's true 'nature' (14), and therefore they denote something else. But it is the author's playing with numbers that leaves us baffled and makes more detailed explanation conjectural or arbitrary.

Dead Ends (*Riddle* 90)

It is true that whenever numbers are involved in the Exeter Book *Riddles*, they tend to obscure rather than elucidate the subject described. So perplexing can numbers be that numerical riddles are often particularly hard to solve, and many of them even defy solution. One of these is *Riddle* 90, the only item in the Exeter collection – and, in fact, in the entire manuscript – that is written in Latin:

---

39 See ASPR 3:341; Dewa, 'Runic Riddles,' 34–5; Orchard, 'Oral Tradition,' 114–17.
40 See Fry, 'Exeter Book Riddle Solutions,' 24; Muir, *Exeter Anthology*, 660.
41 Williamson, *Feast of Creatures*, 185; cf. the more detailed discussion in Williamson, *Old English Riddles*, 248–52. Compare also the figureheads on Noah's ark in Dodwell and Clemoes, *Old English Illustrated Hexateuch*, fols 14r–15v.

Mirum videtur mihi,   lupus ab agno tenetur;
obcubuit agnus   et capit viscera lupi.
Dum starem et mirarem,   vidi gloriam magnam,
duo lupi stantes   et tertium tribulantes;
IIII pedes habebant,   cum septem oculis videbant.[42]   5

It seems amazing to me: a wolf is held by a lamb; the lamb has lain down and seizes the entrails of the wolf. As I stood and wondered, I saw a great glory: two wolves standing and tormenting a third; [5] they had four feet (and) saw with seven eyes.

As 'a single tiny island in an otherwise unbroken sea of Old English poetry,' the riddle raises several questions.[43] Is there a reason why this riddle was composed in Latin, or did the compiler, whose work was almost complete at this point in the manuscript, simply forget to translate it into the vernacular? Is there some wordplay – perhaps an allusion to a name – that works only in Latin and would be lost in translation? Was the Latin language supposed to reflect another (biblical, liturgical) text? Does the riddle also have a Latin answer and, if so, what is it?

Over the years, *Riddle* 90 has generated a number of elaborate and controversial interpretations but found no satisfactory solution. The only consensus among scholars concerns its linguistic eccentricity. The language seems to place it with the Anglo-Latin *enigmata* of Aldhelm, Tatwine, Eusebius, and Boniface; yet despite some stylistic resemblance, there is no analogue. *Riddle* 90 is clearly less accomplished: its second line is metrically incomplete, and from the many errors and blunders in the text, it appears that the copyist (or author) had some difficulties with Latin.[44] However, if we follow the majority of editors and allow for a few emendations, the riddle's syntax and narrative nevertheless become fairly clear. Like Aldhelm and his imitators, the author employs the conventional 'I saw'-formula (*vidi*, 3) and thus participates as an eyewitness in the two strange and surreal scenes he describes. The first of these is a perversion of a natural law: a lamb has slain a wolf (rather than vice versa). The second incident is introduced by the author as 'a great glory' (*gloriam magnam*, 3): there are two

---

42 *Riddle* 90 (ASPR 3:240, except line 2: *rupi* (after *agnus*, not in MS), line 3: *misarem*, and line 4: *dui*).
43 Anderson, 'Exeter Latin Riddle 90,' 73.
44 Compare the scribal errors in the encrypted Latin words in *Riddle* 36. For a detailed discussion of these editorial issues, see Davis and Schlueter, 'Latin Riddle,' 93.

wolves troubling a third one; yet the total number of their feet and eyes again seems contradictory and unnatural, for neither two nor three wolves have four feet and seven eyes.

For a medieval reader, such suggestive images no doubt echoed the apocalyptic scenarios of the Bible and the Church Fathers. The parallels with the Revelation of John and its haunting vision of the heavenly Lamb of God with its 'seven eyes' (Revelation 5.6) are indeed striking and have led some critics to conclude that *Riddle* 90 deals with a Christian subject. For Henry Morley, writing in 1888, the passage is an allegorical description of the triumph of the Agnus Dei (i.e., Christ) over the wolfish devil: the 'four feet' (5) are the four Gospels, and the 'seven eyes' (5) refer to the Revelation of John, 'where the seven eyes of the Lamb are the seven Spirits of God sent forth into all the earth,' while the 'two wolves' (4) are 'the Old and the New Testament troubling the devil, and having the four Gospels upon which their teaching stands.'[45] Morley's 'Lamb of God' is not the only religious solution that has been put forward; other proposals include Whitbread's fanciful 'Crucifixion,' Anderson's equally far-fetched 'two seven-branched candelabra flanking a single candlestick,' and Stanley's tentative 'The Trinity.'[46]

The riddle's almost insistent allusion to Christian symbolism, however, may also be intended to mislead the reader. Rather than being viewed allegorically, the mysterious lamb and the multiple *lupi* or 'wolves' may provide a linguistic clue to the solution, and – as some have conjectured – imply a pun on an Old English compound word or name with *wulf* (OE for *lupus*) as one of its elements. One of these is 'Cynewulf,' an answer first proposed in 1865 by Franz Dietrich and once favoured by those critics who believed that the *Riddles* were composed by the famed and fabled Anglo-Saxon poet of this name, a theory now long since abandoned.[47] More recently, Craig Williamson has proposed the rather unlikely solution 'web and loom,' arguing that the riddle's Latin animal names involve an orthographic wordplay on OE *wulflys* 'fleece of wool,' derived from

---

45 Morley, *English Writers*, 225.
46 See Whitbread, 'Latin Riddle'; Anderson, 'Exeter Latin Riddle 90'; Stanley, 'Heroic Aspects,' 198–9.
47 Dietrich ('Die Räthsel des Exeterbuchs,' 486, 250) assumed that there is a wordplay on the various meanings of Latin *lupus* 'wolf' or 'perch.' For further elaborations on the 'Cynewulf' solution, see Tupper, *Riddles of the Exeter Book*, 230–2. Another early critic, Henry Bradley ('Two Riddles,' 436–40), construed that the riddle recollects the conversion of a certain Wulfstan and the triumph of two other saintly 'Wulfs' over the devil.

OE *wulf* 'wolf' > *wul* 'wool' and *flys* 'fleece.' As he explains: 'the lamb (*agnus*) holds the wolf (*lupus*) and indeed seizes (*capit*) the belly or entrails (*viscera*) of the wolf and thus metaphorically commandeers its last letter,' so that the riddle describes a *wul-flys*, that is 'the woolen web on an Anglo-Saxon vertical loom,' whose parts are likened to feet and eyes.[48]

The most sweeping (and least convincing) attempt to read *Riddle* 90 as a charade is Patricia Davis and Mary Schlueter's double answer 'Augustine and Tertullian,' which also is built upon a doubtful letter game involving several random steps of orthographic rearrangement, letter omission, and substitution. According to Davis and Schlueter, the name of St Augustine (the Church Father, not the missionary to England) can be derived from a combination of the two words *agnus* and *lupus* in the first line of the riddle, which they rearrange from 'agnuslupus' to 'auguslpnus' (*sic*) and change to 'auguslinus,' concluding that the latter 'visually suggests' the name Augustinus; a similar reshuffling of line 4 of the riddle, they propose, yields the second name of their unlikely couple, 'tertllium' (*sic*) or 'tertullium' (for 'Tertullianus') – again, the result is neither an actual name nor an anagram.[49]

Certainly, to take the numbers of *Riddle* 90 as logographic clues is tempting, but doing so has led critics to forced readings and dead ends, even if it is true that there are some Anglo-Latin *enigmata* that actually do use logographs. In these examples, however, the word puzzle is never central but serves as an additional clue or a witty conclusion following the riddle's descriptive part. Moreover, the answer to the logograph can be obtained quite easily if the reader observes the rules of letter substitution (or omission) indicated by the author. In Aldhelm's riddle about the ram (*Aries*) for instance, the solution can be derived from the orthographical clue given in the final line:

Littera quindecima praestat, quod pars domus adsto.

If the fifteenth letter [of the alphabet] stands in front, I am part of a house.[50]

In the Latin alphabet, the fifteenth letter is 'p' - hence: *paries* 'wall,' which yields the solution, *aries* 'ram.' There is a similar play with *orbus* 'without

---

48 Williamson, *Old English Riddles*, 385, and *Feast of Creatures*, 215.
49 Davis and Schlueter, 'Latin Riddle,' 97–9.
50 *Enigma* 86.8 (ed. Glorie, *Collectiones Aenigmatum Merovingicae Aetatis*, 505; trans. Lapidge and Rosier, *Aldhelm: The Poetic Works*, 89).

offspring,' and *corbus* 'raven,' in Aldhelm's riddle about the raven; and the same logogriphic device is used twice by Eusebius.⁵¹ These are by no means singular examples. A series of short prose logogriphs are attributed to Bede in the already mentioned 'Cambridge Songs' manuscript, which also contains the riddle-groups of Symphosius, Aldhelm, Tatwine, Eusebius, and Boniface. These so-called *Joco-seria* of pseudo-Bede consist of nineteen grammatical puzzles, all on one page, each followed by a gloss explaining the answer.⁵² Most of them involve sober word pairs such as *bonus* 'good,' and *onus* 'weight,' *pes* 'foot,' and *apes* 'bees,' but one item is a carnivalesque wordplay on the letter 'o':

Littera queque culum facit ut videat velut oculus?

What letter makes that a bottom [Lat. *culus*] can see like an eye [*oculus*]?⁵³

In a logogriphic riddle, then, it is always clear that there is a conundrum to be solved, as the text expressly refers to 'letters' and 'words' that have to be substituted, eliminated, or else modified. Yet there are no comparable hints in Exeter Book *Riddle* 90 to suggest that its words and numbers actually conceal such a grammatical puzzle.

What the critical attempts to solve *Riddle* 90 in terms of Christian allegory, Latin-English wordplay, or logogriph have in common is the fact that they are either inconsistent in themselves or are strained and too complicated to be plausible. The riddle's stark and disturbing images seem to have diverted most modern readers from searching for a solution as profane as those of many Old English or Latin riddles dealing with everyday objects or tools. Just as animals in the *Riddles* are portrayed as human beings, so are inanimate objects often described in terms of animals. Rather than being linguistic ciphers, the lamb and the wolves in *Riddle* 90 therefore perhaps stand for an object whose inner parts are metaphorically referred to as 'entrails' (*viscera*, 2). As Michael Lapidge has shown, the notion of the *viscera* as 'entrails' or 'womb,' is 'one of the

---

51 Aldhelm, *Enigma* 63 (*Corbus*); Eusebius, *Enigma* 34 (*De flumine*; cf. Isidore, *Differentiae* 1.244) and 44 (*De panthera*).
52 Cambridge, UL Gg.5.35, fol. 418v, edited as the so-called *Joco-seria* of pseudo-Bede by Tupper, 'Riddles of the Bede Tradition,' 565–71; see Rigg and Wieland, 'Canterbury Classbook,' 126 (no. 29b).
53 No. x (ed. Tupper, 'Riddles of the Bede Tradition,' 569).

most striking images' to be found in the riddles of Aldhelm: 'In twenty of the *Enigmata*,' Lapidge writes, 'reference is made explicitly to the object's *viscera*'; these include the sounding 'entrails' of an organ, the hot 'inwards' of a peppercorn, the wick of a candle, the 'inwards' of a cooking-pot, a ciborium, a flour sieve, and a wine cask, or the sacred volumes of a bookcase.⁵⁴ The same conceit also occurs in the anonymous *Berne Riddles* of the seventh century, where a tree and an animal's hide are stripped of their 'entrails' (*viscera*) and turned into a ship and parchment, respectively.⁵⁵ Analogously, the lupine 'entrails' (*viscera lupi*, 2) in *Riddle* 90 may denote the inner parts of an inanimate object, while the 'four feet' (4) perhaps represent the feet on which this object stands.⁵⁶ But what do the seven eyes signify? And why is the 'wolf' first multiplied into two 'wolves' and then into three? Again, the insurmountable obstacle of the riddle lies in its numerical scheme, which is both conspicuous and utterly incomprehensible. Beginning with one (the narrator, the lamb, the wolf) and progressing from two to three, and from four to seven, the numbers seem to follow a hidden strategy that gradually undermines the riddle's narrative and subverts its generic principles. As the beasts perform their apocalyptic and cruel spectacle, the reader is left in a state of wonder and aporia.

---

54 Lapidge and Rosier, *Aldhelm: The Poetic Works*, 65. Cf. Aldhelm, *Enigmata* 13 (*Barbita*), 40 (*Piper*), 52 (*Candela*), 54 (*Cocuma duplex*), 55 (*Chrismal*), 67 (*Cribellus*), 78 (*Cupa vinaria*), 89 (*Arca libraria*).
55 *Berne Riddles* 11 (*De nave*) and 24 (*De membrana*) (ed. Glorie, *Collectiones Aenigmatum Merovingicae Aetatis*, 557, 570).
56 Cf. Tatwine, *Enigmata* 8 (*De ara*), and 29 (*De mensa*), describing the 'four feet' of an altar and a table.

PART II

Codes

4 Runic Strategies

The Exeter Book contains some of the most striking examples of English manuscript runes. These are occasional letters or words written in the Anglo-Saxon runic futhorc or, in two of the *Riddles*, spelled in roman script by their rune-names such as *æsc*, *nyd*, and *rad*. Except for a few runic or pseudo-runic marginalia that were obviously added much later,[1] all runes and runic clues in the manuscript are an integral part of the text and were carefully drawn in ink by the same scribe who single-handedly copied the entire anthology. Where runic and roman scripts occur side by side, the angular futhorc symbols are marked by small dots before and after individual letters or sequences, while the rune-names in roman are not distinguished from the surrounding text.[2] More important, both the futhorc letters, if read by their names, and the runes in roman script are generally integrated into the metrical verse pattern and may thus participate in the alliteration.

Logographic versus Alphabetic

In some instances runes serve as abbreviations; that is, a futhorc graph stands for its rune-name rather than representing a letter or sound. From the evidence in surviving Anglo-Saxon manuscripts, such non-alphabetic, logographic use of runes seems to have been nothing more than a shorthand

---

1 See Chambers, Förster, and Flower, *The Exeter Book*, 64; Derolez, *Runica Manuscripta*, 397–8; Williamson, *Old English Riddles*, 52–5, 59, 147–8, 151, 155–6, 167–8, 181–2, 327.
2 See Chambers, Förster, and Flower, *The Exeter Book*, 62n21; ASPR 3:xxiii; Derolez, *Runica Manuscripta*, 398; Williamson, *Old English Riddles*, 18–19, 188. For a probable exception to this rule, see the discussion of *Riddle* 64 below.

84 Codes

practice, employed only sporadically by some scribes.[3] The three erratic ᛟ-runes for *eþel* 'homeland' in *Beowulf*, all drawn by the first copyist of the codex, are well-known examples, but they are by no means exceptional, for there are also 'eþel'-runes in the *Waldere* fragments and in the Lauderdale manuscript of the Old English *Orosius*.[4] In the Exeter Book, such runic abbreviations occur in *The Ruin* (fol. 124a), where ·ᛗ· stands for 'man,' the first element of *mandreama* 'human delights,' and in *Riddle* 91 (fol. 129b), where *mod*·ᚹ· is short for *modwynn* 'heart's joy.'[5] It is interesting to note that these two runes occur in compounds and that the principle is the same as in *Riddle* 5, where an abbreviated *ond* is used in the compound *ondweorc* (for *hondweorc* 'handiwork').[6]

In all other cases where runes or runic clues are employed in the Exeter Book, they serve as a means of encoding information or, in the *Riddles*, of encrypting solutions. In the two long poems, *Christ II* (fol. 32a) and *Juliana* (fol. 76a), runes encode the signature of the poet Cynewulf – a technique that is also applied in the two other Cynewulfian poems, *The Fates of the Apostles* and *Elene*, both preserved in the Vercelli Book. In each of these four poems, the runes for 'c,' 'y,' 'n,' 'e,' 'w,' 'u,' 'l,' and 'f' are artfully woven into the verse and thus spell the author's name, *Cyn(e)wulf*.[7] Similarly, in *The Husband's Message* (fol. 123b), a runic sequence of five futhorc letters occurs at the end of the poem, though apparently not as a signature. The poem is presented as a message from an exiled lord to his noble wife or lover, who hope to be soon reunited; the woman is told to board a ship and sail south to rejoin her husband in his new-found prosperity. Then follow lines 48–53:

Ofer eald gebeot   incer twega,
gecyre ic ætsomne   ·ᛋ·ᚱ· geador
·ᛠ·ᚹ· ond ·ᛗ·   aþe benemnan,   50
þæt he þa wære   ond þa winetreowe

---

3 See Derolez, *Runica Manuscripta*, 385, 390–402, and '*Runica Manuscripta* Revisited,' 88–9; Page, *Introduction to English Runes*, 77–8, 221–2.
4 Cf. *Beowulf*, 520, 913, 1702. For recent speculations about the origin and supposed significance of the 'eþel'-runes in *Beowulf*, see Senra Silva, 'Rune "Eþel"'; Orchard, *Critical Companion to Beowulf*, 40n113.
5 ASPR 3:228, 241; cf. ibid., 365, 379.
6 ASPR 3:184; see Williamson, *Old English Riddles*, 13.
7 ASPR 2:54, 101; 3:25, 133. See Derolez, *Runica Manuscripta*, 391–6; Frese, 'Cynewulf's Runic Signatures'; Page, *Introduction to English Runes*, 191–7.

be him lifgendum   læstan wolde,
þe git on ærdagum   oft gespræconn.⁸

In addition to the past promise of the two of you, I turn unitedly together *sigel* and *rad*, *ear*, *wynn*, and *man* to declare with an oath that he would keep, as long as he lives, the pledge and the vow of friendship, which in former days you two often voiced.

Traditionally, it has been suggested that, from the context of the poem, we have to imagine the five runes to be inscribed on a wooden stave, similar to the runic sticks or *rúnakefli* surviving from medieval Scandinavia.⁹ The precise meaning of the cryptogram is elusive, but it seems somehow to seal the lovers' pledge of mutual fidelity or to guarantee the man's betrothal vow. As in Cynewulf's signatures, the runes may represent their corresponding roman letters – 's,' 'r,' 'ea,' 'w,' and 'd' (or 'm') – and perhaps mean *sweard* ~ *sweord* 'sword,' as Sedgefield suggested in 1922: 'By this the man shows his mistress that he remembers the vows which once he swore on his sword, the most solemn way of taking an oath.'¹⁰ Alternatively, as some would have it, the runes may denote their runic names (rather than letters), so that ᛋ would stand for *sigel* 'sun'; ᚱ for *rad* 'riding'; ᛠ for *ear* 'sea' or 'earth'; ᚹ for *wynn* 'joy'; and ᛗ (rather than ᛞ) for *man* 'man.' Based on the latter assumption, some rather fanciful readings and interpretations have been proposed. Still the most widely accepted of these is that put forward by Ralph W.V. Elliott, for whom the runic sequence summarizes the man's message. Taking the first two runes as the otherwise unattested compound *sigel-rad* 'the sun's path,' a kenning for the sky, Elliott expands:

Follow the sun's path [ᛋ·ᚱ] south across the sea [ᛠ] to find joy [ᚹ] with the man [ᛗ] who is waiting for you.¹¹

---

8 ASPR 3:227, except line 49: *gehyre* for *Gecyre*; my punctuation. The last rune is not clearly identifiable and may be either ᛞ 'd' or ᛗ 'm.' See Derolez, *Runica Manuscripta*, 398–9; Leslie, *Three Old English Elegies*, 15, 50, 66; Muir, *Exeter Anthology*, 356, 698.
9 Most recently, Schrunck Ericksen, 'Runesticks and Reading.' No Anglo-Saxon rune-staves survive; for Scandinavian *rúnakefli*, see Page, *Introduction to English Runes*, 101–2.
10 Sedgefield, *Anglo-Saxon Verse-Book*, 36–7, 159; supported by Fiocco, 'Le rune ne *Il messagio del marito*.'
11 Elliott, 'Runes in *The Husband's Message*,' 7, and *Runes*, 90; similarly, Leslie, *Three Old English Elegies*, 17. Both Elliott and Leslie follow an earlier suggestion made by Kock, 'Interpretations and Emendations,' 122–3. See Klinck, *Old English Elegies*, 207–8; and Niles (*Old English Enigmatic Poems*, 213–50), who proposes a new logographic reading of the passage.

In a recent essay, Lois Bragg has radically challenged these received interpretations of *The Husband's Message* and its runic content. Arguing that communication by runic sticks was alien to the Anglo-Saxons, she questions the textual evidence for the putative rune-stave in the poem and dismisses the often cited logographic readings of its runes as 'romantic' and wrong. Directing our attention instead to what she calls 'the fundamental principles of the runic writing system,' Bragg correctly points out that 'runic writing is alphabetic writing. In the living, epigraphic tradition, where runes are a genuine alphabet, each rune stands for a phoneme, while in the manuscript tradition, where runes are a dead, cryptographic alphabet, for a roman letter.'[12] This is indeed true for the immediate context of *The Husband's Message*, that is, the other runic poems of the Exeter Book. Apart from the only two examples of non-alphabetic runes used as scribal abbreviations quoted above, all futhorc runes and roman rune-names in these poems are actually to be understood as alphabetic characters.

Treating the runes as alphabetic letters rather than logographs, therefore, is the key not only to the Cynewulfian poems, but also to those *Riddles* in which rune-graphs and rune-names come into play as an additional linguistic code. Of the ninety-five *Riddles* in the Exeter Book, six employ runes in futhorc or rune-names spelled in roman script. Rune-graphs proper occur in *Riddle* 19, the first of two 'ship' riddles, with an impressive sequence of seventeen runes; in *Riddle* 24, the 'jay' (six runes); in *Riddle* 64, the second 'ship' (thirteen runes); and in the short *Riddle* 75, with the most likely answer 'hound' (four runes). Rune-names in roman are used in *Riddle* 42, the 'cock and hen,' and in *Riddle* 58, the 'well-sweep.' Each time, the runes or rune-names have to be transliterated into the roman alphabet in order to spell out a word or several words in Old English that either name the enigmatic subject or describe it. In this linguistically complex process, different modes of encoding require specific strategies of decoding from the erudite reader.[13]

Sea-Horses (*Riddles* 19 and 64)

Arguably the most intricate pattern of this kind of encoding underlies the two 'ship' riddles (nos 19 and 64), whose intermittent strings of futhorc

---

12 Bragg, 'Runes and Readers,' 36.
13 The 'varying degrees and kinds of linguistic integration' of the runes into the text of the *Riddles* and their function in the process of problem-solving are thoroughly discussed by Dewa, 'Runic Riddles.'

letters offer a baffling visual conundrum on the manuscript page. The first of these reads:

Ic seah ᛋᚱᚩ
ᚾ· hygewloncne, heafodbeorhtne,
swiftne ofer sælwong swiþe þrægan.
Hæfde him on hrycge hildeþryþe;
·ᚾᚩᛗ· nægledne rad.   5
·ᚪᚷᛖᚹ· widlast ferede
rynestrong on rade rofne ·ᚳᚩ
ᚠᚩᚩᚾ· For wæs þy beorhtre,
swylcra siþfæt. Saga hwæt ic hatte.[14]   10

Read aloud as *Ic seah sigel, rad, os, hægl, hygewloncne*, and so on, the runes fit more or less perfectly into the verse by metre and alliteration, but in the context of the poem, they do not seem to make sense semantically. Yet the runes beg special attention and signal to the reader that sense can be made of them only through a heuristic act of decoding. As is generally the case in the runic riddles, each rune-graph stands for a letter of the alphabet, and each unit (marked by framing dots) represents a word; but here, things are further complicated by the fact that the encoded words are spelled backwards, so that the runes have to be both transliterated and read in reverse:

·ᛋᚱᚩᚾ· - *sroh* - *hors* 'horse'
·ᚾᚩᛗ· - *nom* - *mon* 'man'
·ᚪᚷᛖᚹ· - *agew* - *wega* 'ways'
·ᚳᚩᚠᚩᚩᚾ· - *cofoah* - *haofoc* 'hawk'

Now the four decoded words fit in neatly with the rest of the poem, both syntactically and semantically:

> I saw a *horse*, proud-minded, with a bright head, run very swiftly over the fair plain. [It] had on its back battle-strength; [5] a *man* rode the nailed one. Over the wide track of the *ways*[15] strong-running on [its] ride, [it] carried a

---

14 *Riddle* 19 (ASPR 3:189–90, except line 1: *Ic seah* (MS) for *Ic on siþe seah*; my punctuation).
15 I follow Pinsker and Ziegler (*Die altenglischen Rätsel*, 41, 183) and take the runic *wega* as a genitive plural of *weg*, and *widlast* as a noun in the accusative singular, used adverbially to express extent of space; see Mitchell, *Old English Syntax*, 1:580, §1382.

brave *hawk*. The journey was the brighter, the voyage of these. Say what I am called.

At this point, however, the riddle still remains unsolved, since the typical concluding formula, *Saga hwæt ic hatte* (9), suggests a single solution that must meet all the terms of the riddle, including its runic clues.[16] As Craig Williamson has convincingly demonstrated, in this poem the runes do not simply spell out an answer, such as 'A man upon horseback with a hawk on his fist,' as proposed by a number of critics who think that this is a riddle about falconry.[17] Rather than being meant literally, the runic words furnish the clues needed to arrive at the ultimate solution, 'ship,' once they are understood as metaphorical references to a sea-going vessel and its crew. The riddle, in fact, 'plays upon the common Old English kenning of the ship as a sea-horse,' as Williamson notes.[18] The 'horse' (1–2) thus signifies the ship, the 'man' (5) is the sailor, the 'ways' (6) are the sea, and the 'hawk' (7–8) stands for the sail. What the riddler describes in terms of a bright-headed and strong-running steed is a stately ship travelling in full sail 'over the fair plain' (3) of the sea – just like the 'sea-horse' (*merehengest*) in *Riddle* 14, which carries an ornamented drinking horn 'over the waves.'[19] Yet even with the runes thus decoded, the description remains vague enough to sustain the governing ambiguity. Hence, the creature is called a 'nailed one' (*nægledne*, 5), not because of its horseshoes, but because of the iron 'clench nails' in the ship's planks – a literal clue that has a parallel in *Riddle* 58, in which the author refers to a boat's

---

16 Dewa, 'Runic Riddles of the Exeter Book,' 32. Strictly speaking, the *ic* in the final challenge, *Saga hwæt ic hatte*, is wrong, or at least inconsistent with the opening formula *Ic seah*. Normally, descriptive riddles of the 'I saw'-type ask *Saga hwæt hio wære* (*Riddle* 36.8) or *saga hwæt hio hatte* (*Riddle* 39.29), but in *Riddle* 86, the manuscript also has *ic* instead of the correct *hio*, referring to the enigmatic *wiht* described in the riddle. Hence Williamson (*Old English Riddles*, 78, 115; followed by Muir, *Exeter Anthology*, 298, 373) emends *hit* and *heo*, respectively, for MS *ic* in *Riddles* 19 and 86, while most other editors retain the manuscript reading. Wilcox's reading of *Riddles* 19 and 86 as 'mock-riddles' parodying the genre by their misleading endings, gives too much weight to what is merely a scribal error (see Wilcox, 'Mock-Riddles in Old English').
17 Williamson, *Old English Riddles*, 186–92; see Fry, 'Exeter Book Riddle Solutions,' 23.
18 Williamson, *Feast of Creatures*, 173; see also DiNapoli, 'Odd Characters,' 152. Olsen ('Animated Ships,' 60–6) lists twenty-one occurrences of ten different OE ship-kennings with 'horse' as their base word.
19 *Riddle* 14.6 (ASPR 3:187): *hwilum merehengest fereð ofer floda*.

'nailed planks' (*nægledbord*).²⁰ Further analogues can be found among the Latin *enigmata*. In Symphosius's 'ship,' for instance, the personified subject, formerly born as a tree in the woods, is an equally elegant traveller in the vast waters that surround it, 'swift' like the nailed horse of the Old English poem:

> Longa feror velox formosae filia silvae.
> Innumeris pariter comitum stipata catervis
> Curro vias multas, vestigia nulla relinquens.

> Long, swift daughter of the beauteous forest am I borne along. With innumerable throng of companions equally encompassed I speed over many paths, leaving no traces behind.²¹

Williamson's reading of *Riddle* 19 as a ship riddle, however, is further supported by additional evidence from the runes: taken together, the four rune-groups conceal a cipher, which has only recently been discovered by Mark Griffith.²² Griffith realized that the initial letters of the four sequences – *sroh*, *nom*, *agew*, and *cofoah* – together spell the acronym *snac*, a variant of OE *snacc*, which occurs in the *Anglo-Saxon Chronicle* and is commonly translated as 'swift-sailing vessel' or 'small vessel, war-ship.'²³ This not only secures the solution 'ship,' but suggests that the author was perhaps thinking more specifically of a swift warship. As Roberta J. Dewa observes, the runic acronym of *snac* thus reveals a 'deeper semantic layer' to the text.²⁴ This layer, however, can be accessed only through several systematic steps of deciphering, rearranging and rereading. Once we understand these hidden strategies, the mysterious sea-horse is stripped of its metaphorical disguise and emerges as a powerful warship, manned by human 'battle-strength' (*hildeþryþe*, 4).

The reader's ability to decode the runes and contextualize their meaning is similarly challenged in the related *Riddle* 64. Its text is somewhat shorter than that of *Riddle* 19, but is even more distorted by its thirteen runic

---

20 *Riddle* 58.5 (ASPR 3:209): *ne hie scip fereð, naca nægledbord*. See Williamson, *Old English Riddles*, 189–90; Hutchinson, 'Ships.'
21 *Aenigma* 13 (ed. Glorie, *Collectiones Aenigmatum Merovingicae Aetatis*, 634; trans. Ohl, ibid.). Cf. *Berne Riddle* 11 (*De nave*; ed. Glorie, ibid., 557), line 6: *Et onusta currens viam nec planta depingo*.
22 Griffith, 'Riddle 19.'
23 See BT, s.v. *snacc*; Roberts, Kay, and Grundy, *Thesaurus of Old English*, 331.
24 Dewa, 'Runic Riddles,' 32.

letters. These form little units or pairs, mostly linked by an abbreviated *ond* in the manuscript and clearly displayed by the usual dots. Again, the author employs the conventional 'I saw'-formula:

> Ic seah ·ᚹ· ond ·ᛁ·   ofer wong faran,
> beran ·ᛒ·ᛖ·;   beam wæs on siþþe
> hæbbendes hyht   ·ᚻ· ond ·ᚫ·
> swylce þryþa dæl,   ·ᚦ· ond ·ᛖ·
> Gefeah ·ᚠ· ond ·ᚫ·   fleah ofer ·ᛠ·   5
> ᛋ· ond ·ᛈ·   sylfes þæs folces.²⁵

While it is generally agreed that the runes here spell not complete words but only their initial letters, opinions differ as to the number of runic units and words they represent. Each pair of runes is to be taken as the first two letters of a word, with the probable exception, however, of the rune ᛠ in line 5 representing a word beginning with the diphthong 'ea': hence, ᚹ and ᛁ stand for *wi(cg)* 'horse'; ᛒ and ᛖ for *be(orn)* 'man'; ᚻ and ᚫ for *ha(foc)* 'hawk'; ᚦ and ᛖ for *þe(ow)* 'servant'; and ᚠ and ᚫ for *fæ(lca)* 'falcon.' The final two lines are obscure, and a number of conjectures and emendations have been put forward. Despite the missing dot after the 'ea'-rune, the sequence ·ᛠᛋ· *ond* ·ᛈ· may represent two words, possibly ᛠ for *ea(rd)* 'earth,' and ᛋ *ond* ᛈ for *sp(or)* 'track.'²⁶ This gives the following translation:

> I saw a *horse* travel over the plain, bearing a *man*; with both on [their] journey was the owner's joy, a *hawk*, [which was] also part of the power; the *servant* [5] rejoiced; the *falcon* flew over the *earth*, [over the] *track* of that same people.

Even without the runes, it is evident that this is in many ways a companion piece to *Riddle* 19, with which it shares the solution 'ship.'²⁷ In both texts, the central clues in the representation of the metaphorical sea-horse are encoded in the runes and connected by the narrative structure of the poem. Again, the runic clusters have to be read 'as elements in the puzzle rather than as ultimate solutions,' as Jonathan Wilcox observes.²⁸ Thus, the 'horse'

---

25 *Riddle* 64 (ASPR 3:230; my punctuation).
26 This interpretation differs from Williamson's. A similar reading of the last three runes as *ea(rd)* and *sp(or)* is proposed by Holthausen, 'Zu altenglischen Dichtungen,' 349.
27 See Williamson, *Old English Riddles*, 325–30.
28 Wilcox, 'Mock-Riddles in Old English,' 186.

(1) is the ship; the 'man' (2) or 'servant' (4) is the sailor; and the 'hawk' (3) or 'falcon' (5) is the sail. Carrying its brave and powerful cargo, the splendid ship travels over the 'plain' (1) or surface of the 'earth' (5), leaving a watery 'track' (6) in its wake.

Once *Riddles* 19 and 64 are decoded and solved, the correspondences as well as the differences between them become apparent. The two poems are structurally identical, but they operate differently in terms of what Dewa calls the 'orthographic variation' employed in the runic clusters: in *Riddle* 19, the letters are reversed, while in *Riddle* 64, they are omitted.[29] In each case, the use of the runes is methodical and consistent, yet the reader is given no clue as to how the orthographic gibberish can be unravelled.

The Barking Bird (*Riddle* 24)

Runic encoding takes further unexpected turns in *Riddle* 24, another bird riddle. The poem consists of a descriptive part (1–7a), in which the enigmatic subject speaks of itself, and a short runic conclusion (7b–10) indicating to the reader how the riddle may be solved:

> Ic eom wunderlicu wiht   wræsne mine stefne,
> hwilum beorce swa hund,   hwilum blæte swa gat,
> hwilum græde swa gos,   hwilum gielle swa hafoc,
> hwilum ic onhyrge   þone haswan earn,
> guðfugles hleoþor,   hwilum glidan reorde   5
> muþe gemæne,   hwilum mæwes song,
> þær ic glado sitte.   ·X· mec nemnað
> swylce ·Ᵽ· ond ·R·   Ᵽ· fullesteð,
> ·N· ond ·I·   Nu ic haten eom
> swa þa siex stafas   sweotule becnaþ.[30]   10

I am a wondrous creature, I change my voice: sometimes I bark like a dog; sometimes I bleat like a goat; sometimes I cry like a goose; sometimes I yell like a hawk; sometimes I imitate the grey eagle, [5] the singing of the war-bird; sometimes I utter from my mouth the language of the kite, sometimes the seagull's song, where I sit cheerfully. 'g' [they] call me, as well as 'æ' and 'r'; 'o' helps, 'h' and 'i.' Now I am named [10] as these six letters clearly show.

---

29 Dewa, 'Runic Riddles,' 31.
30 *Riddle* 24 (ASPR 3:192–3).

Although some of the runes again are linked by an abbreviated *ond* in the manuscript, they are not to be taken as groups but individually, each representing a single letter. Transliterated into the roman alphabet, these letters are 'g,' 'æ,' 'r,' 'o,' 'h,' and 'i.' Although the runes again participate in the alliteration once we read them out by their names (*giefu, æsc, rad, os, hægl,* and *is*), they are to be taken as separate semiotic units that isolate the name of the enigmatic subject.[31] The concluding lines indicate that the six rune-graphs (*þa siex stafas*, 10) alone yield this name, but the difficulty is increased by the fact that, this time, the order of the characters is scrambled (not simply reversed), and that we should actually read them as ᚾᛁᚷᚠᚱᚱ, that is, *higoræ*, a variant form of *higera*, the Old English word for 'jay.'

Elsewhere in the corpus of Old English, the name occurs only in the Anglo-Saxon glossaries, where it mostly translates Latin *picus* 'woodpecker,'[32] evidently a mistake for *pica*, which is the correct Latin name not only for the jay (*Garrulus glandarius*) but also for the related magpie (*Pica pica*), both members of the crow family. This confusion is reflected in the standard Old English dictionaries and, consequently and unfortunately, in the criticism of *Riddle* 24, for which all three bird names – 'jay,' 'magpie,' and 'woodpecker' – have been proposed.[33] While the drumming woodpecker is no mimic of other birds and therefore can be ruled out here, both the common jay and the once rarer magpie have always been notorious for their garrulous song and mimicry. However, as Peter Kitson has conclusively shown, the meaning of *higoræ* is established by its cognates, Old Saxon *higara* and Old High German *hehara* (> Modern German *Häher, Eichelhäher*), meaning 'jay,'[34] while the names for the magpie and the woodpecker in Old English are *agu* and *fina*, respectively,[35] neither of which fits the runes of *Riddle* 24, leaving *higoræ* 'jay' as the only correct solution. This can be further supported by the Latin Old English list of bird names in the so-called Plantin-Moretus / British Library glossary, where *gaia* 'jay,' *pica* 'magpie,' and *picus* 'woodpecker' are clearly distinguished:

---

31 Dewa, 'Runic Riddles,' 29.
32 See *MCOE*, s.v. *higera, higere, higrae, higræ,* and *higre*.
33 BT, s.v. *higera*; Fry, 'Exeter Book Riddle Solutions,' 23.
34 Kitson, 'Old English Bird-Names,' 496. For the etymology and cognates, see Holthausen, *Altenglisches etymologisches Wörterbuch*, s.v. *higera*. Cf. Whitman, 'Birds of Old English Literature,' 161–2 (wrongly identified as 'woodpecker').
35 Cf. OHG *aga* > *agalstra* > ModG *Elster*. See BT, s.v. *agu* and *fina*; DOE, s.v. *agu*; Whitman, 'Birds of Old English Literature,' 152 and 162; Kitson, 'Old English Bird-Names,' 496–7 and 6.

Gaia, vel catanus, higere.
Pica, agu.
Picus, fina.³⁶

Evidently, the *gagia* or *gaia* of the glossaries is nothing other than the late Latin word for the jay, *gaia* ~ *gaius*; it passed into the Romance languages, as in OF *jay* ~ *gai* (> ModF *geai*), and from there into Middle English as *iay* ~ *jay*.³⁷

There is no immediate model for *Riddle* 24 among the earlier Anglo-Latin *enigmata*. The only Latin bird riddle that comes close as an intriguing, if exotic, parallel is Eusebius's loquacious 'parrot' (*De psittaco*), which is drawn entirely from Isidore's *Etymologies*. Eusebius first describes the bird's vivid plumage and then goes on:

> et mea latior instat
> Lingua loquax reliquis avibus: hinc verba sonabo
> Nomina et humanae reddam de more loquelae;
> Nam natura mihi ave est vel iam dicere care,
> Cetera per studium depromam nomina rerum.

and my loquacious tongue surpasses that of other birds so that I speak words and give answers as in human discourse. Nature taught me to say 'ave' or 'care,' study teaches me to say still other words.³⁸

More than the parrot, the jay has a long history as a talking bird in western literature. It was well known to Greek writers by its onomatopoeic name, κισσα ~ κιττα, and it appears prominently in Roman literature, where the *pica* 'jay' and the *pica* 'magpie' were often confounded.³⁹ Pliny the Elder, in his *Natural History*, first seems to refer to both the garrulous jay and the chattering magpie when writing about the birds called *picae*;

---

36 Antwerp, Plantin-Moretus Museum, 47, and London, British Library, Add. 32246 (= Ker, *Manuscripts Containing Anglo-Saxon*, no. 2); Wright and Wülcker, *Anglo-Saxon and Old English Vocabularies*, 1:132; Förster, 'Die altenglische Glossenhandschrift,' 115–17.
37 See André, *Les noms d'oiseaux en latin*, 78; Capponi, *Ornitologia latina*, 245; *MED*, s.v. *jai*; *OED*, s.v. *jay*.
38 *Enigma* 59.3–7 (ed. Glorie, *Collectiones Aenigmatum Merovingicae Aetatis*, 270; trans. Erhardt-Siebold, ibid. Cf. Isidore, *Etym.* 12.7.24.
39 *OLD*, s.v. *pica*; Keller, *Die antike Tierwelt*, 2:112–14; Thompson, *Glossary of Greek Birds*, 146–7; André, *Les noms d'oiseaux en latin*, 127–8; Capponi, *Ornitologia latina*, 414–18; Leitner, *Zoologische Terminologie*, 200. See also Toynbee, *Animals in Roman Life*, 275–6.

but later in the same passage, he clearly speaks of the jay as 'the species that feeds on acorns':

> adamant verba quae loquantur nec discunt tantum, sed diligunt, meditantesque intra semet cura atque cogitatione intentionem non occultant ... satis illis decoris in specie sermonis humani est. verum addiscere alias negant posse quam ex genere earum quae glande vescantur.

> These birds get fond of uttering particular words, and not only learn them but love them, and secretly ponder them with careful reflexion, not concealing their engrossment ... this bird has enough distinction in its power of imitating the human voice. But they say that none of them can go on learning except ones of the species that feeds on acorns.[40]

In early Medieval Latin, too, no clear distinction was generally made between the names for the jay and the magpie; the word for both species was still *pica*, while the name for the jay, *garrulus* 'garrulous,' was introduced only later. In his *Etymologies*, Isidore of Seville explains that *pica* is derived from *poeticae* 'poetic,' because the bird can imitate the sound of the human voice:

> Picae quasi poeticae, quod verba in discrimine vocis exprimant, ut homo. Per ramos enim arborum pendulae inportuna garrulitate sonantes, etsi linguas in sermone nequeunt explicare, sonum tamen humanae vocis imitantur. De qua congrue quidam ait:
>   Pica loquax certa dominum te voce saluto:
>   si me non videas, esse negabis avem.

> *Picae* [jays or magpies] is for 'poetic' (*poeticae*), because they pronounce words with a distinct articulation, like a human. Perching on the branches of trees, they sound out in unmannerly garrulity, and although they are unable to unfold their tongues in meaningful speech, still they imitate the sound of the human voice. Concerning which someone has said, appropriately [Martial, *Epigrams* 14.76]:

---

40 Pliny, *Nat. hist.* 10.118–19 (ed. and trans. Rackham, 368–9). Cf. Aristotle, *Hist. animal.* 9.13 615b 19–23; Plutarch, *De soll. animal.* 19; Aelian, *De nat. animal.* 6.19. Jays mostly feed on insects and seeds, especially acorns, which they bury and cache, whence their scientific name, *Garrulus glandarius* (*Corvus glandarius*, Linné); see Cramp et al., *Birds of Europe*, 8:12–15.

I, a chattering *pica*, salute you as 'master' with a clear voice – if you did not see me, you would deny that I am a bird.[41]

Isidore concludes his explanation with an epigram by the Roman poet Martial, whose *pica loquax* is taken by many Latinists to be a magpie.[42] In Ovid's *Metamorphoses*, the nine Pierides, daughters of the Macedonian king Pierus, lose their singing contest against the Muses and are transformed into *picae* that raucously chatter in the trees, greeting those who pass by and 'imitating everything':

> Musa loquebatur: pennae sonuere per auras,
> voxque salutantum ramis veniebat ab altis.
> Suspicit et linguae quaerit tam certa loquentes
> Unde sonent hominemque putat Iove nata locutum:
> Ales erat! numeroque novem sua fata querentes
> Institerant ramis imitantes omnia picae.

> While the muse was still speaking, the sound of whirring wings was heard and words of greeting came from the high branches of the trees. Jove's daughter looked up and tried to see whence came the sound which was so clearly speech. She thought some human being spoke; but it was a bird. Nine birds, lamenting their fate, had alighted in the branches, picae, which can imitate any sound they please.[43]

It is perhaps no coincidence that the talking jays or magpies in Ovid's *Metamorphoses* and Isidore's *Etymologies* utter their speeches while they perch on the trees, and that the enigmatic creature of *Riddle* 24 delivers its noisy mimicry from where it 'cheerfully' sits (*ic glado sitte*, 7). Their

---

41 Isidore, *Etym.* 12.7.46 (ed. André, 259–61; trans. adapted from Barney et al., 267). The passage was taken over by Hrabanus Maurus, *De rer. nat.* 8.6 (PL 111:247), and Hugh of Fouilloy, *De bestiis et aliis rebus*, 3.32 (PL 177:95–6), and became part of the bestiary tradition; see Rowland, *Birds with Human Souls*, 87–8; George and Yapp, *Naming of the Beasts*, 172–3.
42 Cf. Martial, *Epigrams* 7.87.6 (*pica salutatrix*), and 9.54.9 (*salutatus picae*). For Martial in the Middle Ages and in Anglo-Saxon England, see Reynolds, *Texts and Transmission*, 239–44; Gneuss, *Handlis*, no. 195.
43 Ovid, *Met.* 5.294–9 (ed. and trans. Miller, 258–9, who translates 'magpies' for *picae*); cf. ibid. 5.678: *raucaque garrulitas studiumque immane loquendi*. See further Persius, *Prol.* 9; Petronius, 28.8: the *pica varia* (the black and white magpie?) in a golden cage salutes all who enter; Statius, *Silv.* 2.4.19. Cf. also Eugenius of Toledo, *Carm.* 49.1 (ed. Vollmer, MGH AA 14:259): *garrula pica*.

songs, though, are different, since the jay of the Old English riddle does not include the human voice in its list of those it copies. Rather, what the riddle foregrounds is the Ovidian notion of the *imitantes omnia picae*, the scope and variety of the bird's mimicking song. According to modern ornithologists, the jay is able to produce a remarkably extensive repertoire of sounds. These range from harsh, screeching, husky calls and crooning gurgles to chirruping, bubbling, clicking, knocking, grating, buzzing, and squeaking noises, along with throaty, wheezy, wet and rasping tones, hisses, and chuckles, as well as a medley of mimicked phrases, including not only the calls of wild birds, such as buzzards, kestrels, partridges, cranes, starlings, and crows, but even the sound of motorcycle horns, lawnmowers, barking dogs and – like the Roman *picae* in their golden cages – the human voice.[44]

The Old English riddler's catalogue, taking up two-thirds of the poem, is no less impressive. The creature's mimicry is presented as its main characteristic, leaving no room for a description of the appearance of the colourful jay, which – like the nightingale of *Riddle 8* – is actually more often heard than seen. The sounds mimicked by the jay are now the barking of the dog and the bleating of the goat (1), the cackling noise of the goose (3), the cries of the hawk and the eagle (3–5),[45] and the calls of the kite and the seagull (5–6). The repetitive *hwilum ... swa* of the four half-lines 2a–3b, together with the echoing *hwilum ... hwilum ... hwilum* in lines 4–6, frame and highlight the individual animals and their distinctive calls. Again, each verb is used only once in the poem – *wræsne* (1), *beorce* (2), *blæte* (2), *græde* (3), *gielle* (3), *onhyrge* (4), *gemæne* (6) – and the two pairs, *beorce/blæte* and *græde/gielle*, carry the alliteration. At the same time, the bird sounds are referred to by the three different nouns, *hleoþor* 'sound' or 'singing' (5), *reorde* 'speech' or 'language' (5), and *song* 'song' (6), all copied by the single 'voice' (*stefne*, 1) of this cheerful ventriloquist.

In an archaistic gesture, the 'grey eagle' is invoked in lines 4–5 as the crying 'war-bird' (*guðfugol*) – an ironic allusion to the typical carrion bird that makes its ominous appearance over the battlefields of Old English heroic poetry. In *The Battle of Brunanburh*, for instance, the white-tailed eagle is

---

44 Cramp et al., *Birds of Europe*, 8:7–8, 19–23.
45 More specifically, the 'grey eagle' (4) may be identified as either the white-tailed or sea eagle (*Haliaeetus albicilla*), or the golden eagle (*Aquila chrysaetos*); see Whitman, 'Birds of Old English Literature,' 168; Tupper, *Riddles of the Exeter Book*, 122–3; Biggam, *Grey in Old English*, 281, 302; Kitson, 'Old English Bird-Names,' 7.

the greedy *guðhafoc* or 'war-hawk' that enjoys the carrion left behind by the victorious West Saxons; and in *Judith*, the hungry eagle sings its 'battle-song' before the armies clash.[46] The imposing 'beast of battle' seems a somewhat presumptuous comparison for a small *wiht* that assumes the identities of others in order to hide – and reveal – its own. It is as if it were saying: I do sound like a domestic animal (dog, goat, goose), a bird of prey (hawk, eagle, kite), or a waterbird (seagull), but I am none of these. The rhetorical principle followed is the unwritten rule that, in a successful riddle, the solution is never actually mentioned, but is only vaguely described in terms of something else; or if the literal referent is indeed named in the text, then it is only in an orthographically encrypted form, for instance, spelled backwards as in *Riddle* 23 (*Agob-boga* 'bow') or in a runic cipher, as here.

Far from simply being a playful exercise, the runes here extend the catalogue of the jay's mimicry to the realm of human language. What superficially looks and sounds like some incomprehensible chatter – *giefu, æsc, rad, os, hægl, is* – in fact makes perfect sense, once we realize that the runes spell out a genuine word. Seen in this way, the 'wondrous creature' of *Riddle* 24 not only imitates the voices of its fellow animals, but – like its counterparts in Roman and medieval poetry and animal lore – even speaks the language of man.

---

46 *Battle of Brunanburh*, 63–4 (ASPR 6:20): *earn ... guðhafoc*; *Judith*, 210–11 (ASPR 4:105): *earn ... sang hildeleoð*. Cf. *Exodus*, 162 (ASPR 1:95): *herefugolas*; *Elene*, 29 and 111; *Battle of Maldon*, 107; *Beowulf*, 3026. For the 'Beasts of Battle' (raven, eagle, and wolf) in Old English literature, see Griffith, 'Convention and Originality.'

5 Bits and Pieces

Of the six riddles in the Exeter Book that employ runes, *Riddles* 58 and 75 have elicited comparatively little scholarly interest. It has been argued that the two items are imperfect or fragmentary (although there is no textual loss or gap in the manuscript), and that therefore their solutions are uncertain. The fifteen lines of *Riddle* 58 end rather abruptly, and *Riddle* 75 is so brief that some have taken it for no more than a scrap or opening line of a lost poem. It is most likely, however, that the enigmatic creature of this very short riddle is an animal, probably a hunting dog, while the animal-like object described in *Riddle* 58 is a well-sweep used to lift water from a draw-well. The two poems are quite different in terms of their runic content and technique. *Riddle* 75 features four rune-graphs written in futhorc, apparently to encrypt the solution. *Riddle* 58, on the other hand, uses the roman script to spell one of three runic letters indicating the name of its subject.

Head, Shoulders, Knees, and Toes (*Riddle* 58)

Runes in roman script also occur in the 'cock and hen' riddle (no. 42, discussed in chapter 6, below), and in both cases they are referred to as *runstafas*, that is, 'runic letters.' Yet this time, the author withholds most of his runological register to leave the baffled reader with only a vague cryptographic clue. *Riddle* 58 reads:

> Ic wat anfete   ellen dreogan
> wiht on wonge.   Wide ne fereð,
> ne fela rideð,   ne fleogan mæg
> þurh scirne dæg,   ne hie scip fereð,

naca nægledbord;   nyt bið hwæþre 5
hyre dryhtne   monegum tidum.
Hafað hefigne steort,   heafod lytel,
tungan lange,   toð nænigne,
isernes dæl;   eorðgræf pæþeð.
Wætan ne swelgeþ   ne wiht iteþ, 10
foþres ne gitsað,   fereð oft swa þeah
lagoflod on lyfte;   life ne gielpeð,
hlafordes gifum,   hyreð swa þeana
þeodne sinum.   Þry sind in naman
ryhte runstafas,   þara is rad fruma.[1] 15

I know a one-footed creature, boldly working on the plain. It does not travel far, nor ride much, nor can it fly through the bright day, nor does a ship carry it, [5] a boat with nailed planks; nevertheless it is useful to its master at many times. It has a heavy tail, a small head, a long tongue, no tooth, [and] some iron; it passes through a hole in the earth. [10] It swallows no liquid, nor eats anything, nor craves for fodder, yet it often carries a flood of water into the air. It does not boast of life nor of [its] lord's gifts, but still it obeys its ruler. In [its] name there are three straight runic letters, of which *rad* is the first.

That the one-footed, heavy-tailed, small-headed, long-tongued, and toothless 'creature' (*wiht*, 2) of this riddle is no animate being is clear from the half-line *life ne gielpeð* (12) and from the three negations with *ne* in lines 10–11. Bold and obedient though it is, this creature does not drink or eat like man or like an animal that is given its 'fodder' after a day's work in the field. The author exploits this paradox not only through a string of misleading comparisons to various body parts, but also by alluding to how the object is operated by man. In the anthropomorphizing language of the *Riddles*, this is represented as a master-servant relationship. Here, man appears under the threefold disguise of the controlling 'master' (*dryhtne*, 6), the benevolent 'lord' (*hlafordes*, 13), and the autocratic 'ruler' or 'chief' (*þeodne*, 14). In contrast, the 'hard-working' object is 'useful to its master' (5–6), whom it faithfully obeys (13–14) – just like a draught or pack animal, or a slave – even if it does not enjoy any 'gifts' from its lord (12–14).[2] Such poetic

---

1 ASPR 3:208–9, except line 6: *mondryhtne* for MS *dryhtne*, and line 15: *Rad foran* for MS *rad furum*.
2 Cf. *Elene*, 265 (ASPR 2:73): *hlafordes gifu*.

characterization suggestively evokes the Germanic ethos of companionship and loyalty that determines the social relations between lord and retainer, and that is at the heart of Anglo-Saxon poetry from *Beowulf* to *The Wanderer*. Further paradoxes point to the object's technical nature. It is not moved around (2–5), yet it moves (9); it cannot fly (3), yet it rises into the sky (12); it swallows no liquid (10), yet it carries masses of water (11–12); and, while it passes through a hole in the earth (literally through an 'earth-grave,' 9), it also rises into the 'air' (12).

All of these seemingly contradictory statements concern the object's appearance, its technology, and its function in relation to man. Early critics suggested that the riddle described a draw-well, but the solution 'well-sweep,' first proposed by Ferdinand Holthausen in 1894, more accurately meets all the conditions of the riddle.[3] According to the *OED*, a well-sweep is an 'apparatus for drawing water from a well, consisting of a long pole attached to an upright which serves as a fulcrum.'[4] From the long end of the pole, a bucket on a rope or chain is suspended; at the shorter end, there is a weight that serves as a counterpoise. The person operating the well-sweep pulls down on the rope to lower the bucket into the well and fill it with water, then releases the rope so that the counterweight makes the pole swing back and raise the bucket. The principle is the same as it is in the hand-operated shadoof (or shaduf), a simple water-lifting device known from ancient Egypt and still used in many countries in the East to irrigate land. In Europe, draw-wells with sweeps were widely used from Roman times throughout the Middle Ages and beyond, alongside draw-wells with windlasses used for deeper waterholes.[5] In medieval English towns, rural communities, and monasteries, draw-wells with a wooden or copper bucket and operated with a sweep must have been quite common. Some of them – like the well on the twelfth-century plan of the waterworks at Christ Church monastery, Canterbury – were part of a more sophisticated system of water supply, irrigation, and drainage. Others, especially rural draw-wells, could be simple pits without safety barriers or wellheads, which sometimes posed a hazard to users.[6]

---

3 See Holthausen, 'Beiträge zur Erklärung und Textkritik,' 387.
4 *OED*, s.v. *sweep*, n., 24.
5 See Drower, 'Water-Supply, Irrigation, and Agriculture,' 523–5; Forbes, 'Hydraulic Engineering and Sanitation,' 675–90.
6 See Skelton and Harvey, *Local Maps and Plans*, 43–58; Bond, 'Mittelalterliche Wasserversorgung,' esp. 152–3; Magnusson, *Water Technology*, 136–7 and passim.

The Old English author places his draw-well in the country – literally, 'on the plain' (*on wonge*, 2) – so that he can describe it in terms of an animal working in the field: an ox, for instance, or a horse used for ploughing. Hence, the creature's single foot (1) is the upright support upon which the pole of the sweep pivots or 'rides.' Its 'heavy tail' (7) is the short end of the pole with the counterweight. Its 'small head' (7) is the long and usually thinner end of the pole from which the bucket is hung; and its 'long tongue' (8) is the rope or chain with the bucket. The riddler says that the well-sweep has no teeth (8), but 'some iron' (*isernes dæl*, 9), which obviously denotes the bucket that moves up and down the well shaft or 'earth-grave' (*eorðgræf*, 9). Medieval draw-wells also had wooden buckets with iron rings, and since either ropes or iron chains were used, the *isernes dæl* (9) might equally well refer to the chain, or to both bucket and chain.[7]

The rhetorical device of describing an inanimate object in terms of a living being is as old as riddle-making itself and is characteristic of many popular riddles, conundrums, and riddling questions whose subjects are farm implements, domestic tools, and other objects of everyday life.[8] Conventionally, riddles of this type contain a specific element that is discordant with the rest of the description and suggests that the correct answer cannot be an animal or a person. In *Riddle* 58, the fact that the creature is 'one-footed' (1) is a hint of this kind: there is plainly no real animal with a tail, head, and tongue, but only one foot.[9] In several of the Exeter Book *Riddles*, inanimate objects are described in this way and metamorphosed from ordinary utensils or household tools into living beings. The anchor in *Riddle* 16, for example, is said to have a 'tail' (*steort*); it boldly strives against water and wind – like a restless exile or a wild beast – and yet it is stiff and still. Likewise, the wheel in *Riddle* 32 has many 'ribs' and a 'mouth' (i.e., the spokes and the hub); and while it travels around 'on a single foot' (i.e., the rim), it is blind and without 'hands, shoulders, or arms.' The inkhorn (*Riddle* 93), too, has only 'one foot,' as does the birdlike creature of *Riddle* 81 – possibly a weathercock – with its head, eyes, ears, and hard nose; its steep neck, back, breast, belly, and high

---

7 Compare the ornamented bronze bucket that contained the coin hoard found at Hexham monastery (Northumbria), in Campbell, John, and Wormald, *Anglo-Saxons*, 138.
8 See Taylor, 'Riddle,' 131–2.
9 Cf. Tatwine's 'lectern' (*Enigma* 10 [*De recitabulo*]), which also has a 'single foot' but cannot walk; similarly: Tatwine, *Enigmata* 12.5, 28.3.

tail.[10] The rake in *Riddle* 34 is another such imaginary creature with 'many teeth' and a useful 'nose,' seeking plants and herbs in the field just like a grazing or foraging animal, although it actually 'feeds the cattle.'

All of these lifeless objects thus become part of the animal world of the Exeter Book *Riddles*, assuming identities other than their true nature. The thing that most closely resembles the well-sweep in terms of the author's use of personification, imagery, and setting, however, is the plough in *Riddle* 21:

> Neb is min niþerweard;   neol ic fere
> ond be grunde græfe.   Geonge swa me wisað
> har holtes feond,   ond hlaford min
> woh færeð,   weard æt steorte,
> wrigaþ on wonge,   wegeð mec ond þyð,   5
> saweþ on swæð min.   Ic snyþige forð,
> brungen of bearwe,   bunden cræfte,
> wegen on wægne.   Hæbbe wundra fela.
> Me biþ gongendre   grene on healfe
> ond min swæð sweotol   sweart on oþre.   10
> Me þurh hrycg wrecen   hongaþ under
> an orþoncpil,   oþer on heafde,
> fæst ond forðweard.   Fealleþ on sidan
> þæt ic toþum tere,   gif me teala þenaþ
> hindeweardre,   þæt biþ hlaford min.[11]   15

My nose points downward; low I travel and dig in the ground. I go as the grey enemy of the woods [i.e., the ox] guides me; and my lord walks bent over, the guardian at the tail, [5] presses forward on the plain, moves and urges me, sows in my track. With nose to the ground I move on, brought from the wood, skilfully fastened, carried on a wagon. I have many wondrous things. As I go, there is green on one side of me, [10] and my clear track is dark on the other. Driven through my back there hangs beneath a well-made dart, [and] another on my head, fast and forward. What I tear with my teeth falls to the side, [15] if the one behind me, who is my lord, serves me well.

Like the well-sweep, the wooden plough moves in the field (*on wonge*, 5), its 'nose' down and its 'teeth' in the ground. The pointed coulter and

---

10 See also Sorrell, 'Like a Duck to Water,' 50–1.
11 ASPR 3:191; my punctuation.

share hang from its 'back' and 'head,' as it is operated by its 'lord' (*hlaford*, 3 and 15), who works at its 'tail.'

Given the amount of technical detail that is woven into these poems, the riddle-maker appears to have been familiar with the objects he describes. Wheels, rakes, ploughs, and well-sweeps were, no doubt, a common sight in rural Anglo-Saxon England, and the same applies to the chopping-block (*Riddle* 5), the beehive (no. 17), the churn (no. 54), the bellows (no. 37), the flail (no. 52), and the poker (no. 62).[12] However, the inclusion of farming implements and household objects is less domestic than encyclopedic and traditional: they are already among the stock subjects of the earlier Latin *enigmata*. Even in the case of the well-sweep, the author was not without literary models. Two riddles from the collections of Symphosius and Aldhelm make interesting comparisons, for they deal with two related subjects, namely, the fountain and the well. In Aldhelm's *Enigma* 73 about the fountain (*fons*), the water of the spring tells how it winds its way 'through empty hollows of the earth,' and, although the water itself is 'devoid of life' and has no 'sensation,' it nevertheless gives life to many living creatures.[13] As with his animal riddles, Aldhelm appears to have chosen this particular subject to complement the collection of Symphosius, his predecessor and model, whose riddle about the well (*puteus*) he was undoubtedly familiar with. Read against Aldhelm's 'fountain,' Symphosius's much shorter 'well' in fact perfectly illustrates the difference between the two hydraulic principles involved. The spring water of Aldhelm's fountain keeps moving 'speedily' and restlessly underground without any help from man. The sluggish water of Symphosius's well, on the other hand, reaches the surface of the earth only thanks to human engineering and hard work:

> Mersa procul terris in cespite lympha profundo
> Non nisi perfossis possum procedere venis,
> Et trahor ad superos alieno ducta labore.
>
> Sunk far beneath the ground in the deep soil, I am water that cannot flow forth except when channels are dug through the earth, and I am lifted to the world above, drawn by another's toil.[14]

---

12 The solutions to *Riddles* 5 and 52 are uncertain; alternative answers include 'shield' (no. 5), and 'well-buckets' or 'yoke' (no. 52).
13 Aldhelm, *Enigma* 73 (*Fons*) (trans. Lapidge and Rosier, *Aldhelm: The Poetic Works*, 85–6).
14 Symphosius, *Aenigma* 71 (*Puteus*) (ed. Shackleton Bailey, *Anthologia Latina*, 224; trans. Ohl, *Enigmas of Symphosius*, 103).

The Old English poet makes this very 'toil' the topic of his riddle. Here, the water is equally passive, while the labour is performed by the sweep and its 'master'; but it is their relationship and mutual dependence that enables the author to fully explore the technical side of the beast-like thing he describes. For a contemporary reader (or listener), the poem's descriptive part alone might have sufficed to suggest the solution to the riddle, but the author concludes with what is almost a telltale clue as to the object's name (lines 14b–15):

> Þry sind in naman
> ryhte runstafas, þara is rad fruma.

From these one-and-a-half lines, it would seem easy to work out the Old English name of the well-sweep, but, alas, their exact meaning is obscured by a scribal blunder. In the manuscript, the line ends with the nonsensical word *furum*, which must be a mistake for either *fruma* ~ *forma* (adj., 'first') or *foran* (adv., 'in front') or perhaps *fultum* (n., 'help'). Another problem lies in *rad*, whose syntactic role is ambiguous. While some editors and critics have taken *rad* as a rune, others have interpreted it as the first half of a compound whose second element is three lettered – as in *radpyt*, *radlim*, or *radrod*.[15] None of these compounds, however, is attested in the surviving corpus of Old English. Instead, from what the author says, it seems more likely that the object's name consists of only three letters (*Þry ... runstafas*), the first of which is the *rad*-rune ᚱ, that is, 'r.' With the emendation of *furum* to *fruma* 'first' – as an adjective modifying *runstafas* – the concluding lines may then be translated as follows: 'In [its] name there are three straight runic letters, of which *rad* is the first.'

The Old English word for the well-sweep is not known, but *rod* – as suggested by Holthausen, who translates it as 'pole' - may well be the word in question.[16] OE *rod* normally means 'rood,' 'cross,' or 'gallows.'[17] However, the riddle describes not only the swinging pole ('head' and 'tail') of the sweep, but also its support ('foot') and its rope or chain ('tongue'). The whole apparatus, in fact, resembles a cross or gallows, so

---

15 See Blakeley, 'Riddles 22 and 58,' 247–52; Williamson, *Old English Riddles*, 312; Muir, *Exeter Anthology*, 654; Niles, *Old English Enigmatic Poems*, 89–92.
16 Holthausen, 'Beiträge zur Erklärung und Textkritik,' 387, with the misprint *furma* for *fruma*; cf. Grein, *Bibliothek der angelsächsischen Poesie*, 396.
17 BT, s.v. *rod* and *seglrod*.

that *rod* indeed seems to be the encrypted name to be guessed.[18] A hitherto unnoticed clue to support this interpretation can be found in the adjective *ryhte* (15), whose semantic scope extends from 'right,' 'just,' and 'correct' to 'straight' or 'erect.'[19] The meaning implied here is the more literal 'straight' or 'upright,' which I would suggest refers to the vertical shape of the runes implied: if spelled in the runic futhorc, *rod* indeed consists of three runes with upright vertical strokes, namely, ᚱ 'r,' ᚩ 'o,' and ᛞ 'd.'

The cryptographic puzzle of *Riddle* 58 can be seen as yet another variation of runic encoding employed in the Exeter Book. The 'sea horse' of *Riddle* 19 is hidden in the poem's reversed rune-groups and in the acronym formed by the initial graphs of each group. The runes of *Riddle* 64 also help to identify nouns that denote the subject, but this time only the first two letters of each word are indicated. In *Riddle* 24 (as well as in *Riddles* 75 and 42, as will be demonstrated shortly), the runes spell the full name of the animal to be guessed, but they must be correctly rearranged in order to make sense. In the 'well-sweep' riddle, the principle is again different, albeit similar. Here, the author combines the method of omission with a numeric cipher indicating the total number of letters, while he additionally describes the shape of the rune-graphs to be substituted. The only rune given is ᚱ, or *rad*, whose name means 'riding' or 'journey' (from OE *ridan* 'to ride'). While the rune is primarily an alphabetic clue, the author simultaneously exploits its phonetic and logographic potential insofar as its name, *rad*, provides a pun for *rod*, the possible name of the toiling and 'riding' well-sweep. The word thus sustains the riddle's play of paradox to its conclusion: it is said of the creature that it 'does not travel far, nor ride much' (*Wide ne fereð, ne fela rideð*, 2–3) – yet 'riding' (*rad*) is in its name.

Covered Tracks (*Riddle* 75)

The *hund* 'dog,' whose barking is mimicked by the garrulous jay of *Riddle* 24, must be the animal described in the very short *Riddle* 75, another example of runic encoding. Krapp and Dobbie print it as follows:

Ic swiftne geseah on swaþe feran
·ᛞᚾᛁᛋ·[20]

---

18 Cf. ModG *Galg(en)brunnen*, for a draw-well with sweep.
19 BT, s.v. *riht*, adj.
20 ASPR 3:234.

I saw a swift one go along a track: *dæg, nyd, lagu, hægl*.

In the manuscript, the text consists of only a single line. It is unmistakably marked by the scribe as a separate item, with a capital *I* in the opening *Ic*, and the usual final punctuation mark after the four rune-graphs. Although the non-runic part is metrically intact, the runes do not fit into the verse and merely seem to indicate the solution. Hence, most editors have opted to print the riddle in two lines, with the descriptive part on the first, and the runes on the next. Because of its fragmentary character, some have made a case for printing *Riddle* 75 together with the structurally identical *Riddle* 76, another single-liner that immediately follows on the same manuscript page:

Ic ane geseah   idese sittan.[21]

I saw a woman sit alone.

However, the capitalization and punctuation leave no doubt that, despite their brevity and uniformity, the two entries constitute two individual riddles. While the second of this odd pair of one-liners must remain insoluble, *Riddle* 75 can be solved with the help of its runic clue. Its substance, meagre though it is, consists of a narrated event in which an unknown 'swift one' goes 'along a track' (*swiftne ... on swaþe feran*), as witnessed by the speaker/riddler (*Ic ... geseah*). The riddle thus conforms to the 'I saw'-type of riddles featuring a first-person narrator describing the enigmatic subject, as opposed to the 'I am'-or 'I was'-type, in which the personified subject speaks and describes itself. Both narrative patterns occur almost universally in riddles of all languages and times, including the Latin *enigmata*. In the Exeter Book, most riddles of the first kind typically begin with the *Ic seah*-formula, regularly followed by one or more infinitives. In *Riddle* 75, this stereotypical unit is expanded by the prepositional phrase *on swaþe*, so that the syntactical structure is very much the same as in the opening lines of the two runic ship-riddles (nos 19 and 64) discussed above. Given these parallels, one might assume that *Riddle* 75, too, is about a ship at sea. Yet other riddles in the collection feature similar descriptions of travelling or moving objects, and since the descriptive clues are so vague and so few, it seems reasonable to look for the solution in the four runic letters. Transliterated into the roman alphabet, however, they do not yield a known Old English word, even if the letters are reversed or rearranged: 'd,' 'n,' 'l,' and 'h' are consonants, and it would seem

---

21 Fol. 127r (ibid.).

that there is at least one vowel missing. Several attempts have therefore been made to complete, replace, or emend the four runes. W.S. Mackie, for instance, suggests that the scribe omitted the vowels 'æ' and 'e' to produce an anagram of the consonants of *hælend*, 'saviour,' and proposes the solution: 'Christ as a hunter in pursuit of sin.'[22] Similarly, Craig Williamson postulates a missing 'a' to arrive at his rather eccentric answer, *hland*, 'piss,' taking Riddles 75 and 76 as two contrasting descriptions of male and female urination.[23] Both readings – Mackie's allegorical *hælend* and Williamson's more profane *hland* – try to interpret the runes without emending them, but they are strained and fail to account for the two descriptive clues: the swiftness of the creature and the track it follows. Norman E. Eliason's 'elk hunter' at first seems to fit better, but it is equally farfetched and inconsistent; trying to apply another principle of medieval cryptography, namely, the substitution of consonants for vowels, Eliason believes that the consonants ᛗ 'd' and ᛏ 'n' stand for the vowels 'e' and 'o,' which follow 'd' and 'n' in the alphabet – hence *eolh* 'elk.'[24] As we have seen in chapter 3, the code of vowel substitution is employed in Riddle 36 in its three encrypted Latin words, *homo*, *mulier*, and *equus*. However, roman letters – but not runes – are involved there, and the consonants replace the preceding (rather than the following) vowels.

In search of the missing vowel in the runic clue of Riddle 75, the majority of critics have followed the very first editor of the Exeter Book, Benjamin Thorpe (1842), and emended the third rune, ᛚ 'l,' to ᚢ 'u.' Read backwards, the runes then yield the solution *hund*, the Old English word for a hunting dog or hound, which also occurs in Riddles 24.2 (*hund*) and 36.11 (*hundes*).[25] More radically, René Derolez even suggests that there is no scribal error in Riddle 75 at all. 'Thus far,' he writes, 'all scholars have read the third rune as *l*. Actually the lateral stroke is a broken line, and the whole can only be a poorly made *u*. This gives the reading *hund*, which most scholars in any case obtained through emendation.'[26] *Hund* indeed appears to be the solution to this one-liner; it is a masculine noun and, of course, tallies perfectly with the description of the male 'swift one' that goes 'along a track.'

---

22 Mackie, 'Text of the Exeter Book,' 77.
23 Williamson, *Old English Riddles*, 352–5; Williamson, *Feast of Creatures*, 208.
24 Eliason, 'Old English Cryptographic Riddles,' 554–6.
25 This is the most widely accepted solution; see Fry, 'Exeter Book Riddle Solutions,' 25. For OE *hund* (which is earlier and more common than the late OE *docga*), see BT, s.v.; Jordan, *Die altenglischen Säugetiernamen*, 46–51; Moessner, 'Dog – Man's Best Friend,' 209–10.
26 Derolez, *Runica Manuscripta*, 419.

108   Codes

One thinks of an agile hunting dog pursuing its prey, just like the relentless enemy of the porcupine in *Riddle* 15 or the hounds chasing a stag in *Beowulf* (1368–72). Of all domestic animals, the dog, together with the horse, has always been closest to man. Accordingly, it was given ample space in classical and medieval literature, from natural histories and encyclopedias to fables, beast poems, and hunting manuals. In his *Natural History*, Pliny the Elder praises the dog's fidelity and intelligence at length, illustrating his argument with many anecdotes about famous dogs of antiquity. Concerning dogs used for hunting, Pliny writes:

> plurima alia in his cotidie vita invenit, sed in venatu sollertia et sagacitas praecipua est. scrutatur vestigia atque persequitur, comitantem ad feram inquisitorem loro trahens ...
>
> Experience daily discovers very many other qualities in these animals, but it is in hunting that their skill and sagacity is most outstanding. A hound traces and follows footprints, dragging by its leash the tracker that accompanies it towards his quarry.[27]

Pliny's account was compiled in the third century by Solinus, whose *Collectanea rerum memorabilium* were used, in turn, by Isidore of Seville for his *Etymologies*.[28] More than Pliny and Solinus, Isidore emphasizes not only the fidelity, strength (*fortitudo*), and hunting prowess of the dog, but also its swiftness (*velocitas*) – the very characteristic that is highlighted in *Riddle* 75. Isidore writes:

> Nihil autem sagacius canibus; plus enim sensui ceteris animalibus habent. Namque soli sua nomina recognoscunt; dominos suos diligunt; dominorum tecta defendunt; pro dominis suis se morti obiciunt; voluntarie cum domino ad praedam currunt; corpus domini sui etiam mortuum non relinquunt. Quorum postremo naturae est extra homines esse non posse. In canibus duo sunt: aut fortitudo, aut velocitas.
>
> No animal is smarter than the dog, for they have more sense than the others. They alone recognize their own names; they love their masters; they defend their master's home; they lay down their life for their master; they willingly run after game with their master; they do not leave the body of their master even when he has died. Finally, it is part of their nature not to

---

27 Pliny, *Nat. hist.* 8.147 (ed. Mayhoff, 2:91; trans. Rackham, 103).
28 Cf. Solinus, *Collect.* 15.6–12.

be able to live apart from humans. There are two qualities found in dogs: strength and speed.[29]

Not surprisingly, the dog is also included in the bestiary of Aldhelm's *Enigmata*. For Aldhelm, the dog's unfailing fidelity to its master (*dominus*), which is so much stressed by Isidore, is precisely what characterizes the animal, together with its simultaneous courage and fear of being beaten, even by a child:

> Sic me iamdudum rerum veneranda potestas
> Fecerat, ut domini truculentos persequar hostes;
> Rictibus arma gerens bellorum praelia patro
> Et tamen infantum fugiens mox verbera vito.

> The mighty force of things [i.e., God] long ago created me in such a way that I chase the fierce enemies of my master; bearing arms [as it were] in my mouth I accomplish deeds of war, and yet I'm quick to avoid a beating by fleeing from a child.[30]

For once the Old English *Riddle* and its Latin counterpart may have little in common. Rather than focusing on the animal's fidelity and strength, the Old English riddle-maker took the two aspects of swiftness (*velocitas*) and perhaps its sagacity as the dog's identifying characteristics. The same swiftness, as Frederick Tupper has noted, is also emphasized in Ælfric's *Colloquy* in the dialogue between the master and the pupil playing the huntsman; asked if he knows how to hunt without nets, the pupil replies (in the Latin original and in the Old English gloss):

> Cum velocibus canibus insequor feras.
> Mid swiftum hundum ic betæce wildeor.[31]

> With swift hounds I chase wild animals.

---

29 *Etym.* 12.2.25–6 (ed. André, 111; trans. Barney et al., 253).
30 *Enigma* 10 (ed. Glorie, *Collectiones Aenigmatum Merovingicae Aetatis*, 393; trans. Lapidge and Rosier, *Aldhelm: The Poetic Works*, 72). The subject is not the Molossian dog in particular, but more generally a strong watch- or hunting dog; see Erhardt-Siebold, *Die lateinischen Rätsel*, 173–4.
31 Ælfric, *Colloquy*, 64 (ed. Garmonsway, 24); cf. ibid., line 133. The passage is quoted by Tupper, *Riddles of the Exeter Book*, 215, together with other references to the keeping of hunting dogs in Anglo-Saxon England. See also Hagen, *Anglo-Saxon Food and Drink*, 136–41.

Moreover, both swiftness and sagacity are as typical of the hunting dog as they are essential to the keen reader trying to decipher and solve the riddle. Constructed along a single line, *Riddle* 75 itself describes, as it were, a linguistic 'track' that the reader has to follow, first from left to right and then from right to left.

Loose Ends

Riddles 75 and 76 are not the only items in the collection that seem to be mere fragments. Notably in the third and final sequence of the *Riddles* (fols. 124b–130b), there are – as Wim Tigges notes – 'a few mysterious one- and two-liners [nos 68, 69, 75, 76, and 79] ... which may be evidence of hurried half-recollection as the compilation neared its completion.'[32] We should not forget, however, that in the long history of the riddle as a literary genre, there are many examples of riddling questions and conundrums that consist of only a single line or sentence. For the early Middle Ages, the short prose riddles in Alcuin's *Disputatio Pippini cum Albino* are a case in point. Not only are several of these dialogic puzzles based on verse riddles by Symphosius or otherwise paralleled in medieval riddle collections, but they even follow the traditional 'I saw' pattern, like the riddle about the arrow:

> ALBINUS: Vidi feminam volantem, rostrum habentum ferreum et corpus ligneum et caudam pennatam, mortem portantem.
> PIPPINUS: Socia est militum.[33]
>
> ALCUIN: I saw a woman flying, with an iron beak, a wooden body and a feathered tail, carrying death.
> PIPPIN: That's the companion of the soldiers.

The Latin word for arrow, *sagitta*, is a feminine noun – hence the pun on the enigmatic 'woman,' who is described in terms of a flying bird whose 'beak,' 'body,' and 'tail' recall the lists of body parts in some of the Old English *Riddles*. Typically, the answers in Alcuin's dialogue are not straightforward

---

32 Tigges, 'Snakes and Ladders,' 97.
33 *Disputatio* 104 (ed. Suchier, 'Disputatio Pippini cum Albino,' 142); cf. Symphosius, *Aenigma* 65 (*Sagitta*). The other analogues are Alcuin, *Disputatio*, 93, 95–9 (= Symphosius, *Aenigmata* 76, 30, 14, 98, 12, 99). See Wilmanns, 'Disputatio regalis et nobilissimi iuvenis Pippini cum Albino scholastico,' 542–4; Orchard, *Poetic Art of Aldhelm*, 155–6; Bayless, 'Alcuin's *Disputatio Pippini*.'

solutions naming the subject, but spirited and witty circumlocutions that actually expand the riddle. Laconic diction and the use of the metaphorical language of riddling are equally characteristic of the series of short questions and answers in the first half of the *Disputatio*; highly condensed and often unexpectedly poetic, most of these brief exchanges, in fact, read as if they were inverted riddles, like this definition of spring:

> PIPPINUS: Quid est ver?
> ALBINUS: Pictor terrae.[34]
>
> PIPPIN: What is spring?
> ALCUIN: The earth's painter.

Alcuin's *Disputatio* is just one example of early medieval dialogue literature using riddles for the classroom or for monastic sport. Similar short riddle-questions in prose already existed in the various versions of once widely circulated *Ioca monachorum* and the related wisdom dialogue of *Adrianus et Epictitus*. To this family of Latin texts also belong the lengthier and more disparate *Collectanea* of pseudo-Bede, which perhaps date from the eighth century. The *Collectanea* are a typical miscellany of Bible knowledge, monastic lore, and hagiographic notes, with passages from the *Ioca monachorum* and excerpts from Symphosius's and Aldhelm's *enigmata*, as well as a number of interspersed shorter prose puzzles and paradoxes in conversational form.[35] One of these mini-riddles has been solved as 'a horse drawn by a pen':

> Sedeo super equum non natum, cuius matrem in manu teneo.
>
> I sit on a horse that was not born, and whose mother I hold in my hand.[36]

Another one obviously describes the paradox of the cuckoo. Like the bird of *Riddle* 9, the cuckoo is first 'unborn' in its egg and only brought to life by three 'persons,' that is, its actual parents and its foster mother:

> Vidi filium non natum, sed ex tribus personis suscitatum, et eum nutritum, donec vivus vocaretur.

---

34 *Disputatio* 65 (ed. Suchier, 'Disputatio Pippini cum Albino,' 140).
35 See Bayless, '*Collectanea*.'
36 *Collectanea Pseudo-Bedae*, 19 (ed. and trans. Bayless and Lapidge, 122–3). See Tupper, 'Riddles of the Bede Tradition,' 563.

> I saw a son not born but brought forth from three persons and brought up until he should be called alive.[37]

Related to these Latin tests of knowledge and wit are the riddle-like queries that are woven into the Old English dialogues known as *Solomon and Saturn*. In the two verse and two prose texts bearing this title, the biblical king Solomon (representing Christian wisdom) and the Chaldean prince Saturn (representing the pagan Orient) debate religious questions, discussing the devil and the marvels of the world and exchanging catechetical knowledge and esoteric lore in some sort of riddling contest. The parallels with Old English wisdom literature and the *Riddles* are obvious. In the poetic *Solomon and Saturn I*, for instance, Solomon expounds the apotropaic power of the Lord's Prayer, whose letters are represented by ornamental runes.[38] In the second poem (*Solomon and Saturn II*), the two interlocutors pose and answer several enigmatic questions, including at least two riddles proper whose subjects appear to be 'book' and 'old age.'[39] Unlike these obscure and often bizarre poems, the so-called *Prose Solomon and Saturn* clearly conforms to the question-and-answer pattern of the earlier Latin dialogues. Together with the contemporary Old English *Adrian and Ritheus*, it is rooted in the tradition of the *Ioca monachorum*, sharing their subject matter and humour as well as their biblical, theological, and mystical sources. Many of the fifty-nine questions of the *Prose Solomon and Saturn* read like short riddles or conundrums. Two examples may suffice. Saturn asks, and Solomon answers:

> Sage me hwer god sete þa he geworhte heofonas and eorþan.
> Ic þe secge, he sætt ofer winda feðerum.
>
> Tell me where God sat when He made the heavens and the earth.
> I tell you, he sat on the wings of the winds.

And later:

---

37 *Collectanea Pseudo-Bedae*, 196 (ed. and trans. Bayless and Lapidge, 144–5); solved as 'chick in an egg,' (ibid., 245).
38 The runes occur in only one of the two surviving manuscripts; see Menner, *Solomon and Saturn*, 48–9; Derolez, *Runica Manuscripta*, 419–20; Page, *Introduction to English Runes*, 187–8.
39 *Solomon and Saturn II*, 221–35, 273–92 (ed. Menner, *Solomon and Saturn*, 57–8, 64–5).

Saga me hwæt ys hefogost to berende on eorðan.
Ic þe secge, mannes synna and hys hlafordes yrre.

Tell me what is heaviest to bear on earth.
I tell you, man's sins and his Lord's anger.[40]

Viewed in this context of monastic rhetoric and jocose riddle wisdom, the erratic one- and two-liners among the Exeter Book *Riddles* appear in a different light. Instead of aborted lines from longer poems, they may simply be short riddles: puzzling and tantalizing, but nevertheless complete, even if the solutions to some of them will always elude us.

---

40 *Prose Salomon and Saturn*, 1, 48 (ed. and trans. Cross and Hill, 25, 33, 60, 114).

6 Letter Games

As we have seen in chapter 3, the Anglo-Latin riddle-poets occasionally employed logographs as linguistic clues that help both to obscure and to identify the subjects of their riddles. Aldhelm's and Eusebius's letter games with pairs of words that look and sound similar such as *paries-aries* or *lumen-flumen-fluvius*, however, not only are playful reminiscences from the classroom, but also exhibit a deeper interest in Isidorian concepts of morphology, etymology, and synonymy.[1] It is no surprise, therefore, that even the letters themselves – together or individually – became the subject of medieval riddling, as in Tatwine's and Eusebius's *enigmata* about the alphabet, or the letters *a*, *x*, *v*, and *i*.[2] The model for all these is Aldhelm's riddle about the seventeen characters of the Latin alphabet (*Elementa*); in its opening lines, the letters introduce themselves as the 'seventeen voiceless sisters,' who – paradoxically – are able to produce words:

> Nos decem et septem genitae sine voce sorores
> Sex alias nothas non dicimus annumerandas.
>
> We are born seventeen voiceless sisters; we say that the six other bastards are not to be counted in our number.[3]

---

1 Apart from Isidore's *Etymologies*, his *Differentiae* and *Synonyma* also circulated widely in Anglo-Saxon England, exerting a strong influence on, for instance, Bede's *De orthographia* and Alcuin's work of the same name.
2 Tatwine, *Enigma* 4 (*De litteris*); Eusebius, *Enigmata* 7 (*De littera*), 9 (*De alpha*), 14 (*De x littera*), 19 (*De v littera*), 39 (*De i littera*). See Erhardt-Siebold, *Die lateinischen Rätsel*, 249–56.
3 *Enigma* 30.1–2 (ed. Glorie, *Collectiones Aenigmatum Merovingicae Aetatis*, 413; trans. Lapidge and Rosier, *Aldhelm: The Poetic Works*, 76).

The seventeen sisters are the Latin letters *a, b, c, d, e, f, g, i, l, m, n, o, p, r, s, t,* and *v*. Their six illegitimate siblings are *h, k, q, x, y,* and *z*; they are 'bastards' because they were traditionally considered to be later additions to the original set of seventeen. This distinction – together with the paradox of the 'voiceless,' yet speaking, letters – was known to Aldhelm from Isidore of Seville's *Etymologies*, while the theme of the letters as 'sisters' born from the fingers holding a iron stylus or quill pen likewise occurs in the anonymous, seventh-century *Berne Riddles*.[4]

Ten in All (*Riddle* 13)

Aldhelm's *enigma* about the alphabet has been quoted by some critics in connection with Exeter Book *Riddle* 13, another example where numbers and perhaps a letter puzzle are involved. The riddle describes ten young chickens that have just hatched from their eggs and are making their first steps in the hen yard:

Ic seah turf tredan,   X wæron ealra,
VI gebroþor   ond hyra sweostor mid;
hæfdon feorg cwico.   Fell hongedon
sweotol ond gesyne   on seles wæge
anra gehwylces.   Ne wæs hyra ængum þy wyrs,   5
ne sið þy sarra,   þeah hy swa sceoldon
reafe birofene,   rodra weardes
meahtum aweahte,   muþum slitan
haswe blede.   Hrægl bið geniwad
þam þe ær forðcymene   frætwe leton   10
licgan on laste,   gewitan lond tredan.[5]

I saw [them] treading the turf: they were ten in all, six brothers and their sisters, too; they had lively spirits. [Their] skins hung clear and visible on the wall of each one's hall. [5] None of them was any the worse, nor [their] journey more painful, though they must thus, deprived of their garment [and] roused by the powers of the guardian of the heavens, tear at grey shoots with their mouths. Clothing is renewed [10] to those who before, having come forth, left [their] adornments lying behind [and] went to tread the land.

---

4 Isidore, *Etym.* 1.4.10–15, 1.3.1; *Berne Riddle* 25 (*De litteris*); cf. Eusebius, *Enigma* 39.2.
5 *Riddle* 13 (ASPR 3:187, except line 6: *ne siðe þy sarre*). The MS has *ne side þy sarra*; my emendation follows Cosijn, 'Anglosaxonica,' 128.

The solution, 'ten chickens,' which was first proposed in 1894 by Moritz Trautmann,[6] is sustained by a number of linguistic parallels to other bird riddles of the Exeter Book. First, the half-line *hæfdon feorg cwico* (3) indicates that the ten creatures of this riddle are animate entities; they have 'lively spirits,' like the cuckoo and the barnacle goose in *Riddles* 9 and 10, the water bird in *Riddle* 74, and the ox in *Riddle* 12, all of whom are also endowed with a quick *feorh* or *ferð*.[7] Another hint is given at the beginning of the poem and confirmed in its concluding half-line: treading the 'turf' or 'land' (1 and 11), the ten creatures must be animals. Similarly, in *Riddle* 72, the ox remembers how it 'trod the paths in the Welsh borderland' (*mearcpaþas Walas træd*, 12), while the little birds in *Riddle* 57 'tread the wooded cliffs' (*tredað bearonæssas*, 5), and the swan in *Riddle* 7 says: 'I tread the ground' (*ic hrusan trede*, 1). The same riddle provides a further point of comparison: the swan's plumage is referred to as *hrægl* 'clothing' and *frætwe* 'adornments,' and *hrægl* is again used for the feathers of the barnacle goose in *Riddle* 10.[8] Here, the same terms – *hrægl* (9) and *frætwe* (10) – therefore suggest that the ten treading animals are birds. That they are, in fact, young chickens finally becomes clear when we interpret these lexical clues in the context of the riddle's overall narrative. Like the cuckoo in *Riddle* 9, the embryo birds here are first dead in their eggs and then quickened to life only by 'the guardian of the heavens,' that is, God (7–8). When they have hatched, the young leave their nest and walk around, leaving behind their eggshells and downs. That their 'skins' (*fell*, 3) grotesquely hang 'on the wall of each one's hall' (*on seles wæge anra gehwylces*, 4–5) is part of the riddle's central paradox: the chicks are stripped of their 'skins' and 'garment' (*reafe*, 7), and yet they are alive and unharmed as they walk from their nest. Like *hrægl* and *frætwe*, *fell* and *reafe* are deliberately equivocal terms. As some critics have suggested, the 'skins' are perhaps best interpreted as the shell membranes that are left hanging inside the broken egg or

---

6 Trautmann, 'Die Auflösungen der altenglischen Rätsel,' 48; cf. Trautmann, 'Alte und neue Antworten,' 177–80, 'Zum Streit um die altenglischen Rätsel,' 129, and *Die altenglischen Rätsel*, 76. Alternative solutions are listed by Fry, 'Exeter Book Riddle Solutions,' 23, and Muir, *Exeter Anthology*, 657.
7 Conversely, the subject of *Riddle* 39 ('dream') is no animate being, because 'it has no spirit' (*ne hafað ... feorh*, 16).
8 Similarly, the host bird of the cuckoo (*Riddle* 9) and the hen (*Riddle* 42) are said to wear a feathery 'dress' (OE *wæd*).

'hall' of each chick,⁹ while the metaphorical 'garment' denotes either the eggshell or the chick's down. This is evidenced by a close analogue from the Latin *enigmata*, namely, Eusebius's riddle about the chick or young chicken (*De pullo*). The four-line poem, which also informed the Old English 'cuckoo' (*Riddle* 9), similarly deals with the transformation from lifeless egg to living bird and employs the same metaphors of 'clothing' and 'skin' to describe the protecting eggshell. Eusebius writes:

> Cum corio ante meo tectus vestitus et essem,
> Tunc nihil ore cibi gustabam, oculisque videre
> Non potui; pascor nunc escis, pelle detectus
> Vivo; sed exanimis transivi viscere matris.

> At first I was clothed and protected in a shell, my mouth then tasted no food, my eyes saw nothing; but now, stripped of my skin, I eat and live, though lifeless I once left my mother's womb.¹⁰

Exactly the same theme occurs in a short Latin riddle, which is known in three cognate versions from three different early medieval collections or manuscripts.¹¹ The first is one of the prose puzzles in the pseudo-Bedan *Collectanea*:

> Vidi filium cum matre manducantem, cuius pellis pendebat in pariete.
>
> I saw eating with its mother a son whose skin hung on the wall.¹²

An almost identical version of the same riddle survives in a tenth-century manuscript from St Gallen, together with a handful of other prose riddles that were appended to those of Symphosius; this version reads:

> Vidi hominem ambulantem cum matre sua et pellis eius pendebat in pariete.

---

9 As first suggested by Trautmann, 'Alte und neue Antworten,' 179; see Erhardt-Siebold, 'Old English Riddle 13,' 98, Williamson, *Old English Riddles*, 169. Cf. Aristotle, *Hist. animal.* 6.3 561b.
10 *Enigma* 38 (ed. Glorie, *Collectiones Aenigmatum Merovingicae Aetatis*, 248; trans. Erhardt-Siebold, ibid.). The parallel was first noticed by Trautmann, 'Alte und neue Antworten,' 179.
11 See Lendinara, 'Gli *Aenigmata Laureshamensia*,' 80–4.
12 *Collectanea Pseudo-Bedae*, 18 (ed. and trans. Bayless and Lapidge, 122–3).

118   Codes

I saw a man walking with his mother, and his skin hung on the wall.[13]

A third version, this time in verse, is found among the twelve anonymous *Lorsch Riddles* from the early ninth century. Again, the author uses the same set of phrases and metaphors, recasting them in two hexameters:

> En video sobolem propria cum matre morantem,
> Mandre cuius pellis in pariete pendet adhaerens.
>
> Lo, I see an offspring abiding with his own mother, his skin, by adhering to the stable, hangs on the wall.[14]

The 'mother' in these three mini-riddles is, of course, the hen, while the 'son' or 'man' is the male chick that has just hatched from its egg; the 'skin' (Lat. *pellis*), which is mentioned in all versions (including that of Eusebius), is the down left behind, clinging to the wall of the hen-house. Such striking correspondences suggest that all these Latin riddles and *Riddle* 13 share the same solution and retell a traditional puzzle, which was common enough to be stripped down to a single sentence. It is only in the *Collectanea* and in the Exeter Book, however, that we find the clinching detail that secures the specific solution 'young chicken(s).' In the Latin version, the clue lies in the verb *manducantem*: just hatched, the little bird is eating with its mother. This corresponds to what is said in two half-lines of the Old English riddle, which almost go unnoticed in the long sentence that occupies the middle of the poem (5–9): brought to life by God, the young at once begin to peck the grass or grains, or literally 'tear at grey shoots with their mouths' (*muþum slitan haswe blede*, 8–9).[15] This behaviour is genuinely characteristic of all species of the pheasant family or *Phasianidae*, to which the domestic chicken (*Gallus domesticus*) belongs. Unlike most other birds, young *Phasianidae* immediately leave the nest at hatching and are capable of feeding themselves,

---

13 Suchier, 'Disputatio Pippini cum Albino,' 144. For the manuscript (St Gallen, Stiftsbibliothek, 196), see Scherrer, *Verzeichnis der Handschriften der Stiftsbibliothek von St. Gallen*, 72; Bayless, 'Alcuin's *Disputatio Pippini*,' 159.
14 *Lorsch Riddle* 8 (ed. Glorie, *Collectiones Aenigmatum Merovingicae Aetatis*, 354; trans. adapted from Erhardt-Siebold, 'Old English Riddle 13,' 99). See Bieler, '*Aenigmata Lauresbamensia*,' 14. For MLat. *madra* 'sheepfold,' see *DML*, s.v.
15 For *haswe blede*, see Biggam, *Grey in Old English*, 295, 303; *DOE*, s.v. *bled*, *blæd*.

and only occasionally are they fed bill-to-bill or shown some food by their parents. With their strong bills and claws they eat almost anything they can dig out and pick up, including roots, shoots, seeds, small insects, and cultivated grain and other food they are given by man.[16]

But why does the author of the riddle distinguish male and female chickens: six 'brothers' and four 'sisters'? And why are they 'ten in all' (1)? In the light of Aldhelm's *enigma* about the letters of the alphabet quoted above, it would seem that these numbers involve a logograph, so that the 'brothers' and 'sisters' encode ten letters, which, correctly rearranged or perhaps completed, yield the solution to the riddle. As we have seen, the traditional system that Aldhelm elaborates upon distinguishes 'sisters' from 'bastards'; while the original letters of the Latin alphabet are the seventeen legitimate 'sisters,' all later additions are illegitimate 'bastards.'[17] Obviously, this distinction does not match the six 'brothers' and four 'sisters' of *Riddle* 13, but it may well be that its author, writing in an idiom other than Latin, went one step further and distinguished Old English vowels from consonants. This assumption has led Erika von Erhardt-Siebold to her ingenious proposal to solve *Riddle* 13 as *ten ciccenu* 'ten chickens.' As she argues: 'This solution with its ten letters, of which six are consonants (brothers) and four vowels (sisters), would readily explain the number puzzle. The spelling *ciccen* instead of the usual *ciecen* or *cicen* is characteristic of the Northumbrian dialect; hence, it is another instance corroborating the presumable Northumbrian origin of many of the OE riddles.'[18] *Cicen* (rather than *ciecen*) is indeed the standard West Saxon form for 'chicken' in Old English, its plural being *cicenu* 'chickens.' Both spellings are well recorded in the surviving corpus, while the geminate plural *cicceno* (rather than *ciccenu) occurs only once, namely, in the late tenth-century Northumbrian glosses to the *Lindisfarne Gospels*.[19] The proposed plural *ciccenu is therefore, strictly speaking, a hybrid combining the attested West Saxon *cicenu* and Northumbrian *cicceno*. It is true, though, that we find a number of non West Saxon spellings in the Exeter Book, so that a variant like *ciccenu (or *cicceno*) would be no exception, even though the comparatively few Anglian forms in the *Riddles* appear

---

16 See Cramp et al., *Birds of Europe*, 2:444–5.
17 Aldhelm, *Enigma* 30 (*Elementa*) (trans. Lapidge and Rosier, *Aldhelm: The Poetic Works*, 76).
18 Erhardt-Siebold, 'Old English Riddle 13,' 99.
19 See BT and *DOE*, s.v. *cicen*; Whitman, 'Birds of Old English Literature,' 185–6; Kitson, 'Old English Bird-Names,' 499.

to be no more than occasional archaisms, without necessarily proving any northern origin or influence.[20]

Even without such a possible letter puzzle, however, the solution 'ten chickens' is already suggested strongly enough by the riddle's detailed description and by the various analogues that can be found both within and outside the collection. As in the 'cuckoo' and the 'barnacle goose' (nos 9 and 10), the author describes an ontogenetic evolution, which is represented as a 'journey' (6) from egg to bird. The text enacts this process as it progresses and literally 'treads' from the opening statement to its closing echo in the final half line:

Ic seah turf tredan ...
                    ... gewitan lond tredan.

I saw [them] treading the turf ... [they] went to tread the land.

In this rhetorical scheme, the riddle's conclusion rephrases what has been said at the beginning and thus describes a circular structure.[21] Here, this continuum evokes a vivid picture of a busy hen yard full of scratching and pecking fowl. In this sense, the riddle may also be seen as a complementary piece to the portrayal of the two copulating birds in *Riddle* 42 and its solution, 'cock and hen,' discussed below. While the latter – as we shall see – focuses on the two parent birds, *Riddle* 13 is exclusively concerned with the young. Strikingly, both riddles employ numbers. In *Riddle* 42, they enumerate the runes that must be combined to arrive at the double answer *hana* 'cock' and *hæn* 'hen.' Here, the numbers similarly distinguish male and female birds and perhaps involve a comparable cipher, but the total of ten also conveys the impression of a lively multitude and may indeed simply refer to one mixed brood of male and female chicks.[22] Should this indeed be the only

---

20 For the occasional doubling of consonants and non-West-Saxon spellings in the *Riddles* and in the Exeter Book in general, see Madert, *Die Sprache der altenglischen Rätsel*, 56–8, 126–7; Trautmann, 'Sprache und Versbau,' 356, and 'Zeit, Heimat und Verfasser,' 368–9; Chambers, Förster, and Flower, *Exeter Book*, 66–7; Williamson, *Old English Riddles*, 9–10.
21 This 'envelope pattern' has been observed in a number of *Riddles*, including no. 13; see Bartlett, *Larger Rhetorical Patterns*, 9, 23; Nelson, 'Rhetoric of the Exeter Book Riddles,' 439–40, and 'Time in the Exeter Book Riddles,' 515–16; Lendinara, 'Gli *Aenigmata Laureshamensia*,' 78. For the 'envelope pattern' in *Beowulf*, see Orchard, *Critical Companion to Beowulf*, 58.
22 Meaney, 'Birds on the Stream of Consciousness,' 132.

function of the numbers in this text, then its ten treading siblings have certainly made some modern readers go round in circles.

Fowl Play (*Riddle* 42)

Both runes and numbers are at work in the intriguing *Riddle* 42, which thematizes its use of runes as an archaic linguistic code that is represented in a fictitious context of oral literature and esoteric wisdom practice. The subject to be guessed is first briefly described, before the author goes to lengths to explain how the answer to the riddle may be found by correctly combining the runes that are named and enumerated in the text. As in the runic 'jay' (*Riddle* 24), the order of the runes is scrambled, but now they are spelled in roman script:

> Ic seah wyhte wrætlice twa
> undearnunga ute plegan
> hæmedlaces; hwitloc anfeng
> wlanc under wædum, gif þæs weorces speow,
> fæmne fyllo. Ic on flette mæg 5
> þurh runstafas rincum secgan,
> þam þe bec witan, bega ætsomne
> naman þara wihta. Þær sceal nyd wesan
> twega oþer ond se torhta æsc
> an an linan, acas twegen, 10
> hægelas swa some. Hwylc þæs hordgates
> cægan cræfte þa clamme onleac
> þe þa rædellan wið rynemenn
> hygefæste heold heortan bewrigene
> orþoncbendum? Nu is undyrne 15
> werum æt wine hu þa wihte mid us,
> heahmode twa, hatne sindon.²³

I saw two wondrous creatures openly play the marriage game; if the deed was successful, the fair haired maid, proud under [her] clothes, received [her] fill. By means of runic letters I can tell in the hall to book-wise men the names of both those creatures together. There must be *nyd* twice over, and the bright *æsc* one in the line, two of *ac*, and likewise of *hægel*. Who has

---

23 *Riddle* 42 (ASPR 3:203–4, except lines 8–11: rune-names capitalized, and line 17: *heanmode*; see fn28 below).

unlocked, with the power of the key, the fetters of the treasure-door that guarded the riddle against sharp-witted men skilled in mysteries, its heart concealed by cunning bonds? Now it is revealed to men at [their] wine how those two haughty creatures are called among us.

The use of rune-names, rather than futhorc characters, seems arbitrary and may well be no more than the result of dictation. On the other hand, the syntax requires inflected forms for two of the rune-names (*acas* and *hægelas*, 10–11) and, strictly speaking, the uninflected rune-graphs would render the verse metrically deficient. The runes thus fit both syntactically and metrically, but they are again semantically isolated from the surrounding text, despite the adjective *torhta* (9), which poetically characterizes the runic *æsc* as 'bright' and completes the alliteration of the line.[24]

There are two distinct parts to this riddle: a descriptive and a runic one. The short, descriptive part (1–5a) opens with the typical formula *Ic seah* and describes, in the usual veiled terms, the two 'wondrous creatures' and their love-game in the open. The runic part is much longer, making up more than two-thirds of the poem (5b–17); it spells and enumerates the four runes that yield the solution, and wraps them in the author's convoluted deliberations about how, and by whom, the riddle may be solved. The author thus wittily juxtaposes the lofty mystique of runic cryptography and the lowly instincts of the two creatures whose identity is to be guessed: the subject of the riddle is no more than what 'men at wine' normally talk about.

Since a pair of creatures is described, a two-name solution is required, and therefore the seven 'runic letters' (*runstafas*, 6) in lines 8–11 indicate 'the names of both those creatures' (7–8). The clues are two *nyd*-runes, one *æsc*-rune, two *ac*-runes, and two *hægel*-runes – or, transliterated into the roman alphabet: 'n' (twice), 'æ,' 'a' (twice), and 'h' (twice). The choice of only four different letters seems to defy an answer, but when correctly rearranged and combined, they form *hana* and *hæn*, the Old English words for 'cock' and 'hen.'[25] Once the runic clues are unravelled, the descriptive elements of the first part make full sense: the 'two

---

24 Dewa, 'Runic Riddles,' 28. The *æsc* seems to be called 'bright' because of the silver-grey bark of the ash-tree, as Tupper (*Riddles of the Exeter Book*, 173) suggests.
25 BT, s.v. *hana* and *hæn* ~ *henn*; see Kitson, 'Old English Bird-Names,' 499–500. The solution 'cock and hen' was first proposed by Dietrich ('Die Räthsel des Exeterbuchs,' 473) and has been accepted by all subsequent critics; see Fry, 'Exeter Book Riddle Solutions,' 24, and Muir, *Exeter Anthology*, 661.

wondrous creatures' are a pair of barnyard fowl that openly copulate or – in the author's ironically euphemistic terms – 'play the marriage game' (*plegan hæmedlaces*, 2–3).²⁶ The 'fair-haired' female is the hen, made pregnant by the cock: the 'maid' or 'woman' (*fæmne*, 5) literally receives her 'fill' (*fyllo*, 5). The observant riddle-solver will further identify the maid's 'clothes' (*wædum*, 4) as the hen's white feathers: the same expression, *wedum* (from *wæd* 'clothes,' 'garment'), is used for the plumage of the bird that hatches the cuckoo's egg in *Riddle* 9, while in *Riddles* 7, 10, and 13, the feathers of the swan, the barnacle goose, and the chicken are referred to as *hrægl* 'clothing, dress.'

The fact that the female is 'fair-haired' (*hwitloc*, 3) not only tallies with the actual colour of the plumage of the domestic hen, but also falsely suggests that the subject of the riddle is a woman, and moreover one who belongs to the upper class. In the social world of the *Riddles*, serfs are 'dark-haired' like the Welsh maidservants in *Riddles* 12 and 52, whereas aristocratic ladies have fair locks like the gentlewoman holding a drinking horn:

>   Cwen mec hwilum
> hwitloccedu   hond on legeð,
> eorles dohtor,   þeah hio æþelu sy.²⁷

> Sometimes a fair-haired lady lays hand on me, a nobleman's daughter, though she is noble.

The riddle's anthropomorphisms thus cloak the two fowl as a human couple joined in marriage (OE *hæmed*), and even invest them with human attitudes. While initially only the female is called 'proud' (*wlanc*, 4), at the end of the riddle, both the cock and the hen are referred to as the 'two haughty creatures' (*wihte ... heahmode twa*, 16–17).²⁸ Such a clearly human and rather negative trait recalls the stereotyped characterizations of classical and medieval natural history and beast poetry, where the rooster and the hen typically

---

26 A hapax legomenon, see *MCOE*, s.v.
27 *Riddle* 80.3b–5 (ASPR 3:235); cf. *Riddle* 40.98: *hwite loccas*.
28 I emend MS *heanmode* to *heahmode* (following Grein, *Bibliothek der angelsächsischen Poesie*, 391, and Pinsker and Ziegler, *Die altenglischen Rätsel*, 80 and 256). Both *heanmod* and *heahmod* occur only in the Exeter Book. In *Guthlac B*, 1379 (ASPR 3:88), and *Juliana*, 390 (ASPR 3:124), *heanmod(e)* means 'sad, depressed' or perhaps 'humble' (from OE *hean* 'dejected, wretched'; cf. *The Wanderer*, 23); *heahmod(ne)*, on the other hand, occurs in *The Phoenix*, 112 (ASPR 3:97), and in *Vainglory*, 54 (ASPR 3:148), in the sense of 'proud, haughty,' which is the meaning implied here. Cf. also *Phoenix*, 100 (ASPR 3:96): *fugel feþrum wlonc*.

are portrayed as boastful and salacious animals, behaving like haughty and shameless people. According to Aristotle, for example, the domestic cock is 'specially prone to copulation'; and Pliny, in his *Natural History*, describes at length the royal pride of the watchful and belligerent cock that rules self-assuredly over the 'common herd' of his fellow animals.[29] Such representations mark the beginning of a long tradition that persisted throughout the Middle Ages and well beyond. Chauntecleer and Pertelote, the pair of barnyard fowl in Chaucer's *The Nun's Priest's Tale*, come to mind, as well as the protagonists of numerous fables and folk tales. And since the cock has frequently been the subject of popular riddling, *Riddle* 42 may indeed show – as Patrizia Lendinara suggests – 'some vestige of a folk-riddle' that was 'recast for a bookish audience.'[30]

Men at Wine

Yet the 'cock and hen' riddle gains its comic effect not so much from the direct and sparing description of the copulating fowl as from the contrast between the lewd and coarse world of the two animals on the one hand, and the elevated sphere of book learning conjured up by the riddle-maker on the other. Structurally, the riddle's conclusion (11a–17) may be seen as an expansion of the conventional challenge to the reader to find the solution. In its shortest form, this challenge asks directly: *Saga hwæt ic hatte* 'Say what I am called'; *Frige hwæt ic hatte* 'Ask what I am called'; or *Ræd hwæt ic mæne* 'Guess what I mean.'[31] Alternatively, the riddler may explicitly address the wise or learned reader who is capable of solving the enigma and eager to imbibe its wisdom. Take, for instance, the conclusion of the 'wheel':

> Rece, gif þu cunne,
> wis worda gleaw,   hwæt sio wiht sie.[32]

Explain, if you can, wise [and] skilled in words, what this creature is.

---

29 Aristotle, *Hist. animal.* 1.1 488b, 6.9 564b (ed. and trans. Peck, 1:16–17, 2:254–5). Pliny, *Nat. hist.* 10.46–7 (ed. and trans. Rackham, 320–3). For the classical and medieval tradition, see Thompson, *Glossary of Greek Birds*, 33–44; Rowland, *Birds with Human Souls*, 25–8, 78–9. Compare also Aldhelm's *Enigma* 26 about the cock (*Gallus*).
30 Lendinara, 'World of Anglo-Saxon Learning,' 268. The popular origin of many cock riddles has been noted by Tupper (*Riddles of the Exeter Book*, 172) and others.
31 For a list of the various concluding formulas in the *Riddles* and their parallels in Old English poetry, see Bartlett, *Larger Rhetorical Patterns*, 99–100.
32 *Riddle* 32.13b–14 (ASPR 3:197).

Or the final lines of the 'mailcoat':

> Saga soðcwidum,   searoþoncum gleaw,
> wordum wisfæst,   hwæt þis gewæde sy.³³
>
> Say truly, [you who are] skilled in clever thoughts, wise in words, what this garment is.

Yet for all the 'popular' character of some of these concluding formulas, it is arguable that their rhetorical models are to be found in the earlier Latin *enigmata*. Aldhelm's riddle about the Morning Star (*Lucifer*) is a case in point. The poem describes the bright light of the planet Venus, that is, the Morning Star, heralding the rise of the sun as it moves through the eastern sky. After an allusion to the fall of Lucifer/Satan, Aldhelm closes with a reference to the six remaining planets:

> Sex igitur comites mecum super aethera scandunt,
> Gnarus quos poterit per biblos pandere lector.
>
> Six companions, therefore, climb the heavens with me: the learned reader will be able to disclose [their names] through books.³⁴

Aldhelm uses the same words once more in his culminating 'Creation' riddle, the final and longest piece of his one hundred *Enigmata*, which survives in a close but incomplete Old English version as *Riddle* 40 of the Exeter Book. The poem eloquently sums up the author's theological cosmology and concludes with a fittingly lavish epilogue to the reader:

> Auscultate mei credentes famina verbi,
> Pandere quae poterit gnarus vix ore magister
> Et tamen infitians non retur frivola lector!
> Sciscitor inflatos, fungar quo nomine, sophos.
>
> Pay heed, you who believe the words of my utterance! A learned teacher will scarcely be able to expound them orally; and yet the doubting reader ought not to think them trifles! I ask puffed-up wise men to tell what my name is.³⁵

---

33 *Riddle* 35.13–14 (ASPR 3:198).
34 *Enigma* 81.9–10 (ed. Glorie, *Collectiones Aenigmatum Merovingicae Aetatis*, 499; trans. Lapidge and Rosier, *Aldhelm: The Poetic Works*, 88).
35 *Enigma* 100.79–83 (ed. Glorie, *Collectiones Aenigmatum Merovingicae Aetatis*, 539; trans. Lapidge and Rosier, *Aldhelm: The Poetic Works*, 94).

Unfortunately, in the Old English translation of Aldhelm's *Creatura* riddle, the final portion is missing, owing to the loss of a folio from the manuscript. However, the extant 107 lines render the Latin original so faithfully that it is reasonable to assume that *Riddle* 40 originally concluded with an equally verbose coda addressing the wise and learned. Unlike Aldhelm, the later Anglo-Latin riddle-makers only rarely included remarks about their readers. One notable exception is Tatwine, whose four-line *Conclusio* provides the key to resolving the combined acrostic-telestic that frames his forty *Enigmata*:

> Versibus intextis vatem nunc iure salutat,
> Litterulas summa capitum hortans iungere primas,
> Versibus extremas hisdem, ex minio coloratas;
> Conversus gradiens rursum perscandat ab imo!

> With interlaced verses I now duly greet the wise reader, asking him to join the first letters of the first verses [of each riddle], and of the same the last letters, that is the rubrics. May he, by reversing his course [i.e., by reading backwards] rise again from the bottom![36]

Tatwine's poetic instruction to the reader is particularly interesting here, because it identifies a technique of orthographic decoding that is akin to the methods of systematic decipherment needed to crack the runic *Riddles*. Like their Anglo-Latin counterparts, some of the more elaborate riddle conclusions in the Exeter Book contain an explicit reference to the learned reader, but the *Riddles* repeatedly speak of a group of 'wise men':

> Micel is to hycganne
> wisfæstum menn, hwæt seo wiht sy.[37]

> It is a great thing for wise men to think what this creature is.

There are very similar conclusions in *Riddles* 41 and 67, where again the 'wise' (*wisfæst*) readers are called upon to find the solutions.[38] Such

---

36 'Aenigmata Tatuini' (ed. Glorie, *Collectiones Aenigmatum Merovingicae Aetatis*, 208; trans. Erhardt-Siebold, ibid.).
37 *Riddle* 28.12b–13 (ASPR 3:195).
38 Cf. *Riddles* 41 (*wisfæstum werum*) and 67 (*wisfæstra hwylc*); apart from *Riddles* 2 (*þoncol mon*), 31 (*wisum woðboran*), and the elaborate conclusions of *Riddles* 43 and 55.

challenges show close affinities to some of the texts traditionally referred to as Old English 'wisdom literature' or 'gnomic poetry,' most of which actually survive in the Exeter Book.³⁹ In these poems, the notion that poetry addresses the erudite and book-learned, while concealing esoteric wisdom from the incognizant, conventionally surfaces. The poems *Vainglory*, *Maxims I*, *The Order of the World*, and *Precepts*, all from the Exeter Book, engage the reader in their dialogic strategies in order to offer initiation into hidden knowledge and theological mysteries. It is important to realize that the collection of the *Riddles* opens with precisely such a gesture when, in the first 'storm' poem, the reader is questioned as follows:

Hwylc is hæleþa þæs horsc ond þæs hygecræftig
þæt þæt mæge asecgan, hwa mec on sið wræce.⁴⁰

What man is so clever and so wise that he can say who drives me forth on my journey.

In the 'cock and hen' riddle (no. 42), too, only the 'sharp-witted' (*hygefæste*, literally: 'mind-fast,' 14) are able to find the solution.⁴¹ Here, the author develops the formula into an intricate knot of metaphors and metonyms revolving around the process of enigmatic and runic encoding and decoding. The arcane knowledge of riddling and runology itself is called a sealed treasure (OE *hord*) in a powerful image that is cognate to the biblical 'treasure of wisdom and knowledge' hidden in God.⁴² The metaphorical 'fetters of the treasure-door' (*hordgates clamme*, 11–12) and the 'cunning bonds' (*orþoncbendum*, 15), which guard the riddle against its would-be solvers, are the author's linguistic disguise to conceal the riddle's 'heart' (*heortan*, 14), that is, its solution. In this scheme, the seven runic letters (*runstafas*, 6) provide the powerful 'key' (*cægan*, 12) needed to grasp the mystery and solve the riddle. Yet this interpretative key is available only

---

39 See Lerer, 'Riddle and the Book.'
40 *Riddle* 1.1–2 (ASPR 3:180).
41 I follow Trautmann (*Die altenglischen Rätsel*, 105, 172) and Pinsker and Ziegler (*Die altenglischen Rätsel*, 256) and take *hygefæste* (14) as an accusative plural masculine referring to *rynemenn* (13). The adjective is a synonym of *wisfæst*, which would not metrically fit in here.
42 Colossians 2.3. Tupper (*Riddles of the Exeter Book*, 173) compares Ælfric's preface to his *Grammar* (ed. Zupitza, 2): 'ðe stæfcræft is seo cæg, ðe ðæra boca andgit unlicð'; see also Lerer, 'Riddle and the Book,' 9–11.

to the initiated few: they are sagacious and book-learned – literally: 'men who know books' (7) – and 'men skilled in mysteries' (*rynemenn*, 13), enjoying the riddling-game over their wine. The riddler thus stages himself as a master of ceremonies, who delivers his runic puzzle 'in the hall' (*on flette*, 5)[43] before an audience of drinking men (*werum æt wine*, 16).

Strange 'men at wine' also occur elsewhere in the collection, and these men gathered in the hall often have, as Peter Clemoes has observed, an 'authenticating presence' whenever an enigmatic subject is presented in this setting.[44] In *Riddle* 14, for instance, the enigmatic subject is a horn, which is both an animal's weapon and man's companion: it serves as a drinking horn and hangs on the wall 'where men drink'; as a signal-horn, it summons warriors to battle or invites 'proud men to their wine':

> hwilum hongige   hyrstum frætwed,
> wlitig on wage,   þær weras drincað,
> freolic fyrdsceorp.   Hwilum folcwigan
> on wicge wegað,   þonne ic winde sceal   15
> sincfag swelgan   of sumes bosme;
> hwilum ic gereordum   rincas laðige
> wlonce to wine.[45]

> sometimes I hang, decked with adornments, beautiful, on the wall where men drink, a noble war-ornament. Sometimes warriors carry me on a horse, when, treasure-adorned, [15] I must swallow wind from someone's bosom; sometimes I invite with my sound proud men to [their] wine.

Here, the context is aristocratic and heroic, reminiscent of the social milieu of Heorot, the famed hall in *Beowulf*, where the heroes feast and boast over their drinking horns filled with mead.[46] More explicitly, the hall in *Riddle* 20 is seen as a place where the king and his mead-drinking retainers meet in a courtly environment; the subject to be guessed – perhaps a falcon or a hawk trained as the king's hunting bird – is speaking:

---

43 Cf. *Riddles* 55.2 and 56.12 (*on flet*); literally 'on the floor,' but to be taken metonymically for the hall, as in *Beowulf*, 1025, *Genesis A*, 2449, and *Widsið*, 3. See also Gleißner, *Die 'zweideutigen' altenglischen Rätsel*, 253–4.
44 Clemoes, *Interactions of Thought and Language*, 189.
45 *Riddle* 14.11–17a (ASPR 3:187).
46 See Hume, 'Concept of the Hall'; Earl, *Thinking about 'Beowulf,'* 100–36; Hagen, *Anglo-Saxon Food*, 95–113.

> Cyning mec gyrweð
> since ond seolfre   ond mec on sele weorþað;
> ne wyrneð wordlofes,   wisan mæneð
> mine for mengo,   þær hy meodu drincað.⁴⁷

The king adorns me with treasure and silver, and honours me in the hall; he does not withhold words of praise, relates my merits before the company, where they drink mead.

There are similar allusions to an unspecified assembly of drinking men in *Riddles* 55 and 56. In the first, the enigmatic subject, richly ornamented with gold and silver, is presented in the hall:

> Ic seah in healle,   þær hæleð druncon,
> on flet beran   feower cynna,
> wrætlic wudutreow.⁴⁸

I saw in the hall, where heroes were drinking, a wondrous wood-tree of a fourfold nature being carried on the floor.

The strange 'wood-tree' in this riddle, however, is not a secular object from the wine-hall, but a liturgical cross and thus an image of Christ's cross (which, according to legend, was made from four different kinds of wood). Here, the topos of the hall is ironically employed to mislead the reader, for the assembly of the drinking men, in fact, represents a congregation of monks gathered 'in the hall' – that is, in church – to perform their daily service, just like the 'wise men' in *Riddle* 59, who pass around a golden chalice 'in the hall' (*in healle*, 1) while celebrating the mass.⁴⁹

Such a group of learned religious men also may be implied in the 'cock and hen' riddle, although its setting is clearly profane. Yet of all the riddles that mention the wine- or mead-hall and its drinking men, it is the only one in which the hall becomes the scene of riddle-posing and riddle-solving. Moreover, the notion of the hall as a place of convivial riddling reflects back to the literary embedding of the *Aenigmata* of Symphosius, whose name, as Michael Lapidge notes, is 'a joking pseudonym, meaning "party boy" or

---

47 *Riddle* 20.9b–12 (ASPR 3:190).
48 *Riddle* 55.1–3a (ASPR 3:208).
49 Cf. also *Riddles* 48.1 and 67.14.

the like.'⁵⁰ In the preface to his collection, Symphosius claims that his riddles were composed extemporaneously during the holiday season of the Saturnalia at the 'joyous banquets' and exuberant merry-makings, where the tipsy author joined an after-dinner riddling-contest.⁵¹ From the theatrical stance invoked in the 'cock and hen' riddle, the persona of the riddle-maker likewise engages his audience (or reader) in a social game whose dynamics grotesquely ape the carnal 'marriage game' of the two copulating birds. Just as the cock's deed is 'successful' when the hen has taken her 'fill' (3–5), so the riddle-solver has succeeded once he has unlocked the treasure-door with the riddle's runic key. That said, the metaphorical key carries the erotic connotations that are more fully and straightforwardly exploited in the deliberately ambiguous *Riddles* 44 and 91, with their shared double solution 'key' and 'penis.' The 'cock and hen' poem ironically moves from the sexual act to the handling of the key, while *Riddle* 44, through its playful double entendre, almost conversely describes the handling of the key in terms of a sexual act:

Wrætlic hongað   bi weres þeo,
frean under sceate.   Foran is þyrel.
Bið stiþ ond heard,   stede hafað godne;
þonne se esne   his agen hrægl
ofer cneo hefeð,   wile þæt cuþe hol   5
mid his hangellan   heafde gretan
þæt he efenlang ær   oft gefylde.⁵²

Something wondrous hangs by the man's thigh, under the master's cloak. In front is an aperture. It is stiff and hard, it has a good position; when the fellow lifts his own garment [5] above the knee, he wishes to visit with the head of his hanging thing that well-known hole, which is equally long, and which he has often filled before.

Here, the 'false,' obscene solution ('penis') and the consistent, 'true' solution ('key') are developed alongside each other, and this ambiguity is maintained until the end. The 'master' or 'lord' (*frea*) again turns his suggestive key in *Riddle* 91, and in an image cognate to that employed in the 'cock and

---

50 Lapidge and Rosier, *Aldhelm: The Poetic Works*, 244; see also Orchard, 'Enigmata,' 171.
51 Glorie, *Collectiones Aenigmatum Merovingicae Aetatis*, 621. See Ohl, *Enigmas of Symphosius*, 32–5.
52 *Riddle* 44 (ASPR 3:204–5).

hen' riddle, the lock is referred to as the 'guardian of the treasure' (*hyrde þæs hordes*, 9).⁵³ In all three texts, in *Riddle* 42 as well as the more explicitly sexual *Riddles* 44 and 91, the key thus becomes a metaphor for the initiation into the mysteries of riddle-making and the text's covert linguistic layers. To read and solve the riddle means unlocking the polysemous codes of what is said and what is implied. In the 'cock and hen' riddle, this opposition between what is apparent and what is hidden sustains – as Seth Lerer writes – the 'tension between the public and the private' that governs the poem as a whole.⁵⁴ The riddle enacts this dichotomy as it moves from the exterior world of the barnyard to the interior world of the hall, while simultaneously shifting from one alphabet to another and back. In marked contrast to the actual text of the riddle as it stands in the Exeter Book, however, the runes are presented in an oral context, since the riddle-maker, like the Germanic *scop* in the hall, delivers his runic clues orally:

> Ic on flette mæg
> þurh runstafas   rincum secgan
> þam þe bec witan.⁵⁵

By means of runic letters I can tell in the hall to book-wise men.

Riddle-making and riddle-solving are represented as ritualized and esoteric occupations performed by an intellectual elite familiar with archaic forms of literature, whose imaginary space is the traditional hall of the Germanic warrior class, the wine-hall of heroic poetry.⁵⁶ In this setting, the oral poet in the hall becomes a nostalgic double of the Old English writer at his desk. *Riddle* 42, therefore, reflects the cultural changes that marked early England, as it negotiated the transition from orality to literacy and the shift from one linguistic system to another: from the obsolete practice of runic communication that harked back to the pagan past to the roman alphabet and its use in a Christian scribal culture.

---

53 ASPR 3:241. Note the parallel to Symphosius, *Aenigma* 4 (*Clavis* ['key'] = *Collectanea Pseudo-Bedae*, 239), where the key is also guarded by the 'master.'
54 Lerer, 'Riddle and the Book,' 7, 11.
55 *Riddle* 42.5b–7a (ASPR 3:203).
56 See also DiNapoli, 'Kingdom of the Blind,' 448.

PART III

Tools

7 Silent Speech

The Exeter Book *Riddles* often invite us to think about the very act of riddle-making and riddle-solving, of writing and reading. Some of them can be interpreted as assessing the use of the vernacular within a received literary genre and context that is predominantly Latin, learned and monastic. In *Riddle* 85, for instance, the versatile fish in the river evokes the Old English riddle-maker, who both depends on the 'stream' of Latin riddling and, at the same time, challenges this tradition. Similarly, the warbling nightingale of *Riddle* 8 stands for the Anglo-Saxon poet, whose vernacular song echoes and surpasses the polished verse of his Latin predecessors and models. More obviously, the runic poems – such as the 'jay' (no. 24) and especially the 'cock and hen' (no. 42) – bring into play an obsolete writing system whose archaic character reflects upon notions of orality and literacy and upon the decline of pre-Christian forms of literature, as seen from a nostalgic, late Anglo-Saxon perspective.

Scribal Riddles

By the end of the tenth century, when the Exeter Book was compiled, Old English poetry in many ways had become a bookish pursuit itself, and this is precisely what emerges as the governing theme of a whole group of *Riddles* dealing with the technology of writing and the production of books. These are the 'scribal riddles,' whose subjects range from the making of parchment to the finished codex, including the reed pen, the quill, and the inkhorn.

Unlike the three storm riddles (nos 1–3) or the four bird riddles (nos 7–10) at the beginning of the collection, the scribal riddles do not occur together in the Exeter Book, but are loosely spread over the forty-four pages containing the *Riddles*. As a thematic group, they have been the subject of special study, but since the solutions to some of the *Riddles* are uncertain, critics disagree on the total number of scribal riddles in the collection.[1] Not all proposed solutions, however, have been called into question. There is a general consensus that the subject of both *Riddle* 88 and *Riddle* 93 is a scribe's inkhorn, and that *Riddle* 51 deals with a quill pen held by the three fingers of a writing hand. *Riddle* 26 and the fragmentary no. 67 are commonly solved as 'book' or 'Bible,' and a book perhaps also is the subject of the more obscure *Riddle* 95. In addition to these, *Riddle* 60 tells of a reed plant that is cut and turned into a pen, while *Riddle* 28 describes how a piece of parchment – and utimately a codex – is made from an animal skin. Other riddles are more controversial. While several critics would see the solution of no. 49 as a 'bookcase,' there is no agreement about the subject of the tantalizing *Riddle* 74, which some have interpreted as a variation of no. 51, the 'quill pen.' Another item associated with the medieval scriptorium is *Riddle* 47, the famous 'bookworm': a thievish intruder, it infests the library and eats its way through cover and page, annihilating the scribe's work of art and his labour.

In this third part of my study, I shall discuss the Old English scribal riddles in turn and in context, beginning with the two pen riddles (nos 60 and 51) and moving on to the subject groups 'inkhorn' (chapter 8), 'parchment' and 'book' (chapter 9) – following, so to speak, the transformation of beast to book. I shall conclude with a brief discussion of the subversive 'bookworm,' which will bring us back to the onset of our investigation. All these texts are concerned with the materiality of writing and book-making and thus identify some of the conditions under which Anglo-Saxon literature came to exist. Even more than other thematic groups in the collection, however, the Old English scribal riddles must be seen against the backdrop of the earlier Latin *enigmata*, where the same subjects were first dealt with. Again, it will be apparent that the Anglo-Saxon riddle-makers writing in the vernacular operate from within a basically Latin monastic tradition, which they not only emulate, but also claim for themselves and reassess by means of their own literary strategies and cultural determinants.

---

1 See Baum, *Anglo-Saxon Riddles*, 33–5; Shook, 'Anglo-Saxon Scriptorium'; the most detailed study is Göbel, *Studien zu den altenglischen Schriftwesenrätseln*.

The Mouthless Messenger (*Riddle* 60)

It has long been recognized that those *Riddles* dealing with writing and book-making, in particular, have various analogues and counterparts in the Latin *enigmata*. These riddles are bookish not in terms of their subject matter alone, but also because they are informed by the long-standing practice of composing scribal riddles in Latin, which used to be taught and kept alive in the medieval classroom. Two of the Old English scribal riddles, the 'bookworm' (no. 47) and the 'reed pen' (no. 60), even go back as far as Symphosius, whose collection fittingly opens with two items about the stylus (*Graphium*) and about reed used as a pen (*Harundo*). In the latter, which also occurs in the Latin Apollonius romance, the reed plant relates how it grows in shallow water and how it serves both as a musical instrument (a pan or reed pipe) and a writing tool (a pen); the *amica dei* in the opening line is the nymph Syrinx, who was pursued by the amorous Pan and transformed into reed:

> Dulcis amica dei, semper vicina profundis,
> Suave canens Musis, nigro perfusa colore
> Nuntia sum linguae digitis signata magistris.

> Sweet mistress of a god, always close to deep water, pleasantly singing for the Muses; when suffused with black colour, I am the tongue's messenger, marked by the master's fingers.[2]

By contrast, the Old English 'reed pen' in the Exeter Book is much longer. Again, the reed is the apparent speaker:

> Ic wæs be sonde,   sæwealle neah,
> æt merefaroþe,   minum gewunade
> frumstaþole fæst;   fea ænig wæs
> monna cynnes,   þæt minne þær
> on anæde   eard beheolde,   5
> ac mec uhtna gehwam   yð sio brune
> lagufæðme beleolc.   Lyt ic wende
> þæt ic ær oþþe sið   æfre sceolde

---

2 *Aenigma* 2 (ed. Shackleton Bailey, *Anthologia Latina*, 203); variant readings in line 1 include: *dulcis amica ripae*, 'sweet friend of the bank.' Cf. *Historia Apollonii regis Tyri*, 42 (ed. Schmeling, 34). The source is Ovid, *Met.* 1.689–712.

ofer meodu   muðleas sprecan,
wordum wrixlan.   Þæt is wundres dæl, 10
on sefan searolic   þam þe swylc ne conn,
hu mec seaxes ord   ond seo swiþre hond,
eorles ingeþonc   ond ord somod,
þingum geþydan   þæt ic wiþ þe sceolde
for unc anum twam   ærendspræce 15
abeodan bealdlice,   swa hit beorna ma
uncre wordcwidas   widdor ne mænden.[3]

I was by the sand, near the sea-wall, at the water's edge. I remained firm in my original position; there were but few people [5] who saw my home in the wilderness, but at every dawn, the dark wave played about me with [its] watery embrace. Little did I expect that, sooner or later, I should ever speak mouthless over mead, [10] [and] exchange words. It is a great wonder, marvellous to the mind of the ignorant, how the point of the knife and the right hand, man's intention and the point together, pressed me with the purpose[?] that I should, [15] before the two of us only, boldly announce an errand-speech to you, so that no other men may spread our words more widely.

What is only vaguely touched upon in Symphosius's tristich, the Old English author develops into a detailed narrative revolving around the aquatic origin of the reed plant (1–7a) and its metamorphosis into a writing implement (7b–17).[4] The reed pipe, which is briefly alluded to in line 2 of the Latin poem, may be implied in the fact that the enigmatic creature can speak 'mouthless over mead' (9).[5] The paradox seems to refer to some musical entertainment in the hall, but the author adds that the creature can utter words (*wordum wrixlan*, 10),[6] which can pertain only to the pen. In order to be used for writing, reed stalks had to be cut with a sharp penknife, and this process is described in lines 10b–14a before the author

---

3 *Riddle* 60 (ASPR 3:225, except line 9: *meodubence* for MS *meodu*; my punctuation). In the manuscript, the riddle immediately precedes the text of *The Husband's Message* and has therefore been associated with this poem by some critics in the past; see Muir, *Exeter Anthology*, 694.
4 See Whitman, 'Riddle 60 and Its Source'; Nelson, 'Paradox of Silent Speech,' 612–14.
5 For metrical reasons, most editors emend *ofer meodubence* 'over the meadbench,' but the manuscript has only *meodu* with no gap following.
6 As in *Beowulf*, 366a, 874a, and elsewhere in OE poetry. The half-line *sæwealle neah* (2) also occurs verbatim in *Beowulf* (1924b); further parallels are listed by Tupper, *Riddles of the Exeter Book*, 200, and Göbel, *Studien zu den altenglischen Schriftwesenrätseln*, 324.

further elaborates upon the silent pen that is nevertheless able to deliver a message and produce 'words.'[7] Obviously, the riddle's lengthy conclusion is inspired by Symphosius's notion of the reed pen as the 'marked' (i.e., cut and stained) 'messenger of the tongue' (*nuntia ... linguae*, 3). In the Old English poem, this personification is dramatically expanded by the sudden appearance of an external 'you' (*ic wiþ þe*, 14) and by the use of the dual pronoun (*unc ... uncre*, 15–17), which suggests that there is an intimate dialogue going on between two people exchanging secret information. The two, however, are the pen and the reader, while the 'errand-speech' (*ærendspræce*, 15) denotes the words conveyed in writing. However, the pen also stands metonymically for the writer and thus, likewise, for the riddle-maker, whose written message we are given to interpret.

With the black ink that flows from the pen and the guiding fingers of the writing hand, Symphosius introduced two of the most persistent motifs of scribal riddling. The medieval enigmatists, however, linked these motives with the contemporary quill, rather than the ancient reed pen. Both kinds of pen were known in early medieval Europe. Reed pens had already been utilized in antiquity, and – as Bernhard Bischoff notes – they 'probably continued to be used in the Mediterranean world,' at least initially; but soon the reed was superseded by the novel and more solid quill pen, which became the common instrument for writing with ink, especially in the west.[8] As the basic tool for generations of authors, the quill pen is a virtually ubiquitous subject of pre-modern riddle collections. Not surprisingly, it is treated by Aldhelm, Tatwine, and Eusebius and occurs also in the ninth-century *Lorsch Riddles*.[9] The latter also include a riddle about black ink made from thorns, and the inkhorn is found again in Eusebius's *Enigmata*.[10] Parchment is another common subject, appearing as it does among the riddles of both Tatwine and

---

7 I follow Trautmann (*Die altenglischen Rätsel*, 164) and take *geþydan* (14) as pret. pl. of wv *geðywan ~ geðy(a)n*, 'press, push, oppress.' A sharp penknife was used for both reed and quill pens to form a nib; see Wattenbach, *Das Schriftwesen im Mittelalter*, 228–30. An eleventh-century Anglo-Saxon student sharpening his pen is vividly portrayed in a Latin scholastic *Colloquy* by Ælfric Bata (*Coll.* 14; ed. and trans. Gwara and Porter, *Anglo-Saxon Conversations*, 112–15).
8 Bischoff, *Latin Palaeography*, 18. See Wattenbach, *Das Schriftwesen im Mittelalter*, 222–8; Hamel, *Scribes and Illuminators*, 27–9.
9 Aldhelm, *Enigma* 59 (*Penna*); Tatwine, *Enigma* 6 (*De penna*); Eusebius, *Enigma* 35 (*De penna*); Lorsch Riddle 9. See Erhardt-Siebold, *Die lateinischen Rätsel*, 57–63.
10 Lorsch Riddle 12; Eusebius, *Enigma* 30 (*De atramentorio*). See Erhardt-Siebold, *Die lateinischen Rätsel*, 68–70.

Eusebius as well as in the seventh-century *Berne Riddles*.¹¹ None of the Latin collections, however, includes the complete codex with all its decorative parts among their subjects, but Aldhelm and Eusebius each wrote a riddle about the bookcase or book-cupboard, in which precious volumes were kept.¹² Probably inspired by Symphosius's stylus riddle, Aldhelm likewise wrote an *enigma* whose subject is a pair of wooden wax tablets used for notes and drafts, and the writing tablets are also referred to by Eusebius and the *Berne* poet in their 'wax' riddles.¹³ These topics betray their scholastic origin, and it is no surprise that both the writing tablets and the book container are already addressed in two poems in the Hiberno-Latin *Hisperica Famina*, an anthology of school texts, which circulated in Irish monasteries as early as the seventh century.¹⁴

For the medieval riddle-makers, the scriptorium and its utensils provided a variety of intellectually challenging themes, by which means they could reflect upon the task and purpose of writing and literature. The more common a riddle subject was, the more freely an author would play with certain generic conventions and received images. A subject like the quill pen (OE *feþer*), for instance, was so familiar that it could even be boiled down to a mere ten words, as can be seen in the following entry from the eighth-century *Collectanea* of pseudo-Bede. In this very short prose riddle, the pen is represented by a weeping girl:

> Vidi virginem flentem et murmurantem: viae eius sunt semitae vitae.
>
> I saw a girl weeping and muttering; her ways are the paths of life.¹⁵

The girl's tears are the ink that flows from the pen onto the page, and the murmur denotes the scratching of the pen, while the 'ways' are the words

---

11 Tatwine, *Enigma* 5 (*De membrano*); Eusebius, *Enigma* 32 (*De membrano*); *Berne* Riddle 24 (*De membrana*). See Erhardt-Siebold, *Die lateinischen Rätsel der Angelsachsen*, 67–8.
12 Aldhelm, *Enigma* 89 (*Arca libraria*); Eusebius, *Enigma* 33 (*De scetha*). See Erhardt-Siebold, *Die lateinischen Rätsel*, 70–1.
13 Aldhelm, *Enigma* 32 (*Pugillares*); Eusebius, *Enigma* 31 (*De cera*); *Berne* Riddle 19 (*De cera*). See Erhardt-Siebold, *Die lateinischen Rätsel*, 63–7.
14 *Hisperica Famina*, 513–30 ('De taberna'), and 531–46 ('De tabula') (ed. and trans. Herren, 104–7). For the *Hisperica Famina*, see Lapidge and Sharpe, *Celtic-Latin Literature*, 93–4 (nos 325–30).
15 *Collectanea Pseudo-Bedae*, 198 (ed. and trans. Bayless and Lapidge, 144–5). See ibid., 245; Tupper, 'Riddles of the Bede Tradition,' 565.

and sentences of religious writing that promise salvation. One of several variants of this image occurs among the *Lorsch Riddles*, where the pen is again personified as a weeping girl (*virgo*), who literally 'sows' her 'black tears' across the 'white fields' of the parchment page, pointing out the way to Heaven.[16] The same agricultural metaphor is employed in the tenth-century version from St Gallen; now the pen is accompanied by her five 'sons,' that is, the five fingers of the writing hand:

> Vidi mulierem flentem et cum quinque filiis currentem, cuius semita erat via et pergebat valde plana campestria.
>
> I saw a woman weeping and running with her five sons; her path was a way, and she moved on over very flat fields.[17]

The personification of the enigmatic subject as a girl (*virgo*) or woman (*mulier*) provides a grammatical clue to the solution, since the Latin word for the quill pen, *penna* or *pinna*, is a feminine noun. This excludes the possible alternative *calamus* 'reed pen.' In medieval Latin, both terms, *calamus* and *penna/pinna*, were used for the quill pen,[18] but in his *Etymologies*, Isidore of Seville, still makes a clear distinction between the two kinds of pen. Discussing the terminology for the scribe and his tools, Isidore explains:

> Instrumenta scribae calamus et pinna. Ex his enim verba paginis infiguntur; sed calamus arboris est, pinna avis; cuius acumen in dyade dividitur, in toto corpore unitate servata, credo propter mysterium, ut in duobus apicibus Vetus et Novum Testamentum signaretur, quibus exprimitur verbi sacramentum sanguine Passionis effusum. Dictus autem calamus quod liquorem ponat. Unde et apud nautas calare ponere dicitur. Pinna autem a pendendo vocata, id est volando. Est enim, ut diximus, avium. Foliae autem librorum appellatae sive ex similitudine foliorum arborum, seu quia ex follibus fiunt, id est ex pellibus, qui de occisis pecudibus detrahi solent; cuius partes paginae dicuntur, eo quod sibi invicem conpingantur. Versus autem vulgo vocati quia sic scribebant antiqui sicut aratur terra. A sinistra enim ad dexteram primum deducebant stilum, deinde convertebantur ab inferiore, et rursus ad dexteram versus; quos et hodieque rustici versus vocant.

---

16 *Lorsch Riddle* 9 (ed. Glorie, *Collectiones Aenigmatum Merovingicae Aetatis*, 355).
17 St Gallen, Stiftsbibliothek, 196 (ed. Suchier, 'Disputatio Pippini cum Albino,' 144).
18 See *MLW*, s.v. *calamus*.

The scribe's tools are the reed pen [*calamus*] and the quill pen [*pinna*]. With these, words are fixed onto the pages. The reed pen is from a plant, the quill pen from a bird. Its tip is split into two, while the whole shaft preserves its unity, I think on the account of the mystery that by the two nibs may be signified the Old and New Testament, through which is expressed the sacrament of the word poured forth in the blood of the Passion. The reed pen [*calamus*] is so called because it places liquid, whence among sailors *calare* means 'to place.' The quill pen [*pinna*] is so called from 'hanging' [*pendendo*], that is, 'flying,' for it comes, as we have said, from birds. The leaves [*foliae*] of books are so called either from their likeness to the leaves of trees, or because they are made of leather sacks [*folles*], that is, of the skins that are stripped from slaughtered livestock. The sides of a leaf are called pages [*paginae*] because they are joined [*conpingere*] to one another. Written lines are commonly called verses [*versus*] because the ancients would write in the same way that land is ploughed: they would first guide the stylus from left to right, then reverse direction [*convertere*] in the line below, and back again to right – whence still today country folk call furrows *versus*.[19]

Typically, Isidore relates the scribe's tools and materials to the various plants and animals that provide them, and thus he sees these tools and materials as part of God's Creation, associating the inanimate with the animate and the profane with the divine. For Isidore, God has revealed Himself through the Creation, in His Son, and in the Scriptures, and so the activities of the scriptorium are symbolic of this threefold revelation. Hence, writing is first and foremost religious writing; if those who write resemble ploughmen in the field, leaving on the page their 'furrows' of written language, they do so for the spiritual benefit of their readers. Such an allegorical understanding of the business of writing obviously appealed to the early medieval enigmatists, who developed similar concepts and themes in their scribal riddles. Not surprisingly, several of Aldhelm's *Enigmata* explore Isidorian notions of writing, employing scribal metaphors akin to those in the *Etymologies*, including the traditional topos of ploughing as an image for writing. In his riddle about the wax tablets, for instance, Aldhelm compares the movement of the iron stylus to that of a plough in the

---

19 Isidore, *Etym.* 6.14.3–7 (ed. Lindsay; trans. partly adapted from Barney et al., 142); the writing of alternate lines in opposite directions is the ancient boustrophedon method ('turning like oxen in ploughing'), known from Greek epigraphy. The passage was copied by Hrabanus Maurus, *De rer. nat.* 5.5 (PL 111:123).

field, whose divine crop yields a 'holy harvest' of doctrine.[20] Aldhelm's *Enigma* 59 (*Penna*) is another case in point; its theme is the avian nature and etymology of the quill pen, which travels through the white 'fields' of parchment:

> Me dudum genuit candens onocrotalus albam,
> Gutture qui patulo sorbet de gurgite limphas.
> Pergo per albentes directo tramite campos
> Candentique viae vestigia caerula linquo,
> Lucida nigratis fuscans anfractibus arva.   5
> Nec satis est unum per campos pandere callem,
> Semita quin potius milleno tramite tendit,
> Quae non errantes ad caeli culmina vexit.

> The bright pelican, which swallows the waters of the sea in its gaping throat, once begot me [such that I was] white. I move through whitened fields in a straight line and leave dark-coloured traces on the glistening path, [5] darkening the shining fields with my blackened meanderings. It is not sufficient to open up a single pathway through these fields – rather, the trail proceeds in a thousand directions and takes those who do not stray from it to the summits of heaven.[21]

It is not clear exactly which bird Aldhelm had in mind. Early Christian writers distinguished two kinds of *onocrotalus*; one of them, a sea bird, is the well-known pelican, which, according to Pliny, resembles the swan.[22] An anonymous tenth-century glossator of Aldhelm's *Enigmata* explains the unusual name as *cignus* 'swan.'[23] Even to Aldhelm, *onocrotalus* was perhaps no more than an exotic name for the more familiar swan, as quill pens from pelicans must have been extremely rare – if known at all – in medieval scriptoria. Whatever the species of the water bird in question, it was its shining white plumage that Aldhelm wanted

---

20 Aldhelm, *Enigma* 32 (*Pugillares*) (trans. Lapidge and Rosier, *Aldhelm: The Poetic Works*, 76). The topos is already found in classical Greek and Roman literature; see Curtius, *European Literature*, 313–14; Scott, 'Rhetorical and Symbolic Ambiguity,' 120–3; Milovanovic-Barham, 'Aldhelm's *Enigmata* and Byzantine Riddles,' 57–60.
21 Ed. Glorie, *Collectiones Aenigmatum Merovingicae Aetatis*, 455; trans. Lapidge and Rosier, *Aldhelm: The Poetic Works*, 82.
22 Pliny, *Nat. hist.* 10.131; cf. Isidore, *Etym.* 12.7.32 (*Onocrotalos*) and 12.7.26 (*Pelicanus*). See André, *Les noms d'oiseaux en latin*, 122–3; Capponi, *Ornitologia latina*, 363–7.
23 Paris, Bibliothèque Nationale, MS lat. 2339; see Erhardt-Siebold, *Die lateinischen Rätsel*, 61.

to contrast with the dark ink flowing from the pen onto the light parchment page. From the concrete scribal tool, the riddle progresses to the complex act of writing, and from there to its effect upon the devout reader, describing, as it were, a 'straight line' from bird to page, and from page to Heaven. Similarly, in Aldhelm's riddle about the alphabet, this spiritual instruction is provided by the letters that are written with either an iron stylus (on wax) or a feathery quill pen (on parchment). As the letters declare themselves:

> Nascimur ex ferro rursus ferro moribundae
> Necnon et volucris penna volitantis ad aethram;
> Terni nos fratres incerta matre crearunt.
> Qui cupit instanter sitiens audire docentes,
> Tum cito prompta damus rogitanti verba silenter.

> We are born of iron – and we die once again by iron – or of the feather of a bird flying swiftly in the sky. Three brothers of an unknown mother begot us. Whoever in his eagerness wishes earnestly to hear our instruction, we quickly produce for him silent words.[24]

The potent 'three brothers' are the fingers of the writing hand, while their 'mother' is the feminine *penna*, which is 'unknown' because the script alone does not reveal which bird the feather was taken from. Much of this description appears rather conventional: the quill held by the fingers of the writing hand, often personified as family members, is a frequent theme of medieval scribal riddles. The image already occurs in the early *Berne Riddles*,[25] and Tatwine also uses it in his 'quill pen':

> Nativa penitus ratione heu fraudor ab hoste;
> Nam superas quondam pernix auras penetrabam,
> Vincta tribus nunc in terris persolvo tributum.
> Planos compellor sulcare per aequora campos;
> Causa laboris amoris tum fontes lacrimarum   5
> Semper compellit me aridis infundere sulcis.

---

24 *Enigma* 30.3–7 (ed. Glorie, *Collectiones Aenigmatum Merovingicae Aetatis*, 413; trans. adapted from Lapidge and Rosier, *Aldhelm: The Poetic Works*, 76).
25 *Berne Riddle* 25 (*De litteris*). For further analogues, see Tupper, 'Riddles of the Bede Tradition,' 571 (from Cambridge, UL, Gg.5.35), and *Riddles of the Exeter Book*, 183–4.

Alas, I am wholly cheated of my true nature by an enemy: at one time I used to fly swiftly through the upper air; now, bound by three, I pay tribute on earth. I am forced to plough along the levels of the flat fields and the labour of love always forces me to pour fountains of tears on the dry furrows.[26]

Tatwine conflates several of Aldhelm's scribal themes and metaphors into his own poem, but at the same time he restructures them along the original dyad of master (scribe) and servant (quill). The anthropomorphized quill is cruelly forced into captivity by its 'enemy' (i.e., man), whom it faithfully, if unhappily, serves. Its paradoxical 'labour of love' alludes to what Aldhelm more specifically identified as the edifying effects of writing and reading. This aspect is underscored by Tatwine's follower, Eusebius, who treats the same subject as follows:

Natura simplex stans, non sapio undique quicquam;
Sed mea nunc sapiens vestigia quisque sequetur.
Nunc tellurem habitans, prius aethera celsa vagabar;
Candida conspicior, vestigia tetra relinquens.

Simple by nature, I don't know anything at all; but now every wise man will follow my traces. I live on the earth now, but once I wandered through the heights of heaven; in appearance white, I leave behind black traces.[27]

Eusebius's poem is built upon a series of antithetical statements. Most of them are familiar from elsewhere, including the contrast between the 'wise' readers and the 'simple' quill, whose intellectual business nevertheless leaves it witless – a humorous paradox similarly exploited in Symphosius's bookworm riddle (*Aenigma* 16). With this riddle, it seems, Eusebius tried to introduce something new to a subject that had lost much of its enigmatic character, but little of its attraction to the medieval poet.

The Struggling Warrior (*Riddle* 51)

The Old English 'quill pen' in the Exeter Book takes a similarly novel approach; at first sight, the poem is a composite of matters and themes

---

26 *Enigma* 6 (*De penna*) (ed. Glorie, *Collectiones Aenigmatum Merovingicae Aetatis*, 173; trans. adapted from Allen and Calder, *Sources and Analogues*, 166).
27 *Enigma* 35 (*De penna*) (ed. Glorie, *Collectiones Aenigmatum Merovingicae Aetatis*, 245; trans. adapted from Erhardt-Siebold, ibid., and Allen and Calder, *Sources and Analogues*, 166).

from the earlier Latin scribal riddles, especially those of Aldhelm and Tatwine discussed above. Even its length is comparable to that of the Latin pen riddles:

> Ic seah wrætlice   wuhte feower
> samed siþian;   swearte wæran lastas,
> swaþu swiþe blacu.   Swift wæs on fore,
> fuglum framra;   fleag on lyfte,
> deaf under yþe.   Dreag unstille   5
> winnende wiga   se him wegas tæcneþ
> ofer fæted gold   feower eallum.[28]

> I saw four wondrous creatures travelling together; swarthy were [their] trails, very black tracks. It was swift on [its] journey, bolder than the birds; it flew in the air, dived under the wave. The struggling warrior toiled restlessly, showing the ways to all four over ornamented gold.

The four travelling creatures are, of course, the traditional three fingers plus the quill pen, whose figurative 'journey' leaves a dark track of letters and words on the page (1–3a). The four are represented as a company of travellers; but then, the author singles out the pen to exemplify its avian origin (3b–5a). So swiftly moves the pen in the hands of the scribe that it is even 'bolder' or 'stronger' (*framra*, 4) than the birds, whose movements it mimics as it literally flies over the page and dives into the ink like a water bird. Finally, the focus shifts back to the writing hand (5b–7): the 'four' again denote the three fingers and the pen, while the mysterious 'struggling warrior' is no one other than the scribe – or his personified hand or arm – holding the pen over the decorated (and perhaps partly gilded) manuscript.[29] Although the scribe is said to work 'restlessly' (*unstille*, 5), his toilsome activity is rather static and markedly contrasts with the dexterous excursions of the nimble feather. Indeed, medieval quills were much lighter than our modern writing implements, and it is interesting to note that they were also held differently. As Christopher de Hamel observes:

---

28 *Riddle* 51 (ASPR 3:206).
29 For coloured parchment and gold letters used in medieval deluxe manuscripts, see Wattenbach, *Das Schriftwesen im Mittelalter*, 132–9, 251–61; Bischoff, *Latin Palaeography*, 10–11, 17–18.

The medieval scribe, to judge from pictures, held his pen pointing downwards on the inside of the tips of the middle and forefingers while holding it steady by the very tip of the thumb. The fourth and fifth fingers are curled up out of the way. In this way the quill meets the page much more vertically than a modern pen. Ink seems to flow better when a quill is at right angles to the page. The medieval way of holding the quill gives less finger control than a modern pen and so movement comes from the whole hand. The quill itself, however, is infinitely lighter than a modern pen and it glides across the page without great effort.[30]

In the Middle Ages, quills were taken mostly from geese or swans, and so the riddle's middle passage, describing the scribe's handling of the flying and diving pen, may also be read as a flashback to the time when the quill was still part of a bird's plumage (as in Tatwine's and Eusebius's pen riddles). More important, the image of the bird-like tool also functions as an etymological clue to the riddle's solution, *feþer* 'quill pen.' In Old English, *feþer* denotes both the feather of a bird and the quill pen and thus holds the same ambiguity as Latin *penna*.[31] In the sense of 'quill pen,' the word *feþer* occurs in the eleventh-century *Monasteriales Indicia*. Written in Old English prose, the *Indicia* comprises instructions for monks on how to use manual sign language during the prescribed *silentium* and in certain places of the monastery where strict silence was kept. One such place was the scriptorium, and so the text also includes descriptions of the hand gestures for the scribe's basic tools such as the stylus, the wax tablet, the ruling stick, the inkhorn, and the pen. The latter is explained as follows:

> Fiþere tacen is þæt þu geþeode þine þri fingras tosomne swilce þu feþere hæbbe and hi dype and styre þine fingras swilce þu writan wille.
>
> The sign for a quill is that you join your three fingers together as if you were holding a quill, and dip them, and move your fingers as if you were going to write.[32]

This remarkable piece of silent speech reads almost like a visual riddle. The prosaic instruction precisely names what the Old English riddle

---

30 Hamel, *Scribes and Illuminators*, 29.
31 See *DOE*, s.v. *feþer*; apart from the rarer *pinn* (see BT, s.v.).
32 *Monasteriales Indicia*, 117 (ed. and trans. Banham, 42–3).

expresses in more poetic terms, as though the flying and diving quill of the riddle playfully exhibited the codes of monastic sign language. Yet, while the basic descriptive elements in *Riddle* 51 can be traced to their analogues in the *enigmata*, it is clearly the suggestive warrior figure (*wiga*, 6) that sets the Old English poem apart from its Latin predecessors (5b–7):

                Dreag unstille
winnende wiga   se him wegas tæcneþ
ofer fæted gold   feower eallum.

The struggling warrior toiled restlessly, showing the ways to all four over ornamented gold.

It would be wrong to classify this concluding comparison as merely a poetic hyperbole. Certainly, remarks about the drudgery of copying occur habitually in medieval manuscripts, often in the form of a colophon by the relieved scribe, whose arduous work has come to an end. The following proverbial complaint was quoted by many a copyist throughout the centuries before the invention of the printing press:

Tres digiti scribunt totum corpusque laborat.[33]

Three fingers write, and the whole body labours.

The fact that writing was indeed an act of endurance is further apparent in medieval portraits of authors or scribes at their desks. They typically show the writer in a concentrated yet humble pose, hunched over an open book, often holding a pen between the fingers, as in the famous Romanesque portrait of the Canterbury monk Eadwine, extolled in the inscription as the 'prince of scribes' (*scriptorum princeps*), whose fame will never die.[34] Such visual and verbal representations of the medieval scribe echo what the early Christian writer, Cassiodorus (d. ca. 580), expounded in his once widely disseminated *Institutions of Divine and Secular Learning*. Cassiodorus makes a case for the work of the monastic

---

33 Wattenbach, *Das Schriftwesen im Mittelalter*, 284; cf. ibid., 279–85; the earliest occurrences of the phrase date from the seventh century.
34 Fol. 283v of the Canterbury Psalter (ca. 1150), Cambridge, Trinity College, MS R.17.1; see Clanchy, *Memory to Written Record*, 115–16.

scribe as the noblest of all physical labours; addressing the brethren at the monastery of Vivarium, he writes:

> Ego tamen fateor votum meum, quod inter vos quaecumque possunt corporeo labore compleri, antiquariorum mihi studia, si tamen veraciter scribant, non immerito forsitan plus placere ... felix intentio, laudanda sedulitas, manu hominibus praedicare, digitis linguas aperire, salutem mortalibus tacitum dare, et contra diaboli subreptiones illicitas calamo atramentoque pugnare ... verba caelestia multiplicat homo, et quadam significatione contropabili, si fas est dicere, tribus digitis scribitur quod virtus sanctae Trinitatis effatur.

> Still, I have to admit that of all the tasks that can be achieved among you by physical labour, what pleases me most (not perhaps unjustifiably) is the work of the scribes if they write correctly ... A blessed purpose, a praiseworthy zeal, to preach to men with the hand, to set tongues free with one's fingers and in silence to give mankind salvation and to fight with pen and ink against the unlawful snares of the devil ... A man multiplies the heavenly words and, if such an allegory is permitted, by three fingers is written what the excellence of the holy Trinity speaks.[35]

For Cassiodorus, the scribe's work is a form of silent preaching, of waging a war in the name of God. This very notion reoccurs in the writings of Isidore of Seville, whose inscription or *titulus* for a monastic scriptorium encapsulates the same spiritual understanding of Christian scribal culture:

> Qui calamo certare novit cum mortua pelle
>   Si placet huc veniat hic sua bella gerat.

> He who knows how to fight with the pen against dead hide [i.e., parchment], shall come hither, if he wishes, to wage his wars.[36]

In the Old English 'quill pen' riddle, the scribe's work is seen as equally militant but nonetheless rewarding. As in Isidore's epigram, the act of writing is represented as a restless campaign, as warfare even, the reward for which seems to be some kind of 'gold' or treasure promised to the heroic warlord and his band. Equipped with the arms of the scriptorium, the monastic scribe thus becomes a *miles Christi*, fighting, as it were, for

---

35 Cassiodorus, *Institutiones* 1.30.1 (ed. Mynors, 75; trans. Halporn, 163).
36 Isidore, *Versus* 25 (*Titulus scriptorii*) (ed. Sánchez Martín, 233).

the propagation of literacy, yet well versed in the patterns and modes of native alliterative poetry, which resonate in the riddle's *winnende wiga*.[37] The figure of the 'struggling warrior' thus fuses the early Christian soldier-scribe and the Germanic warlord, and it is with this double recourse to a traditional concept from early Christian writing on the one hand, and to the poetic stock of vernacular literature on the other, that the author conjures up his most powerful trope in a text whose rhetorical strategies are otherwise rather conventional. In this sense, the Old English riddle-maker, too, may be seen under the guise of the 'struggling warrior,' whose poetic endeavours invade and conquer the themes and forms inherited from the bygone golden age of Anglo-Latin riddling.

---

[37] For the *miles Christi* theme in Old English literature, see Hill, 'Soldier of Christ.'

8 Beasts of Battle

Even more than the soldierly 'quill pen,' the two long riddles whose common subject is the scribe's inkhorn (nos 88 and 93) explore traditional generic boundaries and oscillate between the enigmatic, heroic, and elegiac modes of Anglo-Saxon verse.

In the early medieval scriptorium, ink was normally held in simple horns from bovids or deer, such as bulls or stags. The animal horns were hollowed out with a sharp knife and prepared in a similar fashion to the creation of drinking horns described in *Riddles* 14 and 80, but they were commonly smaller and had fewer decorations or fittings, except perhaps for a lid. A scribe often had two inkhorns – one for black and one for red ink – which, in some cases, were inserted into holes at the end of a sloping desk or attached to its edge by metal hoops.[1] Medieval portraits of authors and scribes sometimes show inkhorns with their tips protruding below the desk or stuck into the arm of the chair; but these are rather idealized scenes, and often a scribe may have used a simple stand, or even held the horn in one hand while writing with the other.[2]

In medieval riddle collections, the inkhorn – unlike the quill pen – is rarely addressed. Of the Anglo-Latin enigmatists, only Eusebius includes it; the horn in his tetrastich is taken from a bull:

---

1 Hamel, *Scribes and Illuminators*, 32–3; see also Wattenbach, *Das Schriftwesen im Mittelalter*, 242–3.
2 In his *Vita Columbae*, Adomnán tells how the inkhorn that St Columba (d. 597) kept in his hut at Iona was once knocked over by a visitor: 'eagerly advancing to kiss the saint, he upset and emptied the horn of ink (*atramenti corniculum*) with the border of his garment' (ed. and trans. Anderson and Anderson, *Adomnán's Life of Columba*, 53).

152 Tools

> Armorum fueram vice, meque tenebat in armis
> Fortis, et armigeri gestabar vertice tauri.
> Vas tamen intus habens sum nunc intestina amara
> Viscera, sed ructans bonus ibit nitor odoris.
>
> Once I was used as a weapon: the strong one carried me among his arms, and I was worn on the crest of the warlike bull. But since I have an internal cavity, I now contain a bitter substance inside me; and when I belch, something bright emerges with a good smell.[3]

The use of poetic prosopopoeia, the reference to the function of the horn on the animal's head, the horn's transformation into a container for ink (the 'bitter substance,' 3), and the concluding allusion to writing as something 'good' (4): all these rhetorical and narrative elements reoccur in the two Old English inkhorn riddles of the Exeter Book, but, as we shall see, they are greatly expanded upon and developed into moving accounts of separation, exile, violence, and enslavement.

The Missing Brother (*Riddle* 88)

Owing to a large hole in the manuscript, the texts of *Riddles* 88 and 93 are defective both at the beginning and at the end. Most editors print what remains legible, yet the number of lines that have been lost is uncertain. Below, I follow the transcription of Krapp and Dobbie, while some of the traditionally suggested reconstructions are indicated in brackets in my translation. In *Riddle* 88, the inkhorn says of itself:

> Ic weox þær ic s[......................
> ....] ond sumor mi[................
> ....]me   wæs min ti[.....
> ....
> ...]d ic on staðol[...................   5
> ....]um geong   swa [..........
> ....] seþeana

---

3 *Enigma* 30 (*De atramentorio*) (ed. Glorie, *Collectiones Aenigmatum Merovingicae Aetatis*, 240; trans. Allen and Calder, *Sources and Analogues*, 164). See Erhardt-Siebold, *Die lateinischen Rätsel*, 68–70.

oft geond [....................]fgeaf,
ac ic uplong stod,   þær ic [..........]
ond min broþor;   begen wæron hearde.   10
Eard wæs þy weorðra   þe wit on stodan,
hyrstum þy hyrra.   Ful oft unc holt wrugon,
wudubeama helm   wonnum nihtum,
scildon wið scurum;   unc gescop meotud.
Nu unc mæran twam   magas uncre   15
sculon æfter cuman,   eard oðþringan
gingran broþor.   Eom ic gumcynnes
anga ofer eorþan;   is min bæc
wonn ond wundorlic.   Ic on wuda stonde
bordes on ende.   Nis min broþor her,   20
ac ic sceal broþorleas   bordes on ende
staþol weardian,   stondan fæste;
ne wat hwær min broþor   on wera æhtum
eorþan sceata   eardian sceal,
se me ær be healfe   heah eardade.   25
Wit wæron gesome   sæcce to fremmanne;
næfre uncer awþer   his ellen cyðde,
swa wit þære beadwe   begen ne onþungan.
Nu mec unsceafta   innan slitað,
wyrdaþ mec be wombe;   ic gewendan ne mæg.   30
Æt þam spore findeð   sped se þe se[...
................]   sawle rædes.[4]

I grew where I [stood ...] and summer [with ...] was my [glory ...] [5] in a fixed place I [...] young as [...] nevertheless often over [...] gave [up], but I stood upright where I [...] [10] and my brother; [we] both were hard. [Our] home was the nobler, since we two stood on it, the higher with its trappings. Very often the wood, the shelter of forest trees, covered us on dark nights, shielded us from showers; the Lord created us. [15] Now we two excellent ones shall be succeeded by our kinsmen, younger brothers shall seize [our] home. I am solitary amongst the race of men on earth. My back is dark and wondrous. I stand on wood [20] at the end of a board. My brother is not here; but, brotherless, I must hold my place at the end of a board, stand fast. I do not know in what region of the earth my brother must dwell among

---

4 ASPR 3:239–40, except line 6: *geong, swa*, and line 18: *min agen bæc* for MS *min bæc*.

men's possessions, [25] he who used to dwell high by my side. We two were united in doing battle; neither of us ever displayed his strength unless we both together succeeded in the fight. Now monsters tear at me within, [30] injure me in my belly; I cannot escape. He who [seeks it] will find success in the track [...] benefit for the soul.

Over its more than thirty lines, the riddle makes several shifts in time and space as it moves from past to present and back, alternating between the horn's natural 'home' in the woods and its forced position on the scribe's desk. This creates an almost cinematic narrative, in which the scenes and places of now and then fade in and out, while only the protagonists remain the same. The shifts are signalled by the adverb *nu* 'now,' which occurs twice at the beginning of the verse: first in line 15 and again in line 29, each time triggering the use of the present tense, as opposed to the past tense in each of the two preceding passages (lines 1–14 and 25–8).

The riddle opens with a nostalgic reminiscence of the olden days when the horn was still 'young' (*geong*, 6). Growing up in the woods, the horn's 'fixed place' (*staðol*, 5) and graceful 'home' (*eard*, 11) were the antlers of a deer. There it 'stood upright' and high with its 'brother' (*broþor*, 9–10), that is, the neighbouring horn or tine on the antlers. The repeated use of the dual pronoun and the half-line *unc gescop meotud* 'the Lord created us' (14) suggests that the two brothers are twins.[5] With the first *nu* in line 15, the setting changes from the outdoor 'wood' (*holt*, 12) with its sheltering 'forest trees' (*wudubeama*, 13) to the indoor 'wood' (*wuda*, 19) of the scribe's desk, where the enigmatic speaker now serves as an inkhorn. This dramatic transformation is described in terms of a violent family feud: the usurping 'kinsmen' (*magas*) and 'younger brothers' (*gingran broþor*) who drive the two twin horns from their 'home' (15–17) are the replacements for the antlers, which are shed and renewed every spring. This leaves the speaker 'brotherless' (*broþorleas*, 21) and lonely, as he sadly wonders where in the world his twin 'brother' might be. Again, the difference between past and present is reinforced by a number of expressions that echo the riddle's opening lines and thereby demonstrate how the speaker's fate has been irrevocably changed: just as the horn previously 'stood upright' (*uplong stod*, 9) in its lofty 'place' (*staðol*, 5) on the stag's head, it now must 'stand fast' (*stondan fæste*, 22) and hold its solitary 'place'

---

5 Cf. *Riddle* 85.2–3, about the fish and the river: *unc dryhten scop siþ ætsomne*.

(*stapol*, 22) on the bleak board of the writing desk. In another flashback to the siblings' common past, the speaker then recalls how the two did 'battle' together (*gesome sæcce to fremmanne*, 26)[6] when they still belonged to the stag's headgear, before the second *nu* (29) brings us back to the present: not only is the horn a forlorn exile, but it must also suffer the tortures of some devilish 'monsters' or 'un-beings' (*unsceafta*, 29) from which it cannot escape. Maltreating the inkhorn and injuring its 'belly' (30), these torturers are the sharpened quill pens dipped into the ink by the writing scribe. The latter is not expressly mentioned in the text, but his work is implied in the concluding lines where the promising 'track' (*spore*, 31) denotes the writing left on the page for the spiritual benefit of those who can read. It is the same black track that the quill pen of *Riddle* 51 leaves on its nimble 'journey' across the parchment sheets.

Perhaps the most remarkable element of the riddle's rhetoric is its consistent use of object personification, which works on all narrative levels and includes not only the enigmatic subject itself (the inkhorn) but also the personae of the 'brother' (the second horn), the aggressive 'kinsmen' or 'younger brothers' (the new horns), and the cruel 'monsters' (the quill pens). Of these, the speaker and his brother are the central characters, and the riddle's narrative is essentially the story of their congenial relationship and cruel separation. So consistent is the metaphorical disguise that the whole could indeed be taken as an account of human loss and displacement, and there is nothing in the text that would actually contradict such a reading. Like man, the anthropomorphized horn has a 'back' (*bæc*, 18) and a 'belly' (*wombe*, 30), and even the fact that its back is 'dark' (18) and that it stands on a wooden 'board' (20) is not entirely at odds with human experience.

The story of the missing stag-horn is arguably unique in medieval literature. From the early Christian *Physiologus* to the later encyclopedias, the red deer and its habits are often described in detail; yet the accounts invariably revolve around the stag's enmity with the snake, its manner of crossing rivers in a line with other stags, its sharp hearing, or its eating and breeding habits.[7] The snake-eating stag was frequently depicted in medieval bestiaries and traditionally interpreted as an allegory of Christ or of the penitent sinner defeating the evil of the devil. In the Latin *enigmata*, the stag

---

6 Cf. *Beowulf*, 2499a (ed. Klaeber, 94): *sæcce fremman*.
7 See George and Yapp, *Naming of the Beasts*, 79–81; Bath, *Image of the Stag*, 206–74; Hassig, *Medieval Bestiaries*, 40–51.

is not treated as a separate subject, but in his riddle about the serpent, Aldhelm mentions that snakes 'greatly fear encounters with the antlered stag.'[8] The belief goes back to Greek animal lore and is reported, among others, by Pliny the Elder, who writes that 'even stags are at war with a snake; they track out their holes and draw them out by means of the breath of their nostrils in spite of their resistance.'[9] The victorious 'battle' (*sæcce*, 26) fought by the united stag-horns in *Riddle* 88 may allude to this 'war' (Pliny) with the serpent, although the stag was said to draw out and eat the snakes, not to fight them with the help of its antlers. The red deer, however, does use its antlers to ward off its natural enemies such as the wolf or an intruding male during the rutting season, when rivalling stags clash and lock their antlers.[10] Pliny also says that a stag's right horn, which is believed to contain a 'healing drug,' is never found because the stag buries it when shedding its antlers in spring – a piece of folklore, which perhaps bears a remote resemblance to the riddle's story of the lost twin horn.[11]

In Old English poetry, the stag notably figures in *Beowulf*, where the great hall of the Danish King is somewhat puzzlingly named *Heorot* 'Hart.' In the celebrated passage describing the uncanny mere of Grendel and his mother (lines 1361ff.), the 'strong-antlered stag' (*heorot hornum trum*) is the hunted 'heath-stalker' (*hæðstapa*) that seeks out the forest 'when driven from afar, hard pressed by hounds,' but it would rather give up its life on the bank than take refuge in the monsters' mere.[12] Other names for the stag and the red deer in Old English were *stagga* and *hea(h)deor*, literally 'high deer.'[13] The latter is of particular interest here, since the adjective *heah* occurs in both of the Old English inkhorn riddles and therefore serves as an etymological clue: in *Riddle* 88, where the twin horns are said to 'dwell high' (*heah eardade*, 25) together, as well as at the

---

8 Aldhelm, *Enigma* 88 (*Basiliscus*) (trans. Lapidge and Rosier, *Aldhelm: The Poetic Works*, 89).
9 Pliny, *Nat. hist.* 8.118 (ed. and trans. Rackham, 84–5: 'et his cum serpente pugna: vestigant cavernas nariumque spiritu extrahunt renitentes'). Cf. Isidore, *Etym.* 12.1.18.
10 See Corbet and Harris, *Handbook of British Mammals*, 500.
11 Pliny, *Nat. hist.* 8.115 (ed. and trans. Rackham, 82–3). Cf. Aristotle, *Hist. animal.* 4.11 538b, 9.5 611a–b; Aelian, *De nat. animal.* 6.5. For the stag in antiquity, see Keller, *Die antike Tierwelt*, 1:277–9; Toynbee, *Animals in Roman Life*, 143–5.
12 *Beowulf*, 1368–72 (ed. Klaeber, 52; trans. Swanton, 99). See Metcalf, 'Ten Natural Animals,' 386; Meaney, 'Hunted and the Hunters,' 96.
13 See BT, s.v.; Jordan, *Die altenglischen Säugetiernamen*, 48–9, 183–5, 187–8; *MCOE*, s.v.; Roberts, Kay, and Grundy, *Thesaurus of Old English*, 85.

beginning of *Riddle* 93, where the half-line *heah ond hyht* [...] (4) almost certainly refers to the antlered stag.

The Lost Lord (*Riddle* 93)

Despite its fragmentary text, *Riddle* 93 provides the most extensive description of the red deer in Old English literature. Without the analeptic digressions that characterize *Riddle* 88, its narrative is more linear and chronological. Otherwise, exactly the same linguistic strategies are at work. Again, the speaker is the anthropomorphized stag-horn that is driven from its ancestral 'home' by a 'younger brother' (15–16). Forced to serve as a container for ink on a 'hard board' (*on stið bord*, 31), the horn is harassed by a quill pen that is likened to a 'plundering foe' (32). But instead of the twin 'brother' of *Riddle* 88, now the antlered stag is the horn's most intimate associate. It is represented as the speaker's powerful 'lord' (*frea*, 1), whose sovereign life in the woods is depicted in vivid detail in the long opening scene. The first half of *Riddle* 93 reads:

>   Frea min [...........................
>   ....]de   willum sinum,
>   [..]
>   heah ond hyht[........................
>   ....]rpne,   hwilum [..........   5
>   ....]wilum sohte
>   frea[..............................]s wod,
>   dægrime frod,   deo[...............]s,
>   hwilum stealc hliþo   stigan sceolde
>   up in eþel,   hwilum eft gewat   10
>   in deop dalu   duguþe secan
>   strong on stæpe,   stanwongas grof
>   hrimighearde,   hwilum hara scoc
>   forst of feaxe.   Ic on fusum rad
>   oþþæt him þone gleawstol   gingra broþor   15
>   min agnade   ond mec of earde adraf.[14]

My lord [...] his will [...] high and joy[ful] [...] sometimes [...] [5] [sometimes] my lord sought [...] went, old in years, [deep ...], sometimes he had to climb the steep hills [10] up to his homeland, then again he departed into

---

14 *Riddle* 93.1–16 (ASPR 3:241–2).

deep valleys to seek a host, with strong step; he dug into stony plains that were hard with rime; sometimes he shook the hoar-frost from his hair. I rode upon the swift one, [15] until my younger brother claimed the seat of wisdom for himself and drove me from my home.

The enigmatic 'seat of wisdom' (*gleawstol*, 15; a hapax legomenon) is a periphrastic expression for the head of the stag, whose habitat and behaviour the author describes with amazing accuracy. It is a well-known fact that male and female red deer segregate for most of the year.[15] Whereas the hinds remain in a herd with their young, stags form their own, less stable groups, or sometimes live alone, and seek out the hinds only during the rut. Hence, the 'host' (*duguþe*, 11) that the 'lord' seeks with his 'strong step' (12) denotes the herd of the hinds: the stag joins them in the autumn, defending his harem against rival stags, but leaves the herd again before the cold winter months. During this time, hind populations tend to occupy richer soils and grassland, while stags are generally found on poorer ground; this tallies with the 'stony plains' (12) the stag in the riddle is said to dig into when the ground is 'hard with rime' (13). Then, in spring, the stag's antlers are renewed: the 'younger brother' (*gingra broþor*, 15) drives the old horn from its 'home' (*earde*, 16), which repeats the wording of *Riddle* 88 (*eard ... gingran broþor*, 16–17).

In the middle of the text, the focus changes from the horn's natural 'home' in the woods to the craftsman's workshop (lines 17–24a), and finally to the scriptorium (lines 24b–35). The first of these two passages reads:

Siþþan mec isern   innanweardne
brun bennade;   blod ut ne com,
heolfor of hreþre,   þeah mec heard bite
stiðecg style.   No ic þa stunde bemearn,   20
ne for wunde weop,   ne wrecan meahte
on wigan feore   wonnsceaft mine,
ac ic aglæca   ealle þolie,
þæt [..]e bord biton.[16]

Afterwards the dark iron wounded me within; no blood came out, no gore from my breast, though the hard strong-edged steel bit into me. [20] I by no

---

15 See Corbet and Harris, *British Mammals*, 497–501, summarized in this passage.
16 *Riddle* 93.17–24a (ASPR 3:242); the translation of lines 20–3 follows the reading in *DOE*, s.v. *aglac*.

means mourned the hour, nor did I weep for my wound, nor could I avenge my misfortune on the warrior's life, but I endure all the tortures that [...] bit the board[?].

Again the personified horn is exposed to 'violent and warlike actions'[17] and cruel tortures (*aglæca*, 23), but this time they are inflicted by the craftsman or scribe preparing the inkhorn. Both the 'dark iron' (*isern ... brun*, 17–18) and the 'hard strong-edged steel' (*heard ... stiðecg style*, 19–20) that injure and bite the speaker refer to the knife used to gouge out the horn. In Old English heroic poetry, the terms *isen ~ iren* 'iron' and *ecg* 'cutting edge' (including some compounds with these words) are common metonymies for a warrior's sword, and the adjective *brun* is sometimes used to describe its dark, brownish hue.[18] In *The Battle of Maldon*, for example, Byrhtnoth's sword is 'broad and with a dark edge' (*brad and bruneccg*), and the same formula is used for the dagger of Grendel's mother in *Beowulf*.[19] Later, Beowulf wields his sword (*iren*) in his ill-fated fight with the dragon; yet his blow initially fails, and the 'dark edge' of his blade does not 'bite' deeply enough:

> Hond up abræd
> Geata dryhten,   gryrefahne sloh
> incge-lafe,   þæt sio *ecg* gewac
> *brun* on bane,   *bat* unswiðor,
> þonne his ðiodcyning   þearfe hæfde
> bysigum gebæded.

The leader of the Geats swung up his hand, struck the patterned horror [i.e., the dragon] with the heirloom [i.e., his sword] so that the dark edge failed on the bone, bit less strongly than the people's king had need, hard-pressed by troubles.[20]

Riddle 93 plays with these poetic connotations to conjure up its own horrid battle scene, in which the blameless craftsman (or scribe) appears in

---

17 Orton, 'Technique of Object-Personification,' 6.
18 See Keller, *Anglo-Saxon Weapon Names*, 161–3, 171–4; Davidson, *Sword in Anglo-Saxon England*, 123–50; Roberts, Kay, and Grundy, *Thesaurus of Old English*, 608–10; *DOE*, s.v. *brun*, sense 3, *bruneccg*, and *ecg*, sense 1c.
19 *Battle of Maldon*, 163a (ed. Scragg, 62). Cf. *Beowulf*, 1546a (ed. Klaeber, 58): *brad [ond] brunecg*.
20 *Beowulf*, 2575b–80a (ed. Klaeber, 97 (my italics); trans. adapted from Swanton, 157). For the obscure *incge-lafe* (2577a), see Brady, '"Weapons" in *Beowulf*,' 106–7.

the guise of a relentlessly brutal 'warrior' (*wigan*, 22) whose acts of torture the horn passively endures. The seemingly paradoxical fact that the horn's 'breast' does not bleed (18–19) in this process is an ironic clue to its inanimate nature: being no more than a lifeless horn, the speaker remains inert, unable to mourn or weep (20–1), let alone take revenge on its callous torturer (21–2).

The riddle concludes with a brief account of the horn's present condition and its function as a tool on the scribe's desk, before the text virtually disintegrates on the mutilated last page of the manuscript:

>   Nu ic blace swelge
> wuda ond wætre,   w[..]b[..] befæðme   25
> þæt mec on fealleð   ufan þær ic stonde,
> eorþes nathwæt;   hæbbe anne fot.
> Nu min hord warað   hiþende feond,
> se þe ær wide bær   wulfes gehleþan;
> oft me of wombe   bewaden fereð,   30
> steppeð on stið bord,   [....................]
> ...] deaþes d[...]   þonne dægcondel,
> sunne [...........................
> ....]eorc   eagum wliteð
> ond spe[....................................]²¹   35

Now I swallow black [25] wood and water, [my belly] encloses what falls from above on me where I stand, something dark. I have one foot. Now a plundering foe guards my treasure; he who once widely bore the wolf's companion; [30] often he emerges wet[?] from my belly, steps on the hard board [...] of death[?] [...] when the day-candle, the sun [... work(?)] looks with eyes [35] and [success ...]

Again, the adverb *nu* (24, repeated in 28) and the present tense indicate that at this point, the speaker's transformation is completed: the 'dark' or 'swarthy' thing (*eorþes nathwæt*, 27) the horn now contains is the ink made from 'black wood and water' (*blace ... wuda ond wætre*, 24–5). Numerous recipes for making ink were known in the Middle Ages.²² The black ink employed in most insular manuscripts was iron-gall ink. It

---

21 *Riddle* 93.24b–35 (ASPR 3:242).
22 See Wattenbach, *Das Schriftwesen im Mittelalter*, 233–42; Reed, *Ancient Skins*, 154–6; Bischoff, *Latin Palaeography*, 16; Hamel, *Scribes and Illuminators*, 32–3.

generally consisted of the acids of oak galls infused in rainwater or wine, combined with ferrous sulphate (green vitriol) and mixed with gum arabic and carbon (lamp-black). In another method the bark of blackthorn or hawthorn was soaked in water, boiled down until it thickened, and mixed with wine and carbon to make it darker. This brownish blend of 'prickly thorns' and 'clear water' is also described in one of the ninth-century Latin *Lorsch Riddles*, whose subject is ink.[23] The Old English word for all these kinds of ink was *blæc* (from the adjective *blæc ~ blac* 'black, dark'), and hence the inkhorn was called *blæchorn*.[24] The 'black wood and water' in the riddle, therefore, not only provides a technical detail concerning the making of ink, but participates in the author's conundrum about the identity of the subject to be guessed: 'What has one foot and swallows *blæc* wood?' – 'The *blæc-horn*.'

Interestingly, the word *blæchorn* is attested only in the late Old English *Monasteriales Indicia*, the treastise on monastic sign language that also contains the sign for the quill pen discussed in chapter 7. The following entry describes the gesture a scribe in an Anglo-Saxon scriptorium might have made in order to ask one of his fellow brethren to pass over an inkhorn:

> Đonne þu blechorn habban wille þonne hafa þu þine þri fingras swilce þu dypan wille and awend þine hand adune and clyce þine fingras swilce þu blæchorn niman wille.[25]

> When you would like an inkhorn, hold your three fingers as if were going to dip [a pen], and move your hand down and clench your fingers as if you were going to pick up an inkhorn.

The dipping of the scribe's quill into the inkhorn is also alluded to in the final passage of *Riddle* 93, but here the language is radically oblique and charged with poetic metaphors and kennings. The hideous quill pens of *Riddle* 88 that injure the inkhorn's 'belly' reappear in the persona of the 'plundering foe' (*hiþende feond*, 28), who now 'guards' the speaker's 'treasure' (*hord*, 28), that is, the ink contained within the horn. Old English *feond*

---

23 *Lorsch Riddle* 12 (ed. Glorie, *Collectiones Aenigmatum Merovingicae Aetatis*, 358; mistrans. by Minst, ibid.). A famous recipe for ink from thorns is Theophilus Presbyter, *De diversis artibus* 1.37 (ed. and trans. Dodwell, 34–5).
24 *DOE*, s.v.
25 *Monasteriales Indicia*, 116 (ed. Banham, 42), except *blæc horn* (twice).

means 'enemy,' 'foe,' 'adversary,' and, more specifically, 'fiend' or 'devil.' This semantic potential is most notably exemplified in *Beowulf*, where the term characterizes the devilish ogre Grendel, the 'enemy of mankind' *(feond mancynnes)* and incarnation of Satan.[26] But the riddle's treasure-guarding 'foe' is a refiguration not so much of Grendel as of the monstrous dragon and fire-breathing *hordweard* 'hoard-guard' in the second part of *Beowulf*.[27] The analogy becomes even more striking when we consider the fact that the eponymous hero encounters the treasure-keeping dragon at the end of his life rather than as a young prince – just as the horn in the riddle falls victim to the greedy 'foe' only during the final phase of its equally doomed existence, long after its joyful and glorious youth.

The concluding lines of *Riddle* 93 indeed ring with such intertextual allusions and variations of the heroic mode. Even the 'plundering' writing pen is no ordinary quill from a water bird, but is obscurely described as the one 'who once widely bore the wolf's companion' (29). The line is a literary puzzle and a poetic circumlocution for what is, in fact, the quill of a raven. The implication is that the wolf and the raven, together with the eagle, are the typical carrion animals and so-called 'beasts of battle' of heroic literature. In Old English poetry, the motif of the beasts of battle is formulaic in style and structure and conventionally involves – as M.S. Griffith has shown – the 'dark raven,' the 'dewy-plumaged eagle,' and the 'wolf of the forest' appearing in the wake of an army, eager for carrion food.[28] Here, the kenning of the 'wolf's companion' *(wulfes gehleþan*, 29) almost certainly denotes the raven (OE *hrefn*), since fine raven quills were indeed occasionally used in medieval scriptoria, mainly for thin strokes and drawings.[29] The line, therefore, not only tallies with the material reality of the scriptorium, but sustains the heroic subtext of the riddle, so that the writing pen becomes a carrion bird in a scene of carnage: like a raven plundering the battlefield and circling over the slain, the quill dips into the inkhorn's 'belly' and 'emerges' from it, saturated with ink (30–1).

Most of the remaining lines of *Riddle* 93 are lost, but from the few words and fragments that can be deciphered, it seems that the passage

---

26 *Beowulf*, 164, 725 (ed. Klaeber, 7, 28).
27 *Beowulf*, 2293, 2302, 2554, 2593 (ed. Klaeber, 86–7, 96–7).
28 Griffith, 'Convention and Originality' 184.
29 See Tupper, *Riddles of the Exeter Book*, 238; Erhardt-Siebold, *Die lateinischen Rätsel*, 61; Hamel, *Scribes and Illuminators*, 27; Göbel, *Studien zu den altenglischen Schriftwesenrätseln*, 137.

refers to the completed piece of writing as it appears to the reader's 'eyes' (*eagum*, 34). Similar conclusions, often with an allusion to the moral purpose of writing, are found in the Latin scribal riddles, and the same topos also rounds off the first inkhorn riddle (no. 88), where the reader is promised 'success' (*sped*, 31) and 'benefit' from the string of letters in the manuscript. Here, the incomplete *spe[d?]* (35) at the end of the legible text may express this notion, but any reconstruction of these lines must remain conjectural. Of the few other bits of writing that survive around the large hole in the final folio, however, the words *dægcondel sunne* (32–3) stand out as another example of the riddler's use of poetic compounds and kennings; the powerful candle that paradoxically shines by day is, of course, the sun.[30] Apparently, what has been written with the help of the unfortunate inkhorn is eventually read and judged, while the scribe's work glows under the majestic sun.

Modes

Read against Eusebius's earlier attempt at the same topic, the two Old English inkhorn riddles differ markedly in terms of their atypical length and epic treatment of their subject matter. Their lines, however, are not simply filled with meticulous descriptions of the inkhorn's appearance and function, but are replete with statements about the speaker's emotional condition. From the external anthropomorphisms of 'back,' 'belly,' and 'foot,' the personification is extended into the inner sphere of the mind, so that these texts become sympathetic accounts of human emotion and experience. As several critics have observed, this rhetorical strategy links *Riddles* 88 and 93 with the so-called Old English elegies, while their martial language is strongly reminiscent of heroic poetry with its formulaic expressions and themes.[31] Such affinities come as no surprise when we consider that all nine poems conventionally classified as the Old English elegies – *The Wanderer, The Seafarer, The Rhyming Poem, Deor, Wulf and Eadwacer, The Wife's Lament, Resignation, The Husband's Message*, and *The Ruin* – occur exclusively in the Exeter Book. The elegy has been characterized as 'a relatively short reflective or dramatic poem embodying a contrasting pattern of loss and consolation, ostensibly based upon a specific

---

30 The only other occurrence for this word is in the 'heroic' *Andreas*, 835 (ASPR 2:26), from the Vercelli Book; see *DOE*, s.v.
31 See Williamson, *Feast of Creatures*, 214; DiNapoli, 'Kingdom of the Blind,' 424; Whitehurst, '"An Insight of Form",' 242–52.

personal experience or observation.'[32] According to Anne L. Klinck, its typical themes are 'exile, loss of loved ones, scenes of desolation, the transience of worldly joys,' and 'physical hardship'; these themes 'and the formulae associated with them, cluster in the Exeter Book elegies, but are also to be found lending an "elegiac" colouring to many passages in Old English poetry.' Examples of the latter include Hrothgar's lament for Æschere and the laments of the Last Survivor and the Bereaved Father in *Beowulf*, or the lament of Guthlac's disciple in the Exeter Book. Indeed, these texts share with the two 'elegiac' inkhorn riddles what Klinck identifies (in relation to the elegies) as 'a powerful sense of absence, of separation from what is desired.'[33] There is the same nostalgia for lost kin and companionship in *Riddles* 88 and 93 in their poignant stories of the bereaved brother and retainer, who both are last survivors in their own right. Also, structurally, the two riddles conform to the Old English elegies in their characteristic use of monologue and of what Klinck calls personal introduction and generalising conclusion.[34]

The fact that the nine elegies and the *Riddles* all are preserved in the Exeter Book raises challenging questions about our received definitions of Old English poetic genres and modes. Not surprisingly, the tantalizing and utterly enigmatic *Wulf and Eadwacer*, which immediately precedes the 'storm' riddle (no. 1) in the manuscript, was once grouped with the *Riddles* by most early editors, while more recently, some scholars have argued in favour of discounting *Riddle* 60 (the 'reed pen') and suggest instead that it be read as an introduction to the following *Husband's Message*. More generally, it is true that some of the elegies tend to obscure their narratives to the extent that they could be taken for riddles as well, whereas a number of *Riddles* do not conform to the generic conventions established by the Latin *enigmata* and determined by our modern conception of a 'typical' riddle. Often these texts play with the reader's expectation and understanding of what constitutes a riddle, as their language usurps the territories conventionally held by other literary genres. One such traditional territory or mode that is invaded and explored in the *Riddles* is vernacular heroic poetry, whose themes, formulae and tropes are inscribed in the texts of both *Riddles* 88 and 93.[35]

---

32 Greenfield, 'Old English Elegies,' 143.
33 Klinck, *Old English Elegies*, 11; and 'Elegies,' 164.
34 Klinck, 'Elegies,' 164.
35 For *Riddle* 88, Tupper (*Riddles of the Exeter Book*, 228–9) quotes no fewer than five *loci paralleli* to *Beowulf*.

In fact, a number of the *Riddles* employ a primarily heroic vocabulary to recast their subject in scenes of battle and narratives of 'heroic experience.'[36] This characteristic form of personification is applied equally to animate and inanimate subjects. In *Riddle* 15, for instance, the heroic sphere is adopted for the courageous porcupine, and the author goes to epic lengths to portray the prickly animal as a caring mother trying to rescue her children from a male aggressor before she uses her arrow-like quills to defeat the enemy in a fight described as a veritable battle-scene.[37] The animal world and the literary space of the Germanic warrior figure likewise coalesce in *Riddle* 20: its enigmatic subject is a falcon or hawk trained for hunting and represented in the poem as the king's trusty retainer with a licence to kill, who prefers the battlefield to home and family. Elsewhere in the collection, the sometimes dark, unleashed forces of nature embody the heroic, as in the devastating strife of wind and waters in the three 'storm' riddles (nos 1–3) or in the subject (possibly an ice floe) of *Riddle* 33, which threatens to invade the land from the sea, ready for 'battle-deeds,' shouting its terrible war cries like a band of raiding Vikings. Fire (*Riddle* 50) is another natural phenomenon treated in terms of a powerful warlord who is cruel in combat but generous to those treating him well; and in *Riddle* 29, the rising and setting of sun and moon are seen as a hostile clash of two warriors fighting over some 'booty' (i.e., the stars in the sky).

Heroic personification is further employed in those *Riddles* that deal with actual weapons. Hence, the bow (no. 23) is bent and 'shaped in the course of battle,' where it charges its poisoned arrows; the battering ram (no. 53) is a soldier's fellow that boldly storms forth to clear a way for its human brother in arms; the spear (no. 73), though unwillingly transformed from tree to weapon and driven into exile, intrepidly campaigns with man, breaking into fortresses and putting warriors to flight; and the shield (no. 5), if this is the correct solution, is constantly exposed to blows of 'iron weapons' and 'swords' as it bravely fights in the riddle's metaphorical battle. Even harmless objects and tools may be represented in mini-epics describing the process of their manufacture or their function in everyday life in terms of perilous warfare. The two 'inkhorns' belong to this group, as does *Riddle* 17: its subject is veiled by

---

36 Irving, 'Heroic Experience.' See also Nelson, 'Four Social Functions'; Stanley, 'Heroic Aspects'; Lendinara, 'Aspetti della società germanica negli enigmi del Codice Exoniense.'
37 See Bitterli 'Exeter Book Riddle 15.'

such a martial vocabulary that generations of commentators have taken for a weapon or a besieged fortress what is actually a simple beehive. Similarly, the anchor in *Riddle* 16 is portrayed as an exile and mercenary fighting against wind and waves, while the wooden object of *Riddle* 56 (perhaps a lathe) is engaged in a losing battle comparable to that of the two inkhorns.

Some *Riddles* couch their heroic figurations in the courtly setting of an imaginary Germanic warrior society, sometimes including kings and queens, white-locked ladies, and 'men at wine.' For example, in *Riddle* 55, a ceremonial cross is displaced from its liturgical environment and misleadingly represented by the author as the powerful 'gold-hilted sword' of Christ and an object of desire to the 'heroes' in the drinking hall (who, in fact, signify the community of the faithful soldiers of Christ assembled in church). A more explicitly courtly context is evoked in *Riddles* 14 and 80, whose common subject is also a horn, but probably one taken from a bovid (rather than a stag), which is used as a drinking vessel, a signal horn, or an art object. It is interesting to compare these two 'courtly' horns to those of *Riddles* 88 and 93. Unlike the two suffering inkhorns, which have been forced, as it were, to join the monastic orders of the scriptorium, the horns in *Riddles* 14 and 80 lead a secular life and take pleasure in the *vita activa* of the court. There is almost a sense of cheerfulness in their narratives: the horns enjoy the company of an aristocratic society, to which they proudly offer their useful services. In *Riddle* 14, the animal origin of the horn is briefly mentioned at the beginning, which echoes the 'warlike bull' carrying his horn-weapon featured in Eusebius's inkhorn *enigma*. Then, however, the martial elements are suppressed in favour of a spirited sequence of episodes from courtly life: the horn is richly decorated by a young craftsman and quickly becomes man's comrade as it performs its various functions:

> Ic wæs wæpen wigan. Nu mec wlonc þeceð
> geong hagostealdmon   golde ond sylfore,
> woum wirbogum.   Hwilum weras cyssað,
> hwilum ic to hilde   hleoþre bonne
> wilgehleþan,   hwilum wycg byreþ   5
> mec ofer mearce,   hwilum merehengest
> fereð ofer flodas   frætwum beorhtne,
> hwilum mægða sum   minne gefylleð
> bosm beaghroden; hwilum ic bordum sceal,
> heard, heafodleas,   behlywed licgan,   10

hwilum hongige   hyrstum frætwed,
wlitig on wage,   þær weras drincað,
freolic fyrdsceorp.   Hwilum folcwigan
on wicge wegað,   þonne ic winde sceal
sincfag swelgan   of sumes bosme;   15
hwilum ic gereordum   rincas laðige
wlonce to wine;   hwilum wraþum sceal
stefne minre   forstolen hreddan,
flyman feondsceaþan.   Frige hwæt ic hatte.³⁸

I was a warrior's weapon. Now a proud young bachelor covers me with gold and silver, with twisted ornamental wires. Sometimes men kiss me; sometimes with [my] speech I summon comrades [5] to battle; sometimes a horse bears me over the marches; sometimes a ship carries [me], bright with trappings, over the floods; sometimes a maiden, ring-adorned, fills my bosom; sometimes I must lie on boards, [10] hard, headless, plundered; sometimes I hang, decked with adornments, beautiful, on the wall where men drink, a noble war-ornament. Sometimes warriors carry me on a horse, when, treasure-adorned, [15] I must swallow wind from someone's bosom; sometimes with my sound I invite proud men to [their] wine; sometimes with my voice I must rescue from foes what has been stolen, put enemies to flight. Ask what I am called.

The shorter *Riddle* 80 varies these themes of fellowship, warfare, and feasting in an expressly aristocratic milieu. Now the horn belongs to the royal *comitatus*; it is filled with mead, the luxury drink of the Anglo-Saxon ruling class and the warriors' reward in heroic poetry;³⁹ and it also participates in the entertainments of the hall, where the *scop* delivers his song:

Ic eom æþelinges   eaxlgestealla,
fyrdrinces gefara,   frean minum leof,
cyninges gesclda.   Cwen mec hwilum
hwitloccedu   hond on legeð,
eorles dohtor,   þeah hio æþelu sy.   5

---

38 *Riddle* 14 (ASPR 3:187, except line 1: *wæpenwiga*).
39 Banham, 'Food and Drink,' 190. See also Hagen, *Anglo-Saxon Food and Drink*, 230–4. 'Mead' is the solution to *Riddle* 27, which describes it production and its effects on man in vivid detail.

Hæbbe me on bosme   þæt on bearwe geweox.
Hwilum ic on wloncum   wicge ride
herges on ende;   heard is min tunge.
Oft ic woðboran   wordleana sum
agyfe æfter giedde.   Good is min wise   10
ond ic sylfe salo.   Saga hwæt ic hatte.[40]

I am a nobleman's companion, a warrior's comrade, dear to my lord, a fellow of a king. Sometimes a fair-haired lady lays hand on me, [5] a nobleman's daughter, though she is noble. I have in my bosom what grew in the grove [i.e., mead made from honey]. Sometimes I ride on a proud horse in the van of an army; hard is my tongue. Often I give a singer a reward for [his] words [10] after [his] song. Good is my nature, and I myself am dark. Say what I am called.

Like the monastic inkhorn, the secular horn is described in terms of a human being with a 'bosom,' a 'tongue,' and a 'voice'; yet it is 'headless' and lies 'plundered' on the table board (14.10) after having been emptied at the feast in the hall. The inkhorn, by contrast, stands firmly on the scribe's wooden 'board' (88.19–20), where it is also plundered, but this time by the cruel quill pen dipping into the ink in its 'bosom' (93.28–31).

Certainly, the heroic mode employed in the *Riddles* may occasionally provide unexpected glimpses into the darker sides of Anglo-Saxon life not normally represented in Old English heroic poetry, which tends to glorify the tragic aspects of war, death, and exile.[41] Yet perhaps more important, the traumatic experience of the two inkhorns in *Riddles* 88 and 93 also reflects the Anglo-Saxons' cultural enterprise of negotiating the heroic narratives of their pagan past within a Christian environment of monastic literary practice. The story of the horn's abduction from its natural habitat in the woods to the ascetic confinement of the scriptorium evokes the transformation from the tribal culture of the Dark Ages to the scribal culture of early medieval England. The two displaced horns participate, as it were, in the epistemological battle waged by Anglo-Saxon poets and scribes, whose nostalgic recreations of the imaginary ethos of a Germanic warrior society help to define their own cultural identity as combatant promulgators of the Christian faith and the Word of God. The battlefield of these Christian warriors is the scriptorium, and the weapons in their arsenal are the scribal tools, including

---

40 *Riddle* 80 (ASPR 3:235).
41 See Irving, 'Heroic Experience.'

quill pen, penknife, and inkhorn, as well as parchment and the finished codex. The manufacture of vellum from animal skin, the intricate process of medieval book-making, and the edifying function of books are the subjects of the riddles discussed in chapter 9.

9 The Flesh Made Word

When we talk about books, we tend to personify and anthropomorphize them, referring to their parts in terms of the human body. As if a book had feet, a back, and a head, we speak of its 'footnotes,' its 'spine,' and the 'heading' of its pages. Like living beings, medieval manuscripts survive as families; they are housed in libraries and enshrined in bookcases, sometimes protected by a chemise or dust jacket; they have a long afterlife within a corpus of texts, and they are subjected to an autopsy when codicologists examine them. In the Middle Ages, the notion of the book as body suggested itself in the very physicality of the codex and the organic materials employed in its production: the animal skin turned into parchment; the quill of a bird cut into a pen; the animal horn serving as an inkpot; the tooth of a boar used for polishing parchment to stop the ink running;[1] and the various ingredients and agents for making inks and colours, such as egg-white, milk, honey, skin and fish glue, animal bile, shell, dove's dung, ground bones, and the egg-bearing Kermes insect used to produce red dye and pigment such as the orange-red *vermiculum* 'worm-colour.'[2] Discussing the origin of parchment in his *Etymologies*, Isidore of Seville states:

> Pergameni reges cum carta indigerent, membrana primi excogitaverunt. Unde et pergamenarum nomen hucusque tradente sibi posteritate servatum est. Haec et membrana dicuntur, quia ex membris pecudum detrahuntur.

---

1 Listed among the scribe's tools in Alexander Neckam's *De nominibus utensilium* (ed. Wright, *Volume of Vocabularies*, 116). See Wattenbach, *Schriftwesen*, 312; Clanchy, *Memory to Written Record*, 116.
2 See Reed, *Ancient Skins*, 159; McKitterick, *Carolingians and the Written Word*, 141–6.

Because the kings of Pergamum lacked papyrus sheets, they first had the idea of using skins. From these the name 'parchment' [*pergamena*], passed on by their descendents, has been preserved up to now. These are also called membranes [*membrana*] because they are stripped from the members [*ex membris*] of livestock.[3]

Two of the scribal riddles in the Exeter Book, namely, numbers 26 and 28, take up this very bodiliness and animal origin of the medieval codex; their common subject is the manufacture of parchment and the making of a book: the flesh made word. The two riddles describe how the skin of a living animal is turned into a lifeless material for writing and how it is then bound into a costly manuscript or, more precisely, into a biblical codex (no. 26). In each case, the subject's transformation 'from beast to book'[4] is represented as a torturous murder and mutilation of the body; yet in both texts the desecrated body is reborn as a splendidly decorated codex to enjoy a glorious afterlife among the company of the living and the literate.

Famous, Useful, and Holy (*Riddle* 26)

Riddle 26 has been unanimously solved as describing the manufacture of a book. A close reading of its text, however, reveals that its subject is, more specifically, a Bible or gospel book, as a number of critics have pointed out:[5]

> Mec feonda sum   feore besnyþede,
> woruldstrenga binom;   wætte siþþan,
> dyfde on wætre,   dyde eft þonan,
> sette on sunnan,   þær ic swiþe beleas
> herum þam þe ic hæfde.   Heard mec siþþan   5
> snað seaxes ecg,   sindrum begrunden;
> fingras feoldan,   ond mec fugles wyn
> geond speddropum   spyrede geneahhe,
> ofer brunne brerd,   beamtelge swealg,

---

3 Isidore, *Etym.* 6.11.1 (ed. Lindsay; trans. adapted from Barney et al., 141). Cf. Pliny, *Nat. hist.* 13.70.
4 Williamson, *Feast of Creatures*, 178.
5 See Fry, 'Exeter Book Riddle Solutions,' 23; Muir, *Exeter Anthology*, 659; Niles, *Old English Enigmatic Poems*, 117–19.

streames dæle,   stop eft on mec,   10
siþade sweartlast.   Mec siþþan wrah
hæleð hleobordum,   hyde beþenede,
gierede mec mid golde;   forþon me gliwedon
wrætlic weorc smiþa,   wire bifongen.
Nu þa gereno   ond se reada telg   15
ond þa wuldorgesteald   wide mære
dryhtfolca helm,   nales dol wite.
Gif min bearn wera   brucan willað,
hy beoð þy gesundran   ond þy sigefæstran,
heortum þy hwætran   ond þy hygebliþran,   20
ferþe þy frodran,   habbaþ freonda þy ma,
swæsra ond gesibbra,   soþra ond godra,
tilra ond getreowra,   þa hyra tyr ond ead
estum ycað   ond hy arstafum
lissum bilecgað   ond hi lufan fæþmum   25
fæste clyppað.   Frige hwæt ic hatte,
niþum to nytte.   Nama min is mære,
hæleþum gifre   ond halig sylf.[6]

A certain enemy robbed me of life, deprived me of [my] bodily strengths; then he wetted me, dipped me in water, took me out again, [and] set me in the sun where I quickly lost [5] the hairs that I had. The hard edge of the knife then cut me, ground clean of impurities; fingers folded me, and the bird's joy frequently made tracks across me with prosperous drops, over the brown rim, swallowed tree-dye, [10] a portion of liquid, stepped on me again, travelled leaving a swarthy trail. Then a man clad me in protecting boards, stretched hide over me, adorned me with gold; therefore I am embellished with the wondrous works of smiths, encircled with wire. [15] Now let these ornaments and the red dye and these glorious possessions celebrate widely the peoples' protector – but let no fool find fault. If the children of men will use me, they shall be the safer and the more victorious, [20] the bolder in heart and the gladder in thought, the wiser in spirit; they shall have the more friends, more beloved and related ones, more true and virtuous ones, more good and loyal ones, who will gladly increase their honour and happiness, and kindly [25] envelop them with benevolence, and

---

6 *Riddle* 26 (ASPR 3:193–4; my punctuation).

clasp them fast in embraces of love. Ask what I am called, (who is) beneficial to humans. My name is famous, and I myself useful to men and holy.

In the first half of the riddle, the different steps of medieval book production are described in some detail, following the actual order of the process: from parchment-making (1–6) and the folding of the leaves (7a), to the act of writing (7b–11a) and bookbinding (11b–14). The second half (15–28) is concerned with the assembled and decorated volume and its various advantageous effects upon the reader. The enigmatic speaker and subject is the personified codex, whose leaves once belonged to a living beast killed by man, the speaker's 'enemy' (*feonda*, 1) and murderer.[7] It has been observed that the riddle's dramatic opening resembles that of the Anglo-Latin *enigma* about parchment (*De membrano*) written by Tatwine in the early eighth century. In fact, the whole Old English text may be read as an expansion of Tatwine's six hexameters:

Efferus exuviis populator me spoliavit,
Vitalis pariter flatus spiramina dempsit;
In planum me iterum campum sed verterat auctor.
Frugiferos cultor sulcos mox irrigat undis;
Omnigenam nardi messem mea prata rependunt,   5
Qua sanis victum et lesis præstabo medelam.

A fierce plunderer stripped me of my fur and also removed the pores that gave me vital breath; but an artisan turned me into a level field again. Soon a planter irrigates my fruitful furrows with water, [5] and my meadows return a bountiful harvest of nard. With it I will give the healthy nourishment and the sick a remedy.[8]

In three episodes, the subject of Tatwine's riddle relates its dire fate. The 'plunderer' (*populator*, 1) is the person who slaughters the animal and strips off its skin, while the 'artisan' (*auctor*, 3) is the *pergamenarius*,[9] the parchment maker or parchmenter, who prepares the hairy hide until it is like a clean 'level field' (3) suitable for writing upon. In the scriptorium, the 'cultivator' (*cultor*, 4), that is, the scribe, finally wets the polished sheet

---

7 Cf. *Beowulf*, 2924 (ed. Klaeber, 110), and *Andreas*, 1324 (ASPR 2:39): *ealdre besnyðede*.
8 *Enigma* 5 (ed. Glorie, *Collectiones Aenigmatum Merovingicae Aetatis*, 172; trans. adapted from Erhardt-Siebold, ibid., and Allen and Calder, *Sources and Analogues*, 166).
9 Or *pergamentarius*; see *NGML*, s.v.

with fresh ink, and the result of this allegorical irrigation is the fruitful 'meadows' of the written text, which offers its spiritual nutrition to the eager readers (5–6). The linguistic and structural parallels to *Riddle* 26 are obvious. Tatwine's life-taking 'plunderer' is the Old English robbing 'enemy' (1), who flays the animal whose skin is subsequently processed by the parchmenter before it is used as writing material. Both riddles move from the bloody abattoir to the busy workshop of the parchmenter and from there to the spirited world of the scriptorium, where the dead animal skin regains life as a cornucopia of wisdom and a miraculous helper of man. The correspondences clearly go beyond the riddles' opening lines, yet the two texts also differ markedly in terms of their use of traditional imagery and realistic detail. Tatwine's hexastich elegantly develops a series of interwoven metaphors with almost no literal reference to the subject described. The Old English riddle, on the other hand, typically blends the metaphorical and the literal, requiring nearly five times as many lines as its Latin model to meander along its paratactically interlinked clauses, which are fraught with rare words generating stirring images and filled with meticulous, almost hands-on detail, as if to match the material splendour and spiritual grandeur of the subject in question.

The Old English riddle arguably offers the earliest description in a European vernacular language of the manufacture of parchment and the making of a codex. It is intriguing to note the degree of technical knowledge the author must have had of the various materials, tools and methods involved in the different steps of medieval book production. In the Middle Ages, the hides used for parchment were normally those of cattle, sheep, or goats.[10] On the continent, parchment was mostly made of sheep- and goatskin, while in early Ireland and Anglo-Saxon England, calfskin was often preferred to produce the stronger and finer kind of membrane now called vellum. The term for all these writing materials in Old English was *bocfell* (literally 'book-skin') or *carte* (from Latin *charta*).[11] The manufacture of parchment is a slow and intricate process. First the animal skin is washed and soaked for several days in a bath of lime and water to loosen the remaining fat and hair, which then are scraped away with a knife. This procedure may be repeated several times, before the unhaired pelt is stretched on a wooden frame to be

---

10 See Reed, *Ancient Skins*, 118–73; McKitterick, *Carolingians and the Written Word*, 138–41; Bischoff, *Latin Palaeography*, 8–11; Hamel, *Scribes and Illuminators*, 8–16.
11 *DOE*, s.v.

cleaned and smoothed on both sides. Using a sharp, semi-lunar knife or *lunellum*, the parchmenter scrapes the skin until it is thin and white, before he lets it dry in the sun, as described in the riddle (2b–5a):

> wætte siþþan,
> dyfde on wætre, dyde eft þonan,
> sette on sunnan, þær ic swiþe beleas
> herum þam þe ic hæfde.

then he wetted me, dipped me in water, took me out again, [and] set me in the sun where I quickly lost [5] the hairs that I had.

Next, the dry skin, while still tightly stretched on the frame, is again scraped and shaved to remove irregularities and is sometimes rubbed over with pumice stone to smooth its surface before it is trimmed and cut to size (5b–6):

> Heard mec siþþan
> snað seaxes ecg, sindrum begrunden

The hard edge of the knife then cut me, ground clean of impurities.[12]

Once the parchment sheet is folded into book format, pricked, and ruled, it is ready for writing (7–11a):

> fingras feoldan, ond mec fugles wyn
> geond speddropum spyrede geneahhe,
> ofer brunne brerd, beamtelge swealg,
> streames dæle, stop eft on mec,
> siþade sweartlast.

fingers folded me, and the bird's joy frequently made tracks across me with prosperous drops, over the brown rim, swallowed tree-dye [10], a portion of liquid, stepped on me again, travelled leaving a swarthy trail.

---

12 *sindrum begrunden* relates to the parchment, not the knife (as some have argued) and is appositive to *me* (13b); see Afros, '*Sindrum begrunden*.' Lester ('*Sindrum begrunden*,' 14) translates it as 'ground away with cinders,' that is, rubbed over with pumice; but OE *sinder* means 'dross, impurity' (Lat. *scoria*; see BT, s.v.), and the OE word for pumice was *pumic*. More likely, the expression refers to the fat and hairs that are scraped away with the *lunellum*. See also Marsden, *Cambridge Old English Reader*, 314.

This passage describes the scribe's work in a cluster of metaphors and periphrastic expressions akin to those employed in other scribal riddles (both Latin and Old English). The pen, the ink, and the inkhorn, together with the act of writing and the written text, are referred to, but only obliquely: first, the kenning of the 'bird's joy' (*fugles wyn*, 7) denotes the quill pen, whose avian nature is also alluded to in the riddles about the writing hand (no. 51) and the inkhorn (no. 93); secondly, the 'useful' or 'prosperous drops' (*speddropum*, 8) and the 'tree-dye' (*beamtelge*, 9) are the scribe's ink, which is likewise 'swallowed' by the stag-horn and guarantees benefit (*sped*) to the reader in *Riddles* 88 and 93; thirdly, the 'brown rim' (*brunne brerd*, 9) is that of the inkhorn, stained at its lip from the frequent dipping of the pen, and whose 'dark' colour is also mentioned in *Riddle* 88; finally, the 'swarthy trail' (*sweartlast*, 11) is the freshly written text on the manuscript page, created by the journeying pen. The latter topos is frequently employed in the Latin *enigmata*; moreover, nearly the same wording occurs in *Riddle* 51, where the travelling quill pen leaves behind its 'swarthy trails' (*swearte ... lastas*, 2).

From these metaphorical excursions, the text returns to the technicalities of medieval book-making with a passage describing how the assembled gatherings (or quires) of the folded leaves are sewn together and bound between wooden boards covered with leather (11b–17):

> Mec siþþan wrah
> hæleð hleobordum,   hyde beþenede,
> gierede mec mid golde;   forþon me gliwedon
> wrætlic weorc smiþa,   wire bifongen.
> Nu þa gereno   ond se reada telg   15
> ond þa wuldorgesteald   wide mære
> dryhtfolca helm,   nales dol wite.

Then a man clad me in protecting boards, stretched hide over me, adorned me with gold; therefore, I am embellished with the wondrous works of smiths, encircled with wire. [15] Now let these ornaments and the red dye and these glorious possessions celebrate widely the peoples' protector – but let no fool find fault.

Obviously, this is no ordinary book, but a lavishly decorated volume, whose boards are embellished with leather, gold, and metalwork. Few such costly bindings are extant from Anglo-Saxon England, but judging by what has survived in British and continental libraries, it is clear that in the early Middle Ages, more elaborate decorations were almost exclusively applied to the covers of Bibles and liturgical books, many of which were made for display in churches.[13] Religious manuscripts typically feature various interior and exterior 'ornaments' (*gereno*, 15) as well as 'red dye' (*reada telg*, 15), that is, red ink used for headings, initials, and rubrics.[14] All these decorative elements together render the codex – in the words of the riddle-maker – one of man's 'glorious possessions' (15–16) and help to glorify God, 'the peoples' protector' (*dryhtfolca helm*, 17). The latter notion leads up to the final passage of the riddle, which deals with the edifying effects the finished book has upon its readers, emphasizing the various benefits its contents bring to the Christian community of 'beloved and related ones' (*swæsra ond gesibbra*, 22).[15] The solution, Bible or gospel book, is secured by the concluding characterization (27b–28):

> Nama min is mære,
> hæleþum gifre ond halig sylf.

My name is famous, and I myself useful to men and holy.

A number of books may be deemed useful and famous; yet from a Christian perspective, only the Bible, the 'book of books,' is also holy. As Richard Marsden has observed, 'The long peroration of the riddle (lines 15–28) is a claim for the power of the Gospel among men, predicated on the simple premise, "If men are willing to use me ...," with the verb *brucan* offering a sense of "enjoy" as well as "use." Understatement invests the closing lines with special power: "Ask (or discover) what I am called, of advantage to men ..." The synonym for these men in the last line, *hæleþ*, hints at the idea of the Christian warrior and is used also in *The Dream of the Rood* for the heroic Christ who willingly climbs Calvary.'[16] For the pious author of the riddle, not only does the Bible make its readers happy and wise, but it turns them into successful Christian heroes (*hæleþum*, 28),

---

13 See Pollard, 'Some Anglo-Saxon Bookbindings'; McKitterick, *Carolingians and the Written Word* 147–8; Nixon and Foot, *Decorated Bookbinding in England*, 1–3, 18–20; Szirmai, *Archaeology of Medieval Bookbinding*, 99–139; Gullick, 'Bookbindings.'
14 Hamel, *Scribes and Illuminators*, 33.
15 Cf. *Riddle* 15.22a: *swæse ond gesibbe*. See DiNapoli, 'Kingdom of the Blind,' 428; and the parallels listed by Tupper (*Riddles of the Exeter Book*, 130–1) for what he calls the theme of the 'friendly aid and lofty guidance brought by the Book to men.'
16 Marsden, '"Ask What I Am Called",' 146.

making them 'the more victorious' (*sigefæstran*, 19) and 'the bolder in heart' (*heortum þy hwætran*, 20) once they endorse its wisdom and lore. The same term, *hæleþ*, with its double meaning of both 'hero' and, more generally, 'man,' is also used in line 12 for the craftsman binding the book, another heroic *miles Christi*, who is joined in his noble campaign by the monkish scribe, the 'struggling warrior' (*Riddle* 51).

Yet the true hero and Christian champion of the Bible riddle is its speaker and subject, that is, the hide turned into a book. The riddle's detailed account of this transformation is 'a compunction-inducing drama, in which an animal skin enacts its own story of violence, death, and triumphant rebirth.'[17] As Craig Williamson notes, in this riddle the Bible 'suffers its own form of passion ... but as keeper and conveyor of the Word, it transcends its fate to bring grace, honor, and glory to men. Its inner treasure is reflected in its outer appearance.'[18] In this dramatic process, the subject of *Riddle* 26 indeed resembles the most heroic figure of Christian narrative next to Christ, namely, the martyr, who patiently suffers brutal torture and a violent death to be ultimately glorified in heaven. Like the Bible, the martyr is not only 'holy' (*halig*, 28) but 'famous' (*mære*, 27) among Christians, and 'useful' (*gifre*, 28) to those who pray for his intercessory help.

Under My Skin (*Riddle* 28)

To understand how, in the *Riddles*, the holy book refigures the martyred body of the holy saint, we need only turn to the ninth-century *Old English Martyrology* or Ælfric's *Lives of Saints* (ca. 1000) with their often drastic accounts of the physical harassments and grisly tortures inflicted on the early Christian martyrs venerated in Anglo-Saxon England. Typically in these narratives – as in their Latin antecedents, notably Bede's *Martyrologium* or Aldhelm's *De virginitate* – the saintly men and holy virgins who suffer for their faith are first fetched and 'bound' (*gebunden*) by their heathen enemies before they are commanded to be cast into the water, put into a boiling caldron or a burning oven, roasted alive, or thrown into the fire. Others are hung on a gibbet, tied to a wheel, or stretched on an iron bed over burning coals; they are sprinkled with pitch, oil, or molten lead; they are poisoned, pierced with nails and spears, shot at with arrows, or scratched with iron claws. Others are thrown to the lions, bears, dogs, or snakes; stoned, dragged through the streets and into the wilderness, or

---

17 Ibid., 147.
18 Williamson, *Feast of Creatures*, 178–9.

buried alive; scourged and beaten to death; and many are ultimately slain 'with a hard sword' and beheaded.[19] A particularly cruel torture was chosen for St Cassian of Imola, the fourth-century schoolmaster who instructed his boys in Christian doctrine and would not worship the pagan idols: the Romans tied his hands and 'allowed the children to kill him with their writing tablets (*writbredum*) and to stab him with their styluses (*writeyrenum*) and his martyrdom was the longer and the heavier, as their hands were too weak to kill him.'[20]

More often, however, a saint miraculously survives a series of different tortures before dying as a martyr, encouraged by God, who usually appears in a vision shortly before death. In his *Passio* of the virgin martyr St Eugenia, Ælfric writes that, after refusing to worship the goddess Diana, Eugenia is commanded by the Roman emperor Severus to be thrown into a river and then cast into a burning oven (from which she again emerges unharmed) before she is put into prison for twenty days and eventually executed. When the Christians bury her, Eugenia appears to her mother in a vision, 'adorned with gold' (*mid golde gefrætewode*).[21] The passage reads almost like the description of the decorated volume in *Riddle* 26 (11b–13a):

> Mec siþþan wrah
> hæleð hleobordum, hyde beþenede,
> gierede mec mid golde.

Then a man clad me in protecting boards, stretched hide over me, adorned me with gold.

Many of the practices employed by the saints' torturers are indeed comparable to those described in medieval recipes for making parchment, and vice versa.[22] Both St Victor and St Bartholomew, for instance, whose passions are summarized in the *Old English Martyrology*, are 'flayed

---

19 *Old English Martyrology* (ed. and trans. Herzfeld, passim); Ælfric, *Lives of Saints* (ed. and trans. Skeat, 1:46 (*mid heardum swurde*), 142, 216, 316 (*mid swurdes ecge*), and passim).
20 *Old English Martyrology*, 13 August (ed. and trans. Herzfeld, 146–7 [trans. adapted]). Cf. Bede, *Martyrologium*, 13 August (PL 94:1005–6); Prudentius, *Peristephanon* 9 (ed. Cunningham, CCSL 126:326–9).
21 Ælfric, *Lives of Saints*, 2 (St Eugenia) (ed. and trans. Skeat, 1:48–9).
22 One might also compare these practices to the penalties prescribed by Anglo-Saxon law codes with their horrible lists of physical punishment and mutilation; see Keynes, 'Crime and Punishment,' and O'Brien O'Keeffe, 'Body and Law.'

alive' (*cwicne beflean*) by their heathen persecutors,[23] while St Chrysanthus is treated by his tormentors like a piece of soaked pelt to be dried in the sun: trying to break his miraculous resistance, the Roman soldiers first drench him 'all over with old urine' before exposing him to the heat of the sun, wrapped in an oxhide. As Ælfric writes:

> Hi behyldon þa ardlice ænne oxan mid graman, and besywodon crisantum swa mid þære hyde to his nacodum lice, and ledon hine ongean þa sunnan. He læg swa ealne dæg on þære ormætan hætan, ac seo hyd ne mihte aheardian him abutan, ne þam halgan derian on þære hatan sunnan.
>
> Then they quickly skinned an ox in their fury, and sewed up Chrysanthus with the hide next to his naked body, and placed him facing the sun. He lay thus all day in the overpowering heat, but the hide could not harden about him, nor hurt the saint in the hot sun.[24]

Like an animal skin to be manufactured into parchment, the Sicilian virgin and martyr, St Agatha, is stretched on a rack (*on hencgene astreccan*) and twisted (*ðrawan*), before her breast is cut off (*ofaceorfan*).[25] St Vincent, too, is first fastened onto a rack; then his torturers stretch his limbs 'as a man stretches a web' (*swa swa man web tiht*) and strike him with rods before they hang him on the gallows, scourge, beat, and singe him with torches and red-hot irons until blood flows all over his body. Half-dead, St Vincent is thrown back into his dungeon, where he begins to sing the psalms, telling his perplexed wardens:

> ge gebrohten me on þrystum, and ic blissige nu on leohte; mine bendas sund to-lysede, and ic blissige mid sange.
>
> You brought me into darkness, and I rejoice now in light; my bands are loosened, and I rejoice with song.[26]

---

23 *Old English Martyrology*; 14 May and 25 August (ed. Herzfeld, 82, 152).
24 Ælfric, *Lives of Saints*, 35 (St Chrysanthus and St Daria) (ed. and trans. Skeat, 2:386–7; my punctuation). Cf. Aldhelm, *De virginitate*, 35; *Carmen de virginitate*, 1204–8 (ed. Ehwald, 279, 403).
25 Ælfric, *Lives of* Saints, 8 (St Agatha) (ed. and trans. Skeat, 1:202–3). Similarly, in Cynewulf's *Juliana* (187–8), the eponymous heroine and martyr is ordered 'to be stretched out (*þennan*) naked ... and scourged with whips' (ASPR 3:118).
26 Ælfric, *Lives of Saints*, 37 (St Vincent) (ed. and trans. Skeat, 2:432–39; my punctuation).

There is a similar paradox in *Riddle* 28, whose subject – parchment manufactured into a codex – first endures a series of painful physical attacks and bodily tortures and yet afterwards carries the 'sound of living beings' inside:

> Biþ foldan dæl   fægre gegierwed
> mid þy heardestan   ond mid þy scearpestan
> ond mid þy grymmestan   gumena gestreona;
> corfen, sworfen,   cyrred, þyrred,
> bunden, wunden,   blæced, wæced,   5
> frætwed, geatwed,   feorran læded
> to durum dryhta.   Dream bið in innan
> cwicra wihta   – clengeð, lengeð –
> þara þe ær lifgende   longe hwile
> wilna bruceð   and no wiht spriceð,   10
> ond þonne æfter deaþe   deman onginneð,
> meldan mislice.   Micel is to hycganne
> wisfæstum menn,   hwæt seo wiht sy.[27]

A part of the earth is beautifully prepared with the hardest and with the sharpest and with the fiercest of men's possessions; [it is] cut, rubbed, turned, dried, [5] bound, wound, bleached, softened, adorned, equipped, carried from afar to the doors of men. Inside there is the sound of living beings – it remains [and] lingers – that first, while alive, for a long time [10] enjoy their desires and say nothing, and then, after death, begin to speak, to declare in various ways. It is a great thing for wise men to think what this creature is.

This riddle has found a number of controversial solutions in the past. Most early commentators interpreted it as describing either the preparation of ale, the making of a musical instrument (a harp, lyre, or horn), or even the fabrication of a sword.[28] None of these solutions, however, is actually sustained by the text. A first and ingenious attempt to read *Riddle* 28 as a scribal riddle was made in 1982 by Waltraud Ziegler, who grounded her answer, 'parchment,' in a number of analogues to the Latin *enigmata*, notably the three parchment riddles in the collections of

---

27 *Riddle* 28 (ASPR 3:194–5; my punctuation).
28 See Fry, 'Exeter Book Riddle Solutions,' 23; Muir, *Exeter Anthology*, 659; Niles, *Old English Enigmatic Poems*, 114–17 (advocating 'ale').

Tatwine, Eusebius, and the *Berne* riddler.[29] Yet the subject of *Riddle* 28 is not simply the manufacture of parchment, but rather the entire codex or book, as can be shown by a number of parallels to both the Latin *enigmata* and the closely related *Riddle* 26.

Even the earlier enigmatists writing in Latin did not confine themselves to the description of parchment-making, as we have seen in Tatwine's *De membrano* discussed above. The parchment riddle from the seventh-century *Berne* collection similarly expands its subject in order to review the entire transformation from living beast to finished book:

> Lucrum viva manens toto nam confero mundo
> Et defuncta mirum praesto de corpore quaestum.
> Vestibus exuta multoque uinculo tensa,
> Gladio sic mihi desecta viscera pendent.
> Manibus me postquam reges et visu mirantur, 5
> Miliaque porto nullo sub pondere multa.[30]

> As long as I live, I bring profit all over the world; but dead, I provide amazing wealth from my body. Stripped of my clothes, stretched fast by a rope, my fleshy parts hang down, cut off with a sword. [5] Afterwards kings hold me in their hands and look at me with wonder, I carry many thousands and yet they weigh nothing.

The poem already covers all the main themes that are further elaborated upon in the Exeter Book *Riddles* nos 26 and 28. The first two lines set up a contrast between the living animal and its prepared skin, both of which – as cattle and book – yield a profit to man. The middle lines 3–4 relate to the manufacture of parchment using a stretching-frame and knife, but even here, the process is already described in terms of physical torture and execution by the 'sword' (*gladio*, 4). Nevertheless, the riddle ends on a happy note by referring in its closing couplet to the finished book as a highly esteemed object of art with a lightweight content: the 'many thousands' its pages carry are the letters of the written text, which alone weigh nothing.

It is interesting to compare the parchment riddle from the *Berne* collection to riddles by the Anglo-Saxons Tatwine and Eusebius. While Tatwine

---

29 Ziegler, 'Ein neuer Lösungsversuch für das altenglische Rätsel Nr. 28'; see also Pinsker and Ziegler, *Die altenglischen Rätsel des Exeterbuchs*, 212–14.
30 *Berne Riddle* 24 (*De membrana*) (ed. Glorie, *Collectiones Aenigmatum Merovingicae Aetatis*, 570).

likens the work of the parchmenter and the scribe to an act of murder and the cultivating of a field, respectively, Eusebius is less concerned with the physical and technical aspects of book-making. In his tetrastich, the manuscript pages are speaking:

> Antea per nos vox resonabat verba nequaquam,
> Distincta sine nunc voce edere verba solemus;
> Candida sed cum arva lustramur milibus atris;
> Viva nihil loquimur, responsum mortua famur.
>
> Once a voice did not speak words through us at all; now without a voice we produce distinct words; while we are white fields, we are traversed by thousands of black ones; alive we say nothing, dead we give an answer.[31]

As he frequently does in his *Enigmata*, Eusebius operates with a string of succinct antitheses, which point up the seemingly paradoxical metamorphosis he describes: as long as the enigmatic subjects were part of a living animal, they could not speak, although the animal itself did have a voice (1); but once turned into manuscript pages, the white pieces of parchment carry countless letters written in black ink and thus eloquently 'speak' to their readers (2–4). The image of the 'speaking letters' itself is a traditional one; Aldhelm already uses it in his *Enigma* 30 about the alphabet (*Elementa*), terming the letters 'voiceless sisters' who are nonetheless able to produce 'silent words.' The notion is derived from Isidore's *Etymologies* and is exploited again in Eusebius's *Enigma* 7 about the letters:

> Innumerae sumus, et simul omnes quaeque sonamus,
> Una loqui nequit; nos tetrae ludimus albis.
> Et licet alta loquamur, non sonus auribus instat;
> Praeteritum loquimur, praesens et multa futura.
>
> Innumerable we are, and all together we make a sound, yet one alone cannot speak. Black we are but play on white. Though we may speak of higher things, no sound troubles the ears; we speak of the past, the present and many future things.[32]

---

31 *Enigma* 32 (*De membrano*) (ed. Glorie, *Collectiones Aenigmatum Merovingicae Aetatis*, 242; trans. adapted from Allen and Calder, *Sources and Analogues*, 166).
32 *Enigma* 7 (*De littera*) (ed. Glorie, *Collectiones Aenigmatum Merovingicae Aetatis*, 217; trans. adapted from Erhardt-Siebold, ibid.). Cf. Isidore, *Etym.* 1.3.1.

In the light of these Latin predecessors, the Old English *Riddle* 28 loses much of its obscurity. The riddle opens with a characteristically oblique reference to an unspecified 'part of the earth' (*foldan dæl*, 1), which is subsequently exposed to a torturous process reminiscent of the violent attacks described in the Latin *enigmata*. The key word here is *folde*, which means 'earth,' 'ground,' or 'land.'[33] Together with *wæter* 'water,' *fyr* 'fire,' and *lyft* 'air,' *folde* is part of the traditional tetrad of elements that constitute the Creation (as, for instance, in the Old English *Boethius*, Metre 20.57b–62). The same word, *folde*, also occurs in *Riddle* 7, where the swan is said to be equally at home both 'on water and land' (*flode ond foldan*, 9) as well as in the air (*lyft*, 4). In *Riddle* 28, the word therefore alludes to the natural element and habitat of a terrestrial animal or quadruped such as a calf, sheep, or goat, whose hides were used for the making of parchment. Hence, the *foldan dæl* is the cattle skin that is prepared for writing with the parchmenter's knife, the 'hardest,' 'sharpest' 'fiercest of men's possessions' (2–3).[34] The passive construction of the first line triggers a cascade of appositive past participles, from *corfen* (4) to *læded* (6), all syntactically dependent on the opening *Biþ* and linked by both alliteration and rhyme. They all relate to the various steps of parchment and book-making: first the animal skin is 'cut' (*corfen*, 4), 'rubbed' clean (*sworfen*, 4), and soaked and 'turned' (*cyrred*, 4) in the lime bath before it is 'dried' (*þyrred*, 4) and 'bound' (*bunden*, 5) onto a wooden frame so that it can be stretched and 'wound' (*wunden*, 5); next the parchment sheet is 'bleached' (*blæced*, 5) and 'softened' (*wæced*, 5) with pumice stone, 'adorned' (*frætwed*, 6) with ink by the scribe, and finally 'equipped' (*geatwed*, 6) with a binding. Only then is the assembled codex ready to leave the scriptorium, to be 'carried from afar to the doors of men' (*feorran læded to durum dryhta*, 6–7). These 'doors' are most likely those of the monastery that either commissioned the codex or whose scriptorium will produce a copy of it: ideally, the book travels from door to door, or – in Cassiodorus's words – from one holy place to another, and the work of the copyist travels with it.[35]

The riddle's condensed description of parchment- and book-making echoes not only the fuller account of the same process in *Riddle* 26, but also

---

33 See *DOE*, s.v. *folde*.
34 Cf. *Riddle* 26.5–6: 'Heard mec siþþan snað seaxes ecg.'
35 Cassiodorus, *Institutiones* 1.30.1 (ed. Mynors, 75): 'uno itaque loco situs, operis sui disseminatione per diversas provincias vadit; in locis sanctis legitur labori ipsius … operatur absens de opere suo.'

the rhetoric of the earlier Latin *enigmata*. For instance, there is a strikingly similar use of passive constructions in the parchment riddle from the *Berne* collection, whose tormented subject is 'stripped' (*exuta*) of its clothes and 'stretched' (*tensa*) by a rope before its fleshy parts are 'cut off' (*desecta*). A possible model is Symphosius's riddle about a leather boot made from 'lifeless' oxhide, which is 'lacerated' (*lacerata*), 'bound' (*ligata*), and 'torn' (*revulsa*) in the process.[36] Moreover, the second part of *Riddle* 28 plays on the same double dichotomy of silence and sound and life and death, which is also central to Eusebius's parchment riddle. Paradoxically, 'inside' the codex of *Riddle* 28, there is the sound of ghostly 'living beings,' who 'say nothing' as long as they are alive and yet 'begin to speak' once they are dead (7b–12a):

> Dream bið in innan
> cwicra wihta   – clengeð, lengeð –
> þara þe ær lifgende   longe hwile
> wilna bruceð   and no wiht spriceð,
> ond þonne æfter deaþe   deman onginneð,
> meldan mislice.

Inside there is the sound of living beings – it remains (and) lingers – that first, while alive, for a long time [10] enjoy their desires and say nothing, and then, after death, begin to speak, to declare in various ways.

This stark juxtaposition of life (*lifgende*) and death (*æfter deaþe*) echoes that of *Riddle* 12, the first of the three ox riddles in the collection, where exactly the same words (*lifgende ... æfter deaþe*) are used. In the concluding lines of this riddle, the enigmatic subject summarizes its transformation from a living beast of burden to a dead piece of leather, contrasting its former existence with its current function:

> Saga hwæt ic hatte,
> þe ic lifgende   lond reafige
> ond æfter deaþe   dryhtum þeowige.[37]

Say what I am called, who, while alive, ravage the land, and after death serve men.

---

36 Cf. Symphosius, *Aenigma* 56 (*Caliga*).
37 *Riddle* 12.13b–15 (ASPR 3:186).

In many ways, the account of the ox whose skin is processed into leather fetters, a bottle, a shoe sole, or a washing cloth, can be read as a kind of secular or lay counterpart to the more religious and monastic context that informs the two book riddles, numbers 26 and 28. As we have seen in the previous chapter, the same is true for the 'horn' group of riddles, where the two courtly drinking-horns (nos 14 and 80) complement the two monastic inkhorns (nos 88 and 93) in their different social milieus and functions. The manufacture of leather and parchment is indeed largely identical, the major difference being that leather is tanned and usually thicker than parchment. Yet in the *Riddles* only the animal skin, which is turned into parchment and bound into a book, is 'beautifully prepared' (*fægre gegierwed*, 28.1) and 'adorned' (*frætwed*, 28.6) even 'with gold' (*mid golde*, 26.13), while the leather gained from common oxhide is found merely in the company of the lowly.

What is more, only the codex is able to speak, producing from within the 'sound of living beings' (*deam … cwicra wihta*, 28.7–8). The Old English term *dream* can mean anything from 'joy,' 'bliss,' or 'jubilation,' to 'noise,' 'sound,' 'music,' 'song,' or 'melody,' including the 'jubilant singing of heavenly choirs' and the 'singing of psalms.'[38] Here, the latter may well be implied, since what emerges as the 'sound of living beings' from within the codex is nothing but the words of a (perhaps biblical or liturgical) text, written onto the pages of the book. The written text is the 'sound of living beings' because it is produced with the help of the tools and materials provided by living animals, such as a quill pen, ink, and parchment. Neither a living goose nor a sheep can utter intelligible words, but the lifeless quill pen and the parchment sheet together 'speak' (*deman*) and 'declare' (*meldan*), as it were, thanks to human skill and the power of language.[39] This double paradox of the animal-book, which is silent when alive, but speaks to its reader when dead, is developed in *Riddle* 28 into a meditation on the permanence of the written word. In the end, it is the written text that 'remains' and 'lingers' (*clengeð*, *lengeð*, 8) with its readers, who absorb its lore, so that they become 'wise men' like those who know the solution to the riddle (12b–13):

---

38 *DOE*, s.v.
39 There seems to be a lack of concord between the plural subject (*þe*) and the singular verbs (*bruceþ … spriceþ … onginneð*), but in *Riddles* 5.12, 39.15, and 39.26, *þara þe* is likewise followed by a singular verb (cf. Madert, *Die Sprache der altenglischen Rätsel des Exeterbuches*, 86), and the blurring of sg -eð and pl -að is not uncommon in both Anglian and WS texts; see Mitchell, *Old English Syntax*, §§ 18, 20, and 2344.

> Micel is to hycganne
> wisfæstum menn,   hwæt seo wiht sy.
>
> It is a great thing for wise men to think what this creature is.

In this extraordinary rebirth from violent death to everlasting life, something miraculous seems to happen. As in the longer Bible riddle (no. 26), the poet's account of physical aggression, stoic endurance, and ultimate elevation reflects and rewrites medieval narratives of Christian martyrdom. Even the double paradox of the 'living dead' and 'speaking speechless' can be found in the Old English saints' lives. A case in point is the *passio* of the two Gaulish missionaries St Ferreolus and St Ferrucio, the patron saints of Besançon, who were still able to speak even after their torturers had cut out their tongues. According to the author of the *Old English Martyrology*, the Roman governor Claudius 'ordered their tongues to be cut off (*forceorfan*), but they spoke without tongues as they had done before and praised God.'[40] Even more grisly and macabre is the story of the nine-year-old St Justus of Beauvais, another saint from third-century Gaul whose passion is recorded in the *Martyrology*. Beheaded by his pagan persecutors, Justus – like the cephalophorous Green Knight at Arthur's court – miraculously picks up his head and begins to speak:

> þa aras se lichoma ond genam þæt heafod him on hand, ond seo tunge spræc of þæm heafde ond cwæð þus: 'heofones god ond eorðan, onfoh mine sawle, forðon ic wæs unsceððende ond clænheort.'
>
> then the body arose and took the head into his hand, and the tongue spoke out of the head and said: 'Lord of heaven and earth, receive my soul, for I did no harm and I was pure in heart.'[41]

In both instances, the paradoxical miracle makes the mutilated or dead saint speak and break out in praise of God. Similarly, the tortured books in the *Riddles* miraculously begin to 'speak after death' (*æfter deaþe deman*, 28.11) and to 'celebrate' the Lord (*mære dryhtfolca helm*, 26.16–17). Just as the holy martyr in the saints' lives unerringly suffers his 'glorious martyrdom' (*wuldorfæstne martyrdom*) to be rewarded eternal bliss

---

40 *Old English Martyrology*, 16 June (ed. and trans. Herzfeld, 96–7).
41 Ibid., 18 October (188–9).

and posthumous fame,[42] so is the holy book in the *Riddles* turned into one of man's 'glorious possessions' (*wuldorgesteald*, 26.16) and becomes 'famous' (*mære*, 26.27), only after a torturous process of death and rebirth. Both the saintly martyr and the (biblical) codex thus triumph over death and obtain a glorious afterlife in the Christian community of the living.

Excarnation

However, such a hermeneutical relationship between martyr and book need not surprise us. As Ernst Robert Curtius has shown, even the late Roman poet Prudentius (d. ca. 405) already interprets the martyr's agony as a spiritual form of writing.[43] In Prudentius's *Peristephanon*, a poetic celebration of early Spanish martyrs, the virgin-saint Eulalia, while being scratched and cut by the executioners' iron claws, triumphantly compares her gashes to sacred letters written on her naked body:

'Scriberis ecce mihi, domine.
Quam iuvat hos apices legere,
qui tua, Christe, tropaea notant.
Nomen et ipsa sacrum loquitur
Purpura sanguinis eliciti.'

'See, Lord, your name is being written on me. How I love to read these letters, for they record your victories, O Christ, and the very scarlet of the blood that is drawn speaks your holy name.'[44]

For Prudentius, the martyr even becomes an immortal 'page inscribed by Christ' (*inscripta Christo pagina*),[45] whose mutilated body forever carries the spiritual inscription of the divine *logos*. In a non-verbal act of pre-lettered writing, the martyr thus commemorates both his own passion and that of Christ. As we have seen, this very notion of the writtenness of the sacred body also surfaces in the Old English saints' lives. It is important to note, however, that Anglo-Saxon narratives of martyred saints not

---

42 Ibid., 29 May (88–9); cf. ibid. (112): *wuldorlicne martyrdom*.
43 Curtius, *European Literature*, 311–12.
44 Prudentius, *Peristephanon* 3.136–40 (ed. Cunningham, CCSL 126:282; trans. adapted from Thomson, *Prudentius*, 151).
45 Prudentius, *Peristephanon* 10.1119 (ed. Cunningham, CCSL 126:368).

only deal with those early Christians who were persecuted in the days of the Roman empire, but also include more contemporary martyrs such as St Oswald of Northumbria (d. 642) and St Edmund of East Anglia (d. 869), the two indigenous royal saints, who suffered martyrdom at the hands of their pagan enemies.[46] In other words, for the Christian inhabitants of Anglo-Saxon England, the concept of martyrdom was by no means archaic and remote, but vigorous and productive in their own negotiations of religious and political identity and nation-building. The 'possibility of martyrdom,' writes Harold Remus, discussing the persecution of Christians under the Roman Empire, 'haunted early Christians. It also strongly suggests how important to Christian self-identity, group-loyalty, social cohesion and control, maintenance of boundaries, and evangelism – and thus ultimately to survival itself – was the professing of Christianity exemplified in the person of the martyr, the "witness" (μαρτυς/*martus*) unto death who follows in the steps of the archetypal witness, Jesus himself.'[47] Once we realize that in the *Riddles* the Christian codex refigures the Christian martyr, then the cruel process of parchment- and book-making can be read as a trope for the militant church in Anglo-Saxon England and for the ultimate triumph of Christianity and Christian literacy over Germanic and Celtic paganism. The preciously bound Bible and the enshrined martyr together bear witness to this triumph. Both are powerful visual symbols of the Christian faith and lasting objects of veneration.

In the Middle Ages, the rich binding of a gospel book and its covering of precious stones, metal, and ivory were indeed 'similar in function to a reliquary,' as as Rosamond McKitterick notes.[48] The codex described in *Riddle* 26, with its embellishments of 'gold' (*golde*, 13), 'wire' (*wire*, 14) and 'wondrous works of smiths' (*wrætlic weorc smiþa*, 14), is precisely such a holy book-reliquary, a shrine of the holy word. 'The word of God,' Horst Wenzel writes, 'dwells between the covers of the book like a saint in his shrine ... The costly decorations of the reliquaries with their gold and precious stones, gems and enamel, increased the belief in the saint's power and the effectiveness of his aid. The gospel books are decorated accordingly: they are not intended to resonate the sound of the word, but their primary function is to exhibit the symbolic presence of

---

46 See Ridyard, *Royal Saints*; Rollason, *Saints and Relics*.
47 Remus, 'Persecution,' 433.
48 McKitterick, *Carolingians and the Written Word*, 147; see also Calkins, *Illuminated Books*, 31.

Christ.'⁴⁹ In the Old English *Riddles*, the very bodiliness of the medieval codex and its representation as a medium of passion and holiness likewise suggest such a symbolic presence of the incarnated *logos*. If the making and writing of a book is a form of excarnation, in which the flesh is made word, then this act also suggests its own inversion. Hence, the martyred and transformed bodies in the *Riddles* not only celebrate the book as a powerful vehicle of Christian literacy and doctrine, but also reflect the notion that the scriptures are the written testimony of God and a holy manifestation of the Word made flesh.

---

49 Wenzel, 'Die Schrift und das Heilige,' 33 (my translation).

Coda

The Thievish Guest (*Riddle* 47)

Through a glorifying representation of the codex as a lasting shrine of the Divine Word, the Old English 'book' riddles construct an idealized picture of what is ultimately a frail product of Anglo-Saxon material culture. Even in the most renowned scriptoria and libraries, occasional damage could not be avoided. Symphosius, the late Roman father of all enigmatists, already knew this. His three-line riddle on the damaging bookworm (*Tinea*) is a humorous contemplation of the fragility and ephemerality of human artefacts and of the very medium of literature:

> Littera me pavit, nec quid sit littera novi.
> In libris vixi, nec sum studiosior inde.
> Exedi Musas, nec adhuc tamen ipsa profeci.
>
> Writing has fed me, but I know not what writing is. I have lived in books, but am no more learned thereby. I have consumed the Muses, and yet so far have not myself made progress.[1]

Symphosius's riddle is the ultimate source of *Riddle* 47, the Old English 'bookworm':

> Moððe word fræt.   Me þæt þuhte
> wrætlicu wyrd,   þa ic þæt wundor gefrægn,

---

[1] *Aenigma* 16 (ed. Glorie, *Collectiones Aenigmatum Merovingicae Aetatis*, 637; trans. adapted from Ohl, *Enigmas of Symphosius*, 49, and Allen and Calder, *Sources and Analogues of Old English Poetry*, 170).

> þæt se wyrm forswealg wera gied sumes,
> þeof in þystro, þrymfæstne cwide
> ond þæs strangan staþol. Stælgiest ne wæs   5
> wihte þy gleawra, þe he þam wordum swealg.[2]

A moth ate words. This seemed to me a wondrous event, when I learned about this marvel, that a worm, a thief in darkness, devoured some man's speech, the glorious statement [5] and its strong foundation. The thievish guest was not a whit the wiser in that he had swallowed these words.

There are a number of significant departures from the earlier Latin version. Not only is the Old English poem twice as long as Symphosius's tristich, but the two riddles also differ in terms of their point of view: in the Latin *enigma*, the bookworm is speaking, while the Old English 'bookworm' belongs to the 'I saw'–type of riddles, in which the author/narrator acts as an eyewitness describing the enigmatic subject to be guessed. Unlike Symphosius, the Old English author identifies his subject in the opening line as a voracious 'moth' (*moððe*, 1), as if giving away the solution to the riddle. In what follows, however, the 'moth' becomes a 'worm' (*wyrm*, 3) only to be further anthropomorphized into a stealthy 'thief' (*þeof*, 4) and a 'thievish guest' or intruder (*stælgiest*, 5). From the literal and concrete, the poem thus gradually moves to the metaphorical and abstract, while other expressions – as Fred C. Robinson has demonstrated – equivocally combine the literal and the abstract: *swealg* (6), for instance, can mean 'swallowed' or 'devoured' as well as 'imbibed' or 'understood' and hence participates in the poem's 'pattern of puns' on 'the simultaneous reality and insubstantiality of language.'[3]

Read in the context of the Old English scribal riddles of the Exeter Book, the 'bookworm' strikes us as an ironic reversal and annihilation of the painstaking writing and book-making processes described in the riddles on the pen (nos 51 and 60), the inkhorn (nos 88 and 93), and the codex (nos 26 and 28). While the subject of these riddles exemplify the flesh made word, the subversive bookworm, on the other hand, enacts the word made flesh in its most secular form, reversing the transformation of beast to book. As a 'thievish guest' who eats through the pages of the

---

2 *Riddle* 47 (ASPR 3:205).
3 Robinson, 'Artful Ambiguities,' 356–7, 362; see also Mitchell and Robinson, *Guide to Old English*, 233. Robinson's other examples of 'verbal ambiguities' in *Riddle* 47 are less convincing and have been criticized as strained; see Jacobs, '"Book-moth" Riddle Reconsidered.'

codex, it resembles the fish in the river, whose free, yet confined, life is portrayed in *Riddle* 85, discussed in the first chapter of this book. Moreover, like the 'fish in the river' riddle, the 'bookworm' can be read as a self-ironic parable of the vernacular riddle-poet. In a way, the two 'guests' – the fish and the bookworm – occupy their 'homes' (the river and the book) just as the vernacular text usurps and occupies the inherited Latin *enigmata*. This said, the Old English author himself becomes the nimble occupant and parasitic thief who freely appropriates and consumes the literary model and its established genre – even if he jokingly concedes that he is 'not a whit the wiser' for digesting the glorious speeches and statements of others.

Bibliography

Primary Sources

Allen, Michael J.B., and Daniel G. Calder, trans. *Sources and Analogues of Old English Poetry: the Major Latin Texts in Translation.* Cambridge and Totowa: D.S. Brewer & Rowman and Littlefield, 1976.
Anderson, Alan Orr, and Marjorie Ogilvie Anderson, eds and trans. *Adomnán's Life of Columba.* Oxford Medieval Texts. Oxford: Clarendon, 1991.
André, Jacques, ed. and trans. *Isidore de Séville: Étymologies, livre XII: Des animaux.* Auteurs latin du moyen âge. Paris: Les Belles Lettres, 1986.
Banham, Debby, ed. and trans. *Monasteriales Indicia: the Anglo-Saxon Monastic Sign Language.* 2nd rev. ed. Hockwold-cum-Wilton: Anglo-Saxon Books, 1996.
Banks, S.E., and J.W. Binns, ed. and trans. *Gervase of Tilbury: Otia imperialia: Recreation for an Emperor.* Oxford Medieval Texts. Oxford: Clarendon Press, 2002.
Barney, Stephen A., W.J. Lewis, J.A. Beach, Oliver Berghof, and Muriel Hall, trans. *The 'Etymologies' of Isidore of Seville.* Cambridge: Cambridge University Press, 2006.
Baum, Paull F., trans. *Anglo-Saxon Riddles of the Exeter Book.* Durham, NC: Duke University Press, 1963.
Bayless, Martha, and Michael Lapidge, eds and trans. *Collectanea Pseudo-Bedae.* Scriptores Latini Hiberniae 14. Dublin: School of Celtic Studies, Dublin Institute of Advanced Studies, 1998.
Brandt, S., ed. *L. Caelius Firmianus Lactantius: Opera omnia.* Vol. 2.1. CSEL 27.1. Vienna, 1893.
Brook, G.L., ed. *The Harley Lyrics: the Middle English Lyrics of MS. Harley 2253.* Old and Middle English Texts. 4th ed. Manchester, 1968.
Chambers, R.W., Max Förster, and Robin Flower, eds. *The Exeter Book of Old English Poetry.* Facsilime edition. London: Percy Lund, Humphries, 1933.
Chambry, Emile, ed. *Fables: Esope.* Paris: Belles Lettres, 1967.

Cross, James E., and Thomas D. Hill, eds. *The Prose Solomon and Saturn and Adrian and Ritheus*. McMaster Old English Studies and Texts 1. Toronto: University of Toronto Press, 1982.
Dimock, James F., ed. *Giraldi Cambrensis [Gerald of Wales]: Topographia Hibernica, et Expugnatio Hibernica*. RS 21.5. London, 1867.
Dodwell, C., ed. and trans. *Theophilus: The Various Arts: De Diversis Artibus*. Oxford Medieval Texts. Oxford: Clarendon Press, 1986.
Dodwell, Charles Reginald, and Peter Clemoes, eds. *The Old English Illustrated Hexateuch: British Museum Cotton Claudius B.iv*. Early English Manuscripts in Facsimile 18. Copenhagen: Rosenkilde and Bagger, 1974.
Dümmler, Ernst, ed. *Poetae Latini aevi Carolini*. Vol. 1. MGH PP 1. Berlin: Weidmann, 1881.
Ehwald, Rudolf, ed. *Aldhelmi Opera*. MGH AA 15. Berlin: Weidmann, 1919.
Ettmüller, Ludwig, ed. *Engla and Seaxna Scôpas and Bôceras: Anglosaxonum poetae atque scriptores prosaici*. Bibliothek der gesammten deutschen National-Literatur 28. Quedlinburg and Leipzig: Gottfried Basse, 1850.
Evelyn-White, Hugh G., ed. and trans. *Hesiod: The Homeric Hymns and Homerica*. Rev. ed., Loeb Classical Library 57. Cambridge, MA: Harvard University Press; London: Heinemann, 1936.
Folkerts, Menso. *Die älteste mathematische Aufgabensammlung in lateinischer Sprache: Die Alkuin zugeschriebenen 'Propositiones ad acuendos iuvenes': Überlieferung, Inhalt, Kritische Edition*. Österreichische Akademie der Wissenschaften, Mathematisch-naturwissenschaftliche Klasse, Denkschriften 116.6. Vienna: Springer, 1978.
Fontaine, Jacques, ed. *Isidore de Séville: Traité de la nature [De natura rerum]*. Bibliothèque de l'Ecole des Hautes études Hispanique 28. Bordeaux: Féret, 1960.
Förster, Max. 'Die altenglische Glossenhandschrift Plantinus 32 (Antwerpen) und Additional 32246 (London).' *Anglia* 41 (1917): 94–161.
Garmonsway, G.N., ed. *Ælfric's Colloquy*. Rev. ed. Exeter Medieval English Texts. Exeter: University of Exeter, 1978.
Glorie, F., ed. *Collectiones Aenigmatum Merovingicae Aetatis*. 2 vols. CCSL 133 and 133A. Turnhout: Brepols, 1968. Pages 165–208: 'Aenigmata Tatuini,' English translation by E. von Erhardt-Siebold; 209–71: 'Aenigmata Eusebii,' English translation by E. von Erhardt-Siebold; 273–343: 'Aenigmata Bonifatii,' German translation by K.J. Minst; 345–58: 'Aenigmata 'Laureshamensia' (= *Lorsch Riddles*), German translation by K.J. Minst; 359–540: 'Aenigmata Aldhelmi,' English translation by J.H. Pitman (1925); 541–610: 'Aenigmata Tullii' (= *Berne Riddles*), German translation by K.J. Minst; 611–721: 'Aenigmata Symphosii,' English translation by R.T. Ohl (1928).

Godman, Peter, ed. and trans. *Poetry of the Carolingian Renaissance*. London, 1985.
Goolden, Peter, ed. *The Old English 'Apollonius of Tyre.'* Oxford English Monographs. London: Oxford University Press, 1958.
Grein, Christian W.M., ed. *Bibliothek der angelsächsischen Poesie*. Vol. 2. Göttingen: Georg H. Wigand, 1858.
Gwara, Scott, and David W. Porter, eds and trans. *Anglo-Saxon Conversations: The Colloquies of Ælfric Bata*. Woodbridge: Boydell Press, 1997.
Halm, Carolus, ed. *Fabulae Aesopicae collectae*. [1852]. Leipzig 1868.
Halporn, James W., trans. *Cassiodorus: Institutions of Divine and Secular Learning and On the Soul*. Introduction by Mark Vessey. Translated Texts for Historians 42. Liverpool: Liverpool University Press, 2004.
Hamilton, N.E.S.A., ed. *William of Malmesbury: De Gesta pontificium Anglorum libri quinque*. RS 52. London, Longman, 1870.
Hartel, W., ed. *Paulinus of Nola: Carmina*. CSEL 30.2. 1–338. Vienna, 1894.
Hausrath, August, et al., eds. *Corpus fabularum Aesopicarum*. Vol. 1.1–2. Leipzig: Teubner, 1940–59.
Henel, Heinrich, ed. *Ælfric's De Temporibus Anni*. EETS OS 213. London: Oxford University Press, 1942.
Herford, C.H., P. Simpson, and E. Simpson, eds. *Ben Jonson: The Sad Shepherd, The Fall of Mortimer, Masques and Entertainments*. The Oxford Jonson 7. Oxford: Clarendon Press, 1941; repr. 1970.
Herren, Michael W., ed. and trans. *The Hisperica Famina:* [vol.] *I: the A-Text*. Toronto: Pontifical Institute of Mediaeval Studies, 1974.
Herzfeld, George, ed. and trans. *An Old English Martyrology*. EETS OS 116. London: Kegan Paul, Trench, Trübner, 1900.
Klaeber, F., ed. *Beowulf and The Fight at Finnsburg*. 3rd ed. Boston, 1950.
Klinck, Anne L., ed. *The Old English Elegies: A Critical Edition and Genre Study*. Montreal and Kingston: McGill-Queen's University Press, 1992.
Krapp, George Philip, and Elliott Van Kirk Dobbie, eds. *The Exeter Book*, ASPR 3. New York: Columbia University Press, 1936.
Lapidge, Michael, and Michael Herren, trans. *Aldhelm: The Prose Works*. Cambridge: D.S. Brewer; Totowa, NJ: Rowman and Littlefield, 1979.
Lapidge, Michael, and James L. Rosier, trans. *Aldhelm: The Poetic Works*. Cambridge and Dover, NH: D.S. Brewer, 1985.
Leslie, Roy F., ed. *Three Old English Elegies*. Manchester: Manchester University Press, 1961; rev. ed. 1966; repr. Exeter: University of Exeter Press, 1988.
Lindsay, W.M., ed. *Isidore of Seville: Etymologiarum sive originum libri XX*. 2 vols. Oxford: Clarendon, 1911.
Mackie, W.S., ed. and trans. *The Exeter Book: Part II: Poems IX–XXXII*, EETS OS 194. London: Oxford University Press, 1934; repr. Millwood: Kraus Reprint, 1987.

Marsden, Richard, ed. *The Cambridge Old English Reader.* Cambridge: Cambridge University Press, 2004.

Mayhoff, K., ed. *C. Plinius secundus: Naturalis historiae libri XXXVII.* 5 vols. Bibliotheca scriptorum Graecorum et Romanorum Teubneriana. Stuttgart: Teubner, 1892–1909; repr. 1967–86.

Menner, Robert J., ed. *The Poetical Dialogues of Solomon and Saturn.* The Modern Language Association of America, Monograph Series 13. New York: Modern Language Association of America; London: Oxford University Press, 1941.

Miller, F.J., ed. and trans. *Ovid: Metamorphoses.* 2nd ed. rev. P.G. Goold. 2 vols. Loeb Classical Library 42–3. Cambridge, MA: Harvard University Press; London: Heinemann, 1984.

Muir, Bernard J., ed. *The Exeter Anthology of Old English Poetry: An Edition of Exeter Dean and Chapter MS 3501.* 2 vols. 2nd ed. Exeter: University of Exeter Press, 2000.

Müllenhoff, K., and W. Scherer, eds. *Denkmäler deutscher Poesie und Prosa aus dem VIII–XII Jahrhundert.* 2nd ed. Berlin: Weidmann, 1873.

Mynors, R.A.B., ed. *Cassiodori Senatoris Institutiones.* 3rd ed. Oxford: Clarendon, 1963.

Ohl, Raymond T., ed. and trans. 'The Enigmas of Symphosius,' Diss., University of Pennsylvania, Philadephia, 1928.

Peck, A.L., and D.M. Balme, eds and trans. *Aristotle: History of Animals [Historia animalium].* 3 vols. Loeb Classical Library 437–9. Cambridge, MA: Harvard University Press; London: Heinemann, 1965–91.

Perry, B.E., ed. *Aesopica.* Vol. 1. Urbana: University of Illinois Press, 1952.

Pinsker, Hans, and Waltraud Ziegler, eds and trans. *Die altenglischen Rätsel des Exeterbuchs.* Anglistische Forschungen 183. Heidelberg: Carl Winter, 1985.

Rackham, H., ed. and trans. *Pliny: Natural History.* Vol. 3: *libri VIII–XI.* Loeb Classical Library 353. 2nd ed. Cambridge, MA: Harvard University Press; London: Heinemann, 1983.

Rogers, Benjamin B., ed. and trans. *Aristophanes.* Vol. 2: *The Peace, The Birds, The Frogs.* Loeb Classical Library 179. Cambridge, MA: Harvard University Press; London: Heinemann, 1923.

Sánchez Martín, José Mariá, ed. *Isidori Hispalensis Versus.* CCSL 113A. Turnhout: Brepols, 2000.

Savage, John L., trans. *Ambrose of Milan: Hexameron, Paradise, and Cain and Abel.* The Fathers of the Church 42. New York: Fathers of the Church, 1961.

Schmeling, Gareth, ed. *Historia Apollonii regis Tyri.* Bibliotheca Scriptorum Graecorum et Romanorum Teubneriana. Leipzig: Teubner, 1988.

Schupp, Volker, ed. *Deutsches Rätselbuch.* Stuttgart: Reclam, 1972.

Scragg, Donald G., ed. *The Battle of Maldon.* Old and Middle English Texts. Manchester: Manchester University Press, 1981.

Sedgefield, Walter J., ed. *An Anglo-Saxon Verse-Book*. Manchester: Manchester University Press, 1922.
– *King Alfred's Old English Version of Boethius: De consolatione philosophiae*. Oxford: Clarendon Press, 1899; repr. Darmstadt: Wissenschaftliche Buchgesellschaft, 1968.
Shackleton Bailey, D.R., ed. *Anthologia Latina*. Vol. 1.1. Bibliotheca scriptorum Graecorum et Romanorum Teubneriana. Stuttgart: Teubner, 1982.
Skeat, Walter W., ed. *Ælfric's Lives of Saints*. 4 vols. Repr. in 2 vols. EETS OS 76, 82, 94, 114. [1890–1900]. London: Oxford University Press, 1966.
Smith, A.H., ed. *Three Northumbrian Poems; Cædmon's Hymn, Bede's Death Song and The Leiden Riddle*. Rev. ed. Exeter Medieval English Texts and Studies. Exeter: University of Exeter Press, 1978.
Stanley, Eric Gerald, ed. *The Owl and the Nightingale*, Old and Middle English Texts. Manchester: Manchester University Press, 1972.
Stork, Nancy Porter. *Through a Gloss Darkly: Aldhelm's Riddles in the British Library MS Royal 12.C.xxiii*. Studies and Texts 98. Toronto: Pontifical Institute of Mediaeval Studies, 1990.
Suchier, Walther, ed. 'Disputatio Pippini cum Albino.' In *Die Altercatio Hadriani Augusti et Epicteti Philosophi, nebst einigen verwandten Texten*, ed. L.W. Daly and W. Suchier. Illinois Studies in Language and Literature 24. 134–46. Urbana: University of Illinois Press, 1939.
Swanton, Michael, ed. and trans. *Beowulf*. Manchester Medieval Classics. Manchester: Manchester University Press, 1978.
Thomson, H.J., ed. and trans. *Prudentius*. Vol. 2. Loeb Classical Library 398. Cambridge, MA: Harvard University Press; London: Heinemann, 1953.
Thorpe, Benjamin, ed. *Codex Exoniensis: a Collection of Anglo-Saxon Poetry, from a Manuscript in the Library of the Dean and Chapter of Exeter, with an English Translation, Notes and Indices*. London: Pickering, 1842.
Trautmann, Moritz, ed. *Die altenglischen Rätsel (Die Rätsel des Exeterbuchs)*. Alt- und Mittelenglische Texte 8. Heidelberg: Carl Winter, 1915.
Tupper, Frederick, ed. *The Riddles of the Exeter Book*. Boston: Ginn, 1910; repr. Darmstadt: Wissenschaftliche Buchgesellschaft, 1968.
White, T.H., trans. *The Book of Beasts: Being a Translation from a Latin Bestiary of the Twelfth Century*. Cambridge University Library Ii 4 26. New York: G.P. Putnam's Sons, 1954; repr. New York: Dover, 1984.
Whitman, F.H., ed. and trans. *Old English Riddles*. Canadian Federation for the Humanities Monograph Series 3. Ottawa: Canadian Federation for the Humanities, 1982.
Williamson, Craig, trans. *A Feast of Creatures: Anglo-Saxon Riddle-Songs*. Philadelphia, PA: University of Pennsylvania Press, 1982; London: Scolar Press, 1983.

- ed. *The Old English Riddles of the Exeter Book*. Chapel Hill: University of North Carolina Press, 1977.
Wilmanns, W., ed. 'Disputatio regalis et nobilissimi iuvenis Pippini cum Albino scholastico.' *Zeitschrift für deutsches Altertum* 14 (1869): 530–55.
Wright, Thomas, ed. *Alexander Neckam: De naturis rerum libri duo* and *De laudibus divinae sapientae*. RS 34. London: Longman, Green, Longman, Roberts, and Green, 1863.
- *A Volume of Vocabularies* (Liverpool: privately printed, 1857).
Wright, Thomas, and R.P. Wülcker, eds. *Anglo-Saxon and Old English Vocabularies*. 2 vols. 2nd ed. London: Trübner, 1884. Repr. Darmstadt: Wissenschaftliche Buchgesellschaft, 1968.
Wyatt, A.J., ed. *Old English Riddles*. The Belles-Lettres Series. Boston and London: D.C. Heath, 1912.
Zeydel, E.H., ed. and trans. *Ecbasis cuiusdam captivi per tropologiam: Escape of a Certain Captive Told in a Figurative Manner: an Eleventh-Century Latin Beast Epic*. University of North Carolina Studies in the Germanic Languages and Literatures 46. Chapel Hill: University of North Carolina Press, 1964.
Zupitza, Julius, ed. *Ælfrics Grammatik und Glossar*. 2nd ed. with a preface by H. Gneuss. Berlin: Weidmann, 1880; repr. 1966.

Secondary Sources

Afros, Elena. '*Sindrum begrunden* in Exeter Book *Riddle 26*: The Enigmatic Dative Case.' *Notes and Queries* 249 (2004): 7–9.
Anderson Bankert, Dabney, Jessica Wegmann and Charles D. Wright. *Ambrose in Anglo-Saxon England with Pseudo-Ambrose and Ambrosiaster*. Old English Newsletter: Subsidia 25. Kalamazoo: Medieval Institute, Werstern Michigan University, 1997.
Anderson, James E. 'Exeter Latin Riddle 90: a Liturgical Vision.' *Viator: Medieval and Renaissance Studies* 23 (1992): 73–93.
André, Jacques. *Les noms d'oiseaux en latin* . Etudes et commentaires 66. Paris: Klincksieck, 1967.
Archibald, Elizabeth. *Apollonius of Tyre: Medieval and Renaissance Themes and Variations: Including the Text of the 'Historia Apollonii Regis Tyri' with an English Translation*. Cambridge: D.S. Brewer, 1991.
Autenrieth, Johanne. 'Purcharts Gesta Witigowonis im Codex Augiensis CCV.' In *Studien zur mittelalterlichen Kunst 800–1250: Festschrift für Florentine Mütherich zum 70. Geburtstag*, ed. K. Bierbrauer et al., 101–6. Munich: Prestel, 1985.
Banham, Debby. 'Food and Drink.' In *The Blackwell Encyclopaedia of Anglo-Saxon England*, ed. M. Lapidge et al. 190–1. Oxford: Blackwell, 1999.

Barley Nigel F. 'Structural Aspects of the Anglo-Saxon Riddle.' *Semiotica* 10 (1974): 143–75.

Bartlett, Adeline Courtney. *The Larger Rhetorical Patterns in Anglo-Saxon Poetry.* Columbia University Studies in English and Comparative Literature 122. New York: Columbia University Press, 1935; repr. New York: AMS Press, 1966.

Bath, Michael. *The Image of the Stag: Iconographic Themes in Western Art*, Saecvla Spiritalia 24. Baden-Baden: Valentin Koerner, 1992.

Bayless, Martha. 'Alcuin's *Disputatio Pippini* and the Early Medieval Riddle Tradition.' In *Humour, History and Politics in Late Antiquity and the Early Middle Ages*, ed. G. Halsall. 157–78. Cambridge: Cambridge University Press, 2002.

– 'The *Collectanea* and Medieval Dialogues and Riddles.' In *Collectanea Pseudo-Bedae*, ed. M. Bayless and M. Lapidge. Scriptores Latini Hiberniae 14. 12–24. Dublin: School of Celtic Studies, Dublin Institute of Advanced Studies, 1998.

Bieler, Ludwig. 'Some Remarks on the *Aenigmata Laureshamensia*.' *Romanobarbarica* 2 (1977): 11–15.

Biggam, Carole P. *Grey in Old English: an Interdisciplinary Semantic Study.* London: Runetree, 1998.

Birkhead, Mike, and Christopher Perrins. *The Mute Swan.* London: Croom Helm, 1986.

Bischoff, Bernhard. *Latin Palaeography: Antiquity and the Middle Ages.* Trans. D. ó Cróinín and D. Ganz. Cambridge: Cambridge University Press; corr. ed. 1992.

Bitterli, Dieter. 'Exeter Book Riddle 15: Some Points for the Porcupine.' *Anglia* 120 (2002): 461–87.

– 'The Survival of the Dead Cuckoo: Exeter Book Riddle 9.' In *Riddles, Knights and Cross-dressing Saints: Essays on Medieval English Language and Literature*, ed. T. Honegger. Sammlung/Collection Variations 5. 95–114. Bern amd Berlin: Peter Lang, 2004.

Blakeley, L. 'Riddles 22 and 58 of the Exeter Book.' *Review of English Studies* n.s. 9 (1958): 241–52.

Bond, C. James. 'Mittelalterliche Wasserversorgung in England und Wales.' In *Die Wasserversorgung im Mittelalter*, ed. K. Grewe *et al.*, Geschichte der Wasserversorgung 4. 147–83. Mainz: Philipp von Zabern, 1991.

Bradley, Henry. 'Two Riddles of the Exeter Book.' *Modern Language Review* 6 (1911): 433–40.

Brady, Caroline. '"Weapons" in *Beowulf*: An Analysis of the Nominal Compounds and an Evaluation of the Poet's Use of Them.' *ASE* 8 (1979): 79–141.

Bragg, Lois. 'Runes and Readers: In and Around "The Husband's Message".' *Studia Neophilologica* 71 (1999): 34–50.

Bryant, Mark. *Dictionary of Riddles*. London, New York: Routledge, 1990.
Calkins, Robert G. *Illuminated Books of the Middle Ages*. London: Thames and Hudson, 1983.
Cameron, Esther. 'Leather-work.' In *The Blackwell Encyclopaedia of Anglo-Saxon England*, ed. M. Lapidge et al. 280–1. Oxford: Blackwell, 1999.
Campbell, James, Eric John, and Patrick Wormald. *The Anglo-Saxons*. London: Phaidon, 1982; repr. Harmondsworth: Penguin, 1991.
Capponi, Filippo. *Ornitologia latina*. Pubblicazioni dell' Istituto di Filologia Classica e Medievale 58. Genoa: Istituto di Filologia Classica e Medievale, 1979.
Catalogus codicum manuscriptorum bibliothecae regiae: pars tertia. 2 vols. Paris, 1744.
Clanchy, M.T. *From Memory to Written Record: England 1066–1307*. 2nd ed. Oxford: Blackwell, 1993.
Clemoes, Peter. *Interactions of Thought and Language in Old English Poetry*. CSASE 12. Cambridge: Cambridge University Press, 1995.
Codoñer, C. 'The Poetry of Eugenius of Toledo.' In *Papers of the Liverpool Latin Seminar: Third Volume 1981*, ed. F. Cairns. Arca 7. 323–42. Liverpool: Francis Cairns, 1981.
Conner, Patrick W. *Anglo-Saxon Exeter: a Tenth-century Cultural History*. Studies in Anglo-Saxon History 4. Woodbridge: Boydell Press, 1993.
– 'The Structure of the Exeter Book Codex (Exeter Cathedral Library, MS. 3501).' *Scriptorium* 40 (1986): 233–42. Repr. in *Anglo-Saxon Manuscripts: Basic Readings*, ed. M.P. Richards. Basic Readings in Anglo-Saxon England 2. 301–15. New York, London: Garland, 1994.
Corbet, Gordon B., and Stephen Harris. *The Handbook of British Mammals*. 3rd ed. Oxford, 1991.
Cosijn, P.J. 'Anglosaxonica.' *Beiträge zur Geschichte der deutschen Sprache und Literatur* 23 (1898): 109–30.
Cramp, S., et al., ed. *Handbook of the Birds of Europe, the Middle East and North Africa: The Birds of the Western Palearctic*. 9 vols. Oxford: Oxford University Press, 1977–94.
Curtius, Ernst Robert. *European Literature and the Latin Middle Ages*, trans. W.R. Trask. Berne: Franke, 1948. Bollingen Series 36. Princeton: Princeton University Press, 1953; repr. 1973, 1990.
Davidson, H.R. Ellis. *The Sword in Anglo-Saxon England*. Oxford: Clarendon Press, 1962.
Davis, Patricia, and Mary Schlueter. 'The Latin Riddle of the Exeter Book.' *Archiv für das Studium der neueren Sprachen und Literaturen* 226 (1989): 92–9.
Dekkers, Eligius, and Aemilius Gaar. *Clavis Patrum Latinorum*. 3rd rev. ed. CCSL. Turnhout: Brepols, 1995.
Derolez, René. *Runica Manuscripta: The English Tradition*. Brugge: de Tempel, 1954.

- 'Runica Manuscripta Revisited.' In Old English Runes and their Continental Backgrounds, ed. A. Bammesberger. Anglistische Forschungen 217. 85–106. Heidelberg: Carl Winter, 1991.
Dewa, Roberta J. 'The Runic Riddles of the Exeter Book: Language Games and Anglo-Saxon Scholarship.' Nottingham Medieval Studies 39 (1995): 26–36.
Dietrich, Franz. 'Die Räthsel des Exeterbuchs. Verfasser: weitere Lösungen,' Zeitschrift für deutsches Altertum 12 (1865): 232–52.
- 'Die Räthsel des Exeterbuchs: Würdigung, Lösung und Herstellung.' Ibid. 11 (1859): 448–90.
DiNapoli, Robert. 'In the Kingdom of the Blind, the One-Eyed Man is a Seller of Garlic: Depth-Perception and the Poet's Perspective in the Exeter Book Riddles.' English Studies 81 (2000): 422–55.
- 'Odd Characters: Runes in Old English Poetry.' In Verbal Encounters: Anglo-Saxon and Old Norse Studies for Roberta Frank, ed. A. Harbus and R. Poole. Toronto Old English Series. 145–61. Toronto: University of Toronto Press, 2005.
Donoghue, Daniel. 'An Anser for Exeter Book Riddle 74.' In Words and Works: Studies in Medieval English Language and Literature in Honour of Fred C. Robinson, ed. P.S. Baker and N. Howe. 45–58. Toronto: University of Toronto Press, 1998.
Drower, M.S. 'Water-Supply, Irrigation, and Agriculture.' In A History of Technology, ed. C. Singer et al. Vol. 1. 520–57. Oxford: Clarendon, 1954.
Earl, James W. Thinking about 'Beowulf'. Stanford: Stanford University Press, 1994.
Ebert, Adolf. 'Über die Räthselpoesie der Angelsachsen, insbesondere die Aenigmata des Tatwine und Eusebius,' Berichte über die Verhandlungen der königlichen sächsischen Gesellschaft der Wissenschaften zu Leipzig, philologisch-historische Klasse 29 (1977): 20–56.
Eliason, Norman E. 'Four Old English Cryptographic Riddles.' Studies in Philology 49 (1952): 553–65.
Elliott, Ralph W.V. Runes: An Introduction. 2nd ed. Manchester: Manchester University Press, 1989.
- 'The Runes in The Husband's Message.' Journal of English and Germanic Philology 54 (1955): 1–8.
Erhardt-Siebold, Erika von. Die lateinischen Rätsel der Angelsachsen: ein Beitrag zur Kulturgeschichte Altenglands. Anglistische Forschungen 61. Heidelberg: Carl Winter, 1925; repr. Amsterdam: Swets and Zeitlinger, 1974.
- 'Old English Riddle 13.' Modern Language Notes 65 (1950): 97–100.
Finch, Chauncey E. 'The Bern Riddles in Codex Vat. Reg. Lat. 1553.' Transactions and Proceedings of the American Philological Association 92 (1961): 145–55.
- 'Codex Vat. Barb. Lat. 721 as a Source for the Riddles of Symphosius.' Transactions of the American Philological Association 98 (1967): 173–9.

- 'Symphosius in Codices Pal. lat. 1719, 1753, and Reg. lat. 329, 2078.' *Manuscripta* 13 (1969): 3–11.
Fiocco, Teresa. 'Le rune ne *Il messagio del marito.*' *Linguistica e filologia* 10 (1999): 167–85.
Folkerts, Menso. 'Die Alkuin zugeschriebenen *Propositiones ad acuendos iuvenes.*' In *Science in Western and Eastern Civilization in Carolingian Times*, ed. P.L. Butzer and D. Lohrmann. 273– 81. Basel: Birkhäuser, 1993.
Forbes, R.J. 'Hydraulic Engineering and Sanitation.' In *A History of Technology*, ed. Ch. Singer et al. Vol. 2. 663–94. Oxford: Clarendon, 1956.
Frese, Dolores Warwick. 'The Art of Cynewulf's Runic Signatures.' In *Anglo-Saxon Poetry: Essays in Appreciation for John C. McGalliard*, ed. L.E. Nicolson and D.W. Frese. 312–34. Notre Dame, London: University of Notre Dame Press, 1975.
Fry, Donald K. 'Exeter Book Riddle Solutions.' *Old English Newsletter* 15 (1981): 22–33.
Geerard, Maurice. *Clavis Patrum Graecorum.* 5 vols. Corpus Christianorum. Turnhout: Brepols, 1974–87.
Gellinek-Schellekens, Josepha E. *The Voice of the Nightingale in Middle English Poems and Bird Debates.* New York and Berne: Peter Lang, 1984.
George, Wilma, and Brunsdon Yapp. *The Naming of the Beasts: Natural History in the Medieval Bestiary.* London: Duckworth, 1991.
Gleißner, Reinhard. *Die 'zweideutigen' altenglischen Rätsel des Exeter Book in ihrem zeitgenössischen Kontext.* Sprache und Literatur: Regensburger Arbeiten zur Anglistik und Amerikanistik 23. Frankfurt: Peter Lang, 1984.
Gneuss, Helmut. *Handlist of Anglo-Saxon Manuscripts: A List of Manuscripts and Manuscript Fragments Written or Owned in England up to 1100.* Medieval and Renaissance Texts and Studies 241. Tempe: Arizona Center for Medieval and Renaissance Studies, 2001.
Göbel, Helga. *Studien zu den altenglischen Schriftwesenrätseln.* Epistema: Würzburger wissenschaftliche Schriften: Reihe Literaturwissenschaft 7. Würzburg: Königshausen und Neumann, 1980.
Greenfield, Stanley B. *The Interpretation of Old English Poems.* London and Boston, 1972.
- 'The Old English Elegies.' In *Continuations and Beginnings: Studies in Old English Literature*, ed. E.G. Stanley. 142–75. London: Nelson, 1966. Repr. in Greenfield's *Hero and Exile: the Art of Old English Poetry*, ed. G.H. Brown. 93–123. London, Ronceverte: Hambledon Press, 1989.
Griffith, Mark. 'Riddle 19 of the Exeter Book: *snac*, an Old English Acronym.' *Notes and Queries* 237 (1992): 15–16.
Griffith, M.S. 'Convention and Originality in the Old English "Beasts of Battle" Typescene.' *ASE* 22 (1993): 179–99.

Gropp, Harald. '*Propositio de lupo et capra et fasciculo cauli* – On the History of River-Crossing Problems.' In *Charlemagne and his Heritage: 1200 Years of Civilization and Science in Europe: Karl der Grosse und sein Nachwirken: 1200 Jahre Kultur und Wissenschaft in Europa*. Vol. 2: *Mathematical Arts*, ed. P.L. Butzer et al. 31–41. Turnhout: Brepols, 1998.
Gullick, Michael. 'Bookbindings.' In *The Blackwell Encyclopaedia of Anglo-Saxon England*, ed. M. Lapidge et al. 70– 1. Oxford: Blackwell, 1999.
Hadley, John, and David Singmaster. 'Problems to Sharpen the Young: An Annotated Translation of *Propositiones ad acuendos iuvenes*, the Oldest Mathematical Problem Collection in Latin, Attributed to Alcuin of York.' *Mathematical Gazette* 76 (1992): 102–26.
Hagen, Ann. *A Handbook of Anglo-Saxon Food: Processing and Consumption*. Rev. ed. Hockwold-cum-Wilton: Anglo-Saxon Books, 1998.
– *A Second Handbook of Anglo-Saxon Food and Drink: Production and Distribution*. Hockwold-cum-Wilton: Anglo-Saxon Books, 1995.
Hamel, Christopher de. *Scribes and Illuminators*. Medieval Craftsmen. London: British Museum Press, 1992.
Harrison, Colin. *The History of the Birds of Britain*. London: Collins, 1988.
Hassig, Debra. *Medieval Bestiaries: Text, Image, Ideology*. Cambridge: Cambridge University Press, 1995.
Heron-Allen, Edward. *Barnacles in Nature and Myth*. London: Oxford University Press, 1928.
Higley, Sarah L. 'The Wanton Hand: Reading and Reaching into Grammars and Bodies in Old English Riddle 12.' In *Naked before God: Uncovering the Body in Anglo-Saxon England*, ed. B.C. Withers and J. Wilcox. Medieval European Studies 3. 29–59. Morgantown: West Virginia University Press, 2003.
Hill, Joyce. 'Ælfric's Use of Etymologies.' *ASE* 17 (1988): 35–44.
– 'The Soldier of Christ in Old English Prose and Poetry.' *Leeds Studies in English* n.s. 12 (1982): 57–80.
Holder, Alfred. *Die Reichenauer Handschriften*. Vol. 1: *Die Pergamenthandschriften*. Die Handschriften der Badischen Landesbibliothek in Karlsruhe 5. Leipzig: Teubner, 1906; repr. Wiesbaden: Otto Harrassowitz, 1970.
Holthausen, Ferdinand. *Altenglisches etymologisches Wörterbuch*. Germanische Bibliothek 1.4.7. Heidelberg: Carl Winter, 1934.
– 'Beiträge zur Erklärung und Textkritik altenglischer Dichtungen.' *Indogermanische Forschungen* 4 (1894): 379–88.
– 'Zu altenglischen Dichtungen.' *Anglia* 44 (1920): 346–56.
Howe, Nicholas. 'Aldhelm's *Enigmata* and Isidorian Etymology.' *ASE* 14 (1985): 37–59.
Hume, Kathryn. 'The Concept of the Hall in Old English Poetry.' *ASE* 3 (1974): 63–74.

Hutchinson, Gillian R. 'Ships.' In *The Blackwell Encyclopaedia of Anglo-Saxon England*, ed. M. Lapidge et al. 419– 20. Oxford: Blackwell, 1999.

Irving, Edward B. 'Heroic Experience in the Old English Riddles.' In *Old English Shorter Poems: Basic Readings*, ed. Katherine O'Brien O'Keeffe. Basic Readings in Anglo-Saxon England 3. 199–212. New York: Garland, 1994.

Jacobs, Nicolas. 'The Old English "Book-moth" Riddle Reconsidered.' *Notes and Queries* 233 (1988): 290–2.

Jordan, Richard. *Die altenglischen Säugetiernamen*. Anglistische Forschungen 12. Heidelberg: Carl Winter, 1903; repr. Amsterdam: Swets & Zeitlinger, 1967.

Jullien, Marie-Hélène, and Françoise Perelman. *Clavis des auteurs latins du moyen âge: territoire français, 735–987*. Vol. 2: *Alcuin*. CCCM: Clavis scriptorum Latinorum medii aevi 2. Turnhout: Brepols, 1999.

Kelber, Werner H. 'Language, Memory, and Sense Perception in the Religious and Technological Culture of Antiquity and the Middle Ages.' *Oral Tradition* 10 (1995): 409–50.

Keller, May Lansfield. *The Anglo-Saxon Weapon Names Treated Archaeologically and Etymologically*. Anglistische Forschungen 15. Heidelberg: Carl Winter, 1906; repr. Amsterdam: Swets and Zeitlinger, 1967.

Keller, Otto. *Die antike Tierwelt*. 2 vols. Leipzig 1909–13; repr. Hildesheim: Olms, 1963.

Ker, N.R. *Catalogue of Manuscripts Containing Anglo-Saxon*. Oxford: Clarendon Press, 1957.

Keynes, Simon. 'Crime and Punishment in the Reign of King Æthelred the Unready.' In *People and Places in Northern Europe, 500–1600: Essays in Honour of Peter Hayes Sawyer*, ed. I. Wood and N. Lund. 67–81. Woodbridge: Boydell Press, 1996.

Kitson, Peter. 'Old English Bird-Names.' *English Studies* 78 (1997): 481–505, and ibid. 79 (1998): 2–22.

– 'Swans and Geese in Old English Riddles.' *Anglo-Saxon Studies in Archaeology and History* 7 (1994): 79–84.

Klinck, Anne L. 'Elegies.' In *The Blackwell Encyclopaedia of Anglo-Saxon England*, ed. M. Lapidge et al. 164–5. Oxford: Blackwell, 1999.

Kock, Ernst A. 'Interpretations and Emendations of Early English Texts.' *Anglia* 45 (1921): 105–31.

Lapidge, Michael. 'Aldhelm.' In *The Blackwell Encyclopaedia of Anglo-Saxon England*, ed. M. Lapidge et al. 25–7. Oxford: Blackwell, 1999.

– *Anglo-Latin Literature: 600–899*. London and Rio Grande: Hambledon Press, 1996.

– 'The Career of Aldhelm.' *ASE* 36 (2007): 15–69.

– 'Stoic Cosmology and the Source of the First Old English Riddle.' *Anglia* 112 (1994): 1–25.

Lapidge, Michael, and Richard Sharpe. *A Bibliography of Celtic-Latin Literature: 400–1200.* Dictionary of Medieval Latin from Celtic Sources: Ancillary Publications 1. Dublin: Royal Irish Academy, 1985.
Leitner, Helmut. *Zoologische Terminologie beim Älteren Plinius.* Hildesheim: Gerstenberg, 1972.
Lendinara, Patrizia. 'Aspetti della società germanica negli enigmi del Codice Exoniense.' In *Antichità germaniche I Parte, I Seminario avanzato in filologia germanica*, ed. V. Dolcetti Corazza and R. Genere. Bibliotheca Germanica: Studi e Testi 10. 3–41. Alessandria: Edizioni dell'Orso, 2001.
– 'Gli *Aenigmata Laureshamensia*.' *Pan: Studi dell'Instituto di Filologia Latina* 7 (1981): 73–90.
– 'The World of Anglo-Saxon Learning.' In *The Cambridge Companion to Old English Literature*, ed. M. Godden and M. Lapidge. 264–81. Cambridge: Cambridge University Press, 1991.
Lerer, Seth. *Literacy and Power in Anglo-Saxon Literature.* Regents Studies in Medieval Culture. Lincoln and London: University of Nebraska Press, 1991.
– 'The Riddle and the Book: Exeter Book Riddle 42 in Its Contexts.' *Papers on Language and Literature* 25 (1989): 3–18.
Lester, G.A. '*Sindrum begrunden* in Exeter Book Riddle no. 26.' *Notes and Queries* 236 (1991): 13–15.
Levison, Wilhelm. *England and the Continent in the Eighth Century.* Oxford: Clarendon Press, 1946.
Mackie, W.S. 'Notes on the Text of the Exeter Book.' *Modern Language Review* 28 (1933): 75–8.
Madert, August. *Die Sprache der altenglischen Rätsel des Exeterbuches und die Cynewulffrage.* Marburg: Heinrich Brauer, 1900.
Magnusson, Roberta J. *Water Technology in the Middle Ages: Cities, Monasteries, and Waterworks after the Roman Empire.* Johns Hopkins Studies in the History of Technology. Baltimore and London: Johns Hopkins University Press, 2001.
Manitius, Max. 'Zu Aldhelm und Baeda.' *Sitzungsberichte der philologisch-historischen Classe der Kaiserlichen Akademie der Wissenschaften* 112 (1886): 535–634.
Marsden, Richard. '"Ask What I Am Called": The Anglo-Saxons and their Bibles.' In *The Bible as Book: the Manuscript Tradition*, ed. J.L. Sharpe and K. van Kampen. 145–76. London: The British Library and Oak Knoll Press, 1998.
McGowan, Joseph P. 'An Introduction to the Corpus of Anglo-Latin Literature.' In *A Companion to Anglo-Saxon Literature*, ed. P. Pulsiano and E. Treharne. 11–49. Oxford: Blackwell, 2001.
McKitterick, Rosamond. *The Carolingians and the Written Word.* Cambridge: Cambridge University Press, 1989.

Meaney, Audrey L. 'Birds on the Stream of Consciousness: Riddles 7 to 10 of the Exeter Book.' *Archaeological Review from Cambridge* 18 (2002): 120–52.
– 'The Hunted and the Hunters: British Mammals in Old English Poetry.' *Anglo-Saxon Studies in Archaeology and History* 11 (2000): 95–105.
Metcalf, Allan. 'Ten Natural Animals in *Beowulf*.' *Neuphilologische Mitteilungen* 64 (1963): 378–89.
Milovanovic-Barham, Celica. 'Aldhelm's *Enigmata* and Byzantine Riddles.' *ASE* 22 (1993): 51–64.
Mitchell, Bruce. *Old English Syntax*. 2 vols. Oxford: Clarendon Press, 1985.
Mitchell, Bruce, and Fred C. Robinson. *A Guide to Old English*. 6th ed. Oxford: Blackwell, 2001.
Moessner, Lilo. 'Dog – Man's Best Friend: a Study in Historical Lexicology.' In *English Historical Linguistics 1992: Papers from the 7th International Conference on English Historical Linguistics: Valencia, 22–26 September 1992*, ed. F. Fernández, M. Fuster, and J.J. Calvo. Amsterdam Studies in the Theory and History of Linguistic Science: Current Issues in Linguistic Theory 113. 207–18. Amsterdam: John Benjamins, 1994.
Morley, Henry. *English Writers: An Attempt Towards a History of English Literature*. Vol. 2: *From Caedmon to the Conquest*. London: Cassell, 1888.
Murphy, Patrick J. 'The Riders of the Celestial Wain in Exeter Book *Riddle 22*.' *Notes and Queries* 22 (2006), 401–7.
Nelson, Marie. 'Four Social Functions in the Exeter Book Riddles.' *Neophilologus* 75 (1991): 445–50.
– 'The Paradox of Silent Speech in the Exeter Book Riddles.' *Neophilologus* 62 (1978): 609–15.
– 'The Rhetoric of the Exeter Book Riddles.' *Speculum* 49 (1974): 421–40.
– 'Time in the Exeter Book Riddles.' *Philological Quarterly* 54 (1975): 511–18.
Niles, John D. *Old English Enigmatic Poems and the Play of the Texts*. Studies in the Early Middle Ages 13. Turnhout: Brepols, 2006.
Nixon, Howard M., and Mirjam M. Foot. *The History of Decorated Bookbinding in England*. Oxford: Clarendon Press, 1992.
O'Brien O'Keeffe, Katherine. 'Body and Law in Late Anglo-Saxon England.' *ASE* 27 (1998): 209–32.
– 'The Text of Aldhelm's Enigma no. C in Oxford, Bodleian Library, Rawlinson C. 697 and Exeter Riddle 40.' *ASE* 14 (1985): 61–73.
Ogilvy, J.D.A. *Books Known to the English: 597–1066*. Cambridge, MA.: Medieval Academy of America, 1967.
Olsen, Karin. 'Animated Ships in Old English and Old Norse Poetry.' In *Animals and the Symbolic in Mediaeval Art and Literature*, ed. L.A.J.R. Houwen. Mediaevalia Groningana 20. 53–66. Groningen: Egbert Forsten, 1997.
Orchard, Andy. *A Critical Companion to Beowulf*. Cambridge: Brewer, 2003.

- 'Enigma Variations: The Anglo-Saxon Riddle Tradition.' In *Latin Learning and English Lore: Studies in Anglo-Saxon Literature for Michael Lapidge*, ed. K. O'Brien O'Keeffe and A. Orchard. Vol. 1. Toronto Old English Series. 284–304. Toronto: University of Toronto Press, 2005.
- 'Enigmata.' In *The Blackwell Encyclopaedia of Anglo-Saxon England*, ed. M. Lapidge et al. 171– 2. Oxford: Blackwell, 1999.
- 'Oral Tradition.' In *Reading Old English Texts*, ed. K. O'Brien O'Keeffe. 101– 23. Cambridge: Cambridge University Press, 1997.
- *The Poetic Art of Aldhelm*, CSASE 8. Cambridge: Cambridge University Press, 1994.
- *Pride and Prodigies: Studies in the Monsters of the 'Beowulf'-Manuscript*. Cambridge: Brewer, 1995.

Orton, Peter. 'The Technique of Object-Personification in *The Dream of the Rood* and a Comparison with the Old English *Riddles*.' *Leeds Studies in English* n.s. 11 (1980): 1–18.

Page, R.I. *An Introduction to English Runes*. 2nd ed. Woodbridge: Boydell Press, 1999.

Parker, A.J. 'The Birds of Roman Britain.' *Oxford Journal of Archaeology* 7 (1988): 197–226.

Pavlovskis, Zoja. 'The Riddler's Microcosm: from Symphosius to St. Boniface.' *Classica et Medievalia* 39 (1988): 219–51.

Petsch, Robert. 'Rätselstudien.' *Zeitschrift des Vereins für Volkskunde* 26 (1916): 1–18.

Pfeffer, Wendy. *The Change of Philomel: the Nightingale in Medieval Literature*. American University Studies 3.14. New York, Berne, Frankfurt: P. Lang, 1985.

Polara, Giovanni. 'Aenigmata,' in *Lo spazio letterario del medioevo latino*. Vol. 1: *Il medioevo latino*, ed. G. Cavallo et al. Vol. 1, part 2. 197–216. Rome: Salerno Editrice, 1993.

Pollard, Graham. 'Some Anglo-Saxon Bookbindings.' *Book Collector* 24 (1975): 130–59.

Poole, Russell. *Old English Wisdom Poetry*. Annotated Bibliographies of Old and Middle English Literature 5. Cambridge: D.S. Brewer, 1998.

Prehn, A. *Komposition und Quellen der Rätsel des Exeterbuches*. Paderborn: Ferdinand Schöningh, 1883.

Reed, R. *Ancient Skins, Parchments and Leathers*. Studies in Archaeological Science. London and New York: Seminar Press, 1972.

Remus, Harold. 'Persecution.' In *Handbook of Early Christianity: Social Science Approaches*, ed. A.J. Blasi, J. Duhaime and P.-A. Turcotte. 431–52. Walnut Creek etc.: Altamira Press, 2002.

Reynolds, L.D. ed., *Texts and Transmission: A Survey of the Latin Classics*. Oxford: Clarendon Press, 1983.

Ridyard, Susan J. *The Royal Saints of Anglo-Saxon England: A Study of West Saxon and East Anglian Cults.* Cambridge Studies in Medieval Life and Thought. 4th Series. 9. Cambridge: Cambridge University Press, 1988.

Rigg, A.G., and G.R. Wieland. 'A Canterbury Classbook of the Mid-Eleventh Century (The "Cambridge Songs" Manuscript).' *ASE* 4 (1975): 113–30.

Roberts, Jane, Christian Kay, and Lynne Grundy, eds. *A Thesaurus of Old English.* 2 Vols. 2nd rev. ed. Costerus, n.s. 131–2. Amsterdam and Atlanta: Rodopi, 2000.

Robinson, Fred C. 'Artful Ambiguities in the Old English "Book-Moth" Riddle.' In *Anglo-Saxon Poetry: Essays in Appreciation for John C. McGalliard*, ed. L.E. Nicholson and D. Warwick Frese. 355–62. Notre Dame: University of Notre Dame Press, 1975.

Rollason, David. *Saints and Relics in Anglo-Saxon England.* Oxford: Basil Blackwell, 1989.

Rowland, Beryl. *Birds with Human Souls: A Guide to Bird Symbolism.* Knoxville: University of Tennessee Press, 1978.

Rulon-Miller, Nina. 'Sexual Humour and Fettered Desire in Exeter Book Riddle 12.' In *Humour in Anglo-Saxon England*, ed. J. Wilcox. 99–126. Cambridge: D.S. Brewer, 2000.

Salvador Bello, Mercedes. 'The Evening Singer of Riddle 8 (K-D).' *Selim: Journal of the Spanish Society for Medieval English Language and Literature* 9 (1999): 57–68.

Salvador [Bello], Mercedes. 'The Oyster and the Crab: A Riddle Duo (nos. 77 and 78) in the *Exeter Book*.' *Modern Philology* 101 (2004): 400–19.

Scherrer, Gustav. *Verzeichnis der Handschriften der Stiftsbibliothek von St. Gallen.* Halle: Verlag der Buchhandlung des Waisenhauses, 1875; repr. Hildesheim and New York: Georg Olms, 1975.

Schrunck Ericksen, Janet. 'Runesticks and Reading *The Husband's Message*.' *Neuphilologische Mitteilungen* 99 (1998): 31–7.

Scott, Peter Dale. 'Rhetorical and Symbolic Ambiguity: the Riddles of Symphosius and Aldhelm.' In *Saints, Scholars, and Heroes: Studies in Medieval Culture in Honor of Charles W. Jones*, ed. M.H. King and W.M. Stevens. 2 vols. 1:117–44. Collegeville, MI: Hill Monastic Manuscript Library, Saint John's Abbey and University, 1979.

Senra Silva, Inmaculada. 'The Rune "Eþel" and Scribal Writing Habits in the Beowulf MS.' *Neuphilologische Mitteilungen* 99 (1998): 241–7.

Shook, Laurence K. 'Riddles Relating to the Anglo-Saxon Scriptorium.' In *Essays in Honour of Anton Charles Pegis*, ed. J.R. O'Donnell. 215–36. Toronto: Pontifical Institute of Mediaeval Studies, 1974.

Singmaster, David. 'The History of Some of Alcuin's Propositions.' In *Charlemagne and His Heritage: 1200 Years of Civilization and Science in*

Europe: Karl der Grosse und sein Nachwirken: 1200 Jahre Kultur und Wissenschaft in Europa. Vol. 2: *Mathematical Arts,* ed. P.L. Butzer et al. 11–29. Turnhout: Brepols, 1998.
Skeat, W.W. *An Etymological Dictionary of the English Language,* rev. ed (Oxford, 1910).
Skelton, R.A., and P.D.A. Harvey, eds. *Local Maps and Plans from Medieval England.* Oxford: Clarendon, 1986.
Sorrell, Paul. 'Like a Duck to Water: Representations of Aquatic Animals in Early Anglo-Saxon Literature and Art.' *Leeds Studies in English* n.s. 25 (1994): 29–68.
Stanley, Eric Gerald. 'Heroic Aspects of the Exeter Book Riddles.' In *Prosody and Poetics in the Early Middle Ages: Essays in Honour of C.B. Hieatt,* ed. M.J. Toswell. 197–218. Toronto: University of Toronto Press, 1995.
Stewart, Ann Harleman. 'Old English Riddle 47 as Stylistic Parody.' *Papers on Language and Literature* 11 (1975): 227–41.
Swaen, A.E.H. 'Riddle 9 (6, 8): Facts and Fancies.' *Studia Neophilologica* 14 (1941/42): 67–70.
Szirmai, J.A. *The Archaeology of Medieval Bookbinding.* Aldershot: Ashgate, 1999.
Tanke, John W. 'Ideology and Figuration in the Sexual Riddles of the Exeter Book.' In *Class and Gender in Early English Literature: Intersections,* ed. B.J. Harwood and G.R. Overing. 21–42. Bloomington and Indianapolis: Indiana University Press, 1994.
Taylor, Archer. *The Literary Riddle before 1600.* Berkeley and Los Angeles: University of California Press, 1948.
– 'The Riddle.' *California Folklore Quarterly* 2 (1943): 129–47.
Thompson, D'Arcy W. *A Glossary of Greek Birds.* London and Oxford: Oxford University Press, 1936; repr. Hildesheim: Olms, 1966.
Ticehurst, Norman F. *The Mute Swan in England: its History, and the Ancient Custom of Swan Keeping.* London: Cleaver-Hume Press, 1957.
Tigges, Wim. 'Snakes and Ladders: Ambiguity and Coherence in the Exeter Book Riddles and Maxims.' In *Companion to Old English Poetry,* ed. H. Aertsen and R.H. Bremmer. 95–118. Amsterdam, 1994.
Tilliette, Jean-Yves. 'Etymology.' In *Encyclopedia of the Middle Ages,* ed. A. Vauchez et al. Trans. A. Walford. 503. Cambridge: James Clarke, 2000. [1st publ. in French, Paris: Cerf, 1997].
Tomasek, Tomas. *Das deutsche Rätsel im Mittelalter.* Hermaea 69. Tübingen: Niemeyer, 1994.
Toynbee, J.M.C. *Animals in Roman Life and Art.* London: Thames and Hudson, 1973; repr. Baltimore: Johns Hopkins University Press, 1996.
Trautmann, Moritz. 'Alte und neue Antworten auf altenglische Rätsel.' *Bonner Beiträge zur Anglistik* 19 (1905): 167–215.

- 'Die Auflösungen der altenglischen Rätsel.' *Anglia Beiblatt* 5 (1894): 46–51.
- 'Das Geschlecht in den altenglischen Rätseln.' *Anglia Beiblatt* 25 (1914): 324–7.
- 'Sprache und Versbau der altenglischen Rätsel.' *Anglia* 38 (1914): 355–64.
- 'Zeit, Heimat und Verfasser der altengl[ischen] Rätsel.' *Anglia* 38 (1914): 365–73.
- 'Zum Streit um die altenglischen Rätsel.' *Anglia* 36 (1912): 127–33.

Tupper, Frederick. 'The Comparative Study of Riddles.' *Modern Language Notes* 18 (1903): 1–8.
- 'Riddles of the Bede Tradition.' *Modern Philology* 2 (1905): 561–72.

Walde, A., and J.B. Hofmann. *Lateinisches etymologisches Wörterbuch*. Indogermanische Bibliothek I.2.1. 3 vols. 3rd ed. Heidelberg, 1938–56.

Wattenbach, Wilhelm. *Das Schriftwesen im Mittelalter* [1871]. 3rd ed. Leipzig: S. Hirzel, 1896; repr. Graz: Akademische Druck- und Verlagsanstalt, 1958.

Wells, Richard. 'The Old English Riddles and their Ornithological Content.' *Lore and Language* 9 (1978): 57–67.

Wenzel, Horst. 'Die Schrift und das Heilige.' In *Die Verschriftlichung der Welt: Bild, Text und Zahl in der Kultur des Mittelalters und der Frühen Neuzeit*. Schriften des Kunsthistorischen Museums 5. 14–57. Vienna: Kunsthistorisches Museum Wien, 2000.

Whitbread, Leslie. 'The Latin Riddle in the Exeter Book.' *Notes and Queries* 190 (1946): 156–58; and ibid. 194 (1949): 80–2.

Whitehurst Williams, Edith. '"An Insight of Form": New Genres in Four Exeter Book Riddles.' In *Essays on Old, Middle, Modern English and Old Icelandic in Honour of Raymond P. Tripp, Jr.*, ed. L.C. Gruber et al. 231–61. Lewiston: The Edwin Mellen Press, 2000.

Whitman, Charles H. 'The Birds of Old English Literature.' *Journal of Germanic Philology* 2 (1898): 149–98.

Whitman, F.H. 'Aenigmata Tatwini.' *Neuphilologische Mitteilungen* 88 (1987): 8–17.
- 'Riddle 60 and Its Source.' *Philological Quarterly* 50 (1971): 108–15.

Wilcox, Jonathan. 'Mock-Riddles in Old English: Exeter Riddles 86 and 19.' *Studies in Philology* 93 (1996): 180–7.
- 'Transmission of Literature and Learning: Anglo-Saxon Scribal Culture.' In *A Companion to Anglo-Saxon Literature*, ed. P. Pulsiano and E. Treharne. 50–70. Oxford: Blackwell, 2001.

Ziegler, Waltraud. 'Ein neuer Lösungsversuch für das altenglische Rätsel Nr. 28.' *Arbeiten aus Anglistik und Amerikanistik* 7 (1982): 185–90.

Ziolkowski, Jan M. *Talking Animals: Medieval Latin Beast Poetry, 750–1150*. Philadelphia: University of Pennsylvania Press, 1993.

Index

Ademar of Chabannes, 57
Adomnán: *Vita Columbae*, 151n2
Adrian and Ritheus, 112
Adrianus et Epictitus, 111
Ælfric, 45n29; *Colloquy*, 31n54, 109; *De temporibus anni*, 65; *Grammar*, 127n42; *Lives of Saints*, 178–80
Ælfric Bata: *Colloquy*, 139n7
Aelian: *De natura animalium*, 94n40, 156n11
Aesop: *Fables*, 41n19, 68n23
Agatha, Saint, 180
Alcuin, 25, 42, 72; *Carmina*, 53, 55n63; *De orthographia* 114n1; *Disputatio Pippini cum Albino*, 4, 13–15, 16n10, 17, 57, 65–6, 110–11; *Epistolae*, 66n20; *Propositiones ad acuendos iuvenes*, 4, 57–60, 73
Aldhelm, 20, 30, 42, 51, 67; *Carmen de virginitate*, 180n24, *De virginitate*, 178, 180n24; *Enigmata*, 4–5, 14, 16, 19–26, 36, 52, 67, 73, 75, 78–9, 111, 142; *Enigma* 1 ('earth'), 36; *Enigma* 2 ('wind'), 36; *Enigma* 3 ('cloud'), 36; *Enigma* 4 ('nature'), 36; *Enigma* 10 ('dog'), 109; *Enigma* 13 ('organ'), 79; *Enigma* 22 ('nightingale'), 52–4;

Enigma 26 ('cock'), 124n29; *Enigma* 30 ('alphabet'), 114–15, 119, 144–6, 183; *Enigma* 32 ('writing-tablets'), 140, 142–3; *Enigma* 33 ('mail-coat'), 25n38; *Enigma* 40 ('pepper'), 79; *Enigma* 52 ('candle'), 79; *Enigma* 53 ('Arcturus'), 63–5; *Enigma* 54 ('double cooking-pot'), 79; *Enigma* 55 ('ciborium'), 79; *Enigma* 59 ('quill pen'), 139, 143–6; *Enigma* 63 ('raven'), 77–8; *Enigma* 67 ('flour sieve'), 79; *Enigma* 73 ('fountain'), 103; *Enigma* 78 ('wine cask'), 79; *Enigma* 81 ('Morning Star'), 125; *Enigma* 83 ('young ox'), 27–8, 33; *Enigma* 84 ('pregnant sow'), 70–1; *Enigma* 86 ('ram'), 77; *Enigma* 88 ('serpent'), 156; *Enigma* 89 ('bookcase'), 79, 140; *Enigma* 90 ('woman giving birth to twins'), 69–70; *Enigma* 100 ('Creation'), 19, 25n38, 36, 73, 125–6; *Epistolae*, 67n21
Alfred, King: *Boethius*, 64–5, 184
Ambrose of Milan: *Hexaemeron*, 51
anagrams. *See* logographs
Andreas, 163n30, 173n7
Anglo-Saxon Chronicle, 89

214   Index

Apollonius of Tyre, Old English, 15–16. See also *Historia Apollonii regis Tyri*
Aristophanes: *The Birds*, 41
Aristotle: *Historia animalium*, 94n40, 117n9, 124, 156n11
Augustine of Hippo, 77
Avian: *Fables*, 68n23

Bartholomew, Saint, 179–80
Battle of Brunanburh, The, 96–7
Battle of Maldon, The, 97n46, 159
Bede, 42, 51; *De orthographia* 114n1; *De temporum ratione*, 66; *De natura rerum*, 66; *Historia ecclesiastica gentis Anglorum*, 67; *Martyrologium*, 178, 179n20. See also *Collectanea Pseudo-Bedae*; *Jocoseria Pseudo-Bedae*
Beowulf, 9, 33n58, 38–9, 62n11, 84, 97n46, 100, 108, 120n21, 128, 138n6, 155n6, 156, 159, 162, 164, 173n7
Beowulf manuscript (London, British Library, Cotton Vitellius A.xv), 71, 84
Berne Riddles (Aenigmata Tullii), 4, 21–2, 24; *Berne Riddle* 11 ('ship'), 79, 89n21; *Berne Riddle* 19 ('wax'), 140; *Berne Riddle* 24 ('parchment'), 79, 140, 182, 185; *Berne Riddle* 25 ('letters'), 115, 144
bestiaries, 19, 38, 42n23, 51, 95, 155
Boethius, *Consolatio philosophiae*, 64–5. See also Alfred, King
Boniface, 72; *Enigmata*, 24, 75, 78

Cassian of Imola, Saint, 179
Cassiodorus: *Institutiones*, 148–9, 184
Charlemagne, 4, 13, 57, 66
Chaucer, Geoffrey, 124

Collectanea Pseudo-Bedae, 4, 16, 25, 27–9, 70, 111–12, 117–18, 131n53, 140–1
cryptograms. See logogriphs
Cynewulf, 76, 84–6; *Christ II*, 84; *Elene*, 84, 97n46, 99n2; *Fates of the Apostles*, 84; *Juliana*, 84, 123n28, 180n25

Dream of the Rood, The, 177

Eadwine of Canterbury, 148
Ecbasis captivi, 52n51
Edgar, King, 39
Edmund of East Anglia, King, 189
elegies, Old English, 5, 9, 34, 163–4. See also *Husband's Message*; *Ruin*; *Wanderer*; *Wulf and Eadwacer*
envelope pattern, 120n21
etymology, 4, 6, 19, 38, 44–6, 49, 54–6, 65, 114, 143, 147, 156, 161. See also Isidore of Seville: *Etymologies*
Eugenia, Saint, 179
Eugenius of Toledo: *Carmina*, 51–2, 95n43
Eulalia, Saint, 188
Eusebius, 30; *Enigmata*, 4–5, 14, 23–5, 36, 75, 78; *Enigma* 1 ('God'), 36; *Enigma* 2 ('Angel'), 36; *Enigma* 3 ('devil'), 36; *Enigma* 4 ('man'), 36; *Enigma* 5 ('heaven'), 36; *Enigma* 6 ('earth'), 36; *Enigma* 7 ('letters'), 36, 114, 183; *Enigma* 9 ('alpha'), 114; *Enigma* 12 ('ox'), 34; *Enigma* 14 ('letter x'), 114; *Enigma* 19 ('letter v'), 114; *Enigma* 30 ('inkhorn'), 139, 151–2, 163, 166; *Enigma* 31 ('wax'), 140; *Enigma* 32 ('parchment'), 140, 182–3, 185; *Enigma* 33 ('bookcase'), 140; *Enigma* 34 ('river'),

78n51; *Enigma* 35 ('quill pen'), 139, 145, 147; *Enigma* 37 ('calf'), 28–9, 33; *Enigma* 38 ('chick'), 117–18; *Enigma* 39 ('letter *i*'), 114, 115n4; *Enigma* 44 ('panther'), 78n51; *Enigma* 59 ('parrot'), 93

Exeter Book (Exeter, Cathedral Library, MS 3501): manuscript, 3, 26, 32, 35, 47, 75, 83–4, 110, 126, 135–6, 152, 160, 164; *Riddle* 1 ('storm'), 26, 35–6, 127, 135, 164–5; *Riddle* 2 ('storm'), 26, 35–6, 126n38, 135, 165; *Riddle* 3 ('storm'), 26, 35–6, 135, 165; *Riddle* 4 ('flail'?), 26, 35; *Riddle* 5 ('shield' or 'chopping block'?), 35, 84, 103, 165, 186n39; *Riddle* 6 ('sun'), 35; *Riddle* 7 ('swan'), 5–6, 19, 35–8, 40–7, 55, 116, 123, 135, 184; *Riddle* 8 ('nightingale'), 5–6, 19, 35–8, 44–56, 96, 135; *Riddle* 9 ('cuckoo'), 19, 35–8, 43n25, 44, 116–17, 120, 123, 135; *Riddle* 10 ('barnacle goose'), 19, 35–8, 43, 116, 120, 123, 135; *Riddle* 11 ('wine'), 43n24; *Riddle* 12 ('ox'), 5, 19, 27, 30–2, 34, 44, 116, 123, 185–6; *Riddle* 13 ('ten chickens'), 7, 19, 37, 43, 115–21, 123; *Riddle* 14 ('horn'), 26, 43n24, 88, 128, 151, 166–8, 186; *Riddle* 15 ('porcupine'), 19, 43n26, 108, 165, 177n15; *Riddle* 16 ('anchor'), 18, 101, 166; *Riddle* 17 ('beehive'), 19, 103, 165–6; *Riddle* 19 ('ship'), 7, 19, 26, 74, 86–91, 105; *Riddle* 20 ('falcon'?), 19, 128–9, 165; *Riddle* 21 ('plow'), 102–3; *Riddle* 22 ('Charles's Wain'), 6, 19, 60–5, 67–8; *Riddle* 23 ('bow'), 97, 165; *Riddle* 24 ('jay'), 7, 19, 37, 47–8, 86, 91–7, 105, 107, 121, 135; *Riddle* 25 ('onion'), 26; *Riddle* 26 ('Bible'), 9, 26, 136, 171–9, 182, 184, 186–9, 192; *Riddle* 27 ('mead'), 167n39; *Riddle* 28 ('codex'), 9, 26, 126, 136, 171, 181–8, 192; *Riddle* 29 ('moon and sun'), 165; *Riddle* 31 ('bagpipes'?), 43n24, 126n38; *Riddle* 32 ('wheel'), 101, 124; *Riddle* 33 ('ice floe?'), 165; *Riddle* 34 ('rake'), 102; *Riddle* 35 ('mail-coat'), 25, 125, *Riddle* 36 ('ship'?), 6, 71–4, 75n44, 88n16, 107; *Riddle* 37 ('bellows'), 18, 26, 103; *Riddle* 38 ('ox'), 5, 19, 27, 29–30, 33–4; *Riddle* 39 ('dream'), 88n16, 116n7, 186n39; *Riddle* 40 ('Creation'), 19, 25, 123n27, 125–6; *Riddle* 41 ('water'?), 126; *Riddle* 42 ('cock and hen'), 7, 19, 37, 86, 98, 105, 116n8, 120–31, 135; *Riddle* 43 ('soul and body'), 126n38; *Riddle* 44 ('key'), 26, 130–1; *Riddle* 46 ('Lot and his offspring'), 6, 58–9; *Riddle* 47 ('bookworm'), 9, 18–19, 136–7, 191–3; *Riddle* 48 ('chalice'), 26, 55n63, 129n49; *Riddle* 49 ('bookcase'?), 136; *Riddle* 50 ('fire'), 165; *Riddle* 51 ('quill pen'), 8, 136, 145–50, 155, 176, 178, 192; *Riddle* 52 ('flail'?), 26, 31, 103, 123; *Riddle* 53 ('battering ram'), 165; *Riddle* 54 ('churn'?), 103; *Riddle* 55 ('cross'), 126n38, 128n43, 129, 166; *Riddle* 56 ('lathe'?),128n43, 129, 166; *Riddle* 57 ('swallows'?), 19, 37, 116; *Riddle* 58 ('well-sweep'), 7, 86, 88–9, 98–105; *Riddle* 59 ('chalice'), 26, 129; *Riddle* 60 ('reed pen'), 8, 18, 136–9, 164, 192; *Riddle* 62 ('poker'), 103; *Riddle* 64 ('ship'), 7, 19, 26, 74, 86, 89–91, 105; *Riddle* 65 ('onion'), 26;

Riddle 66 ('water'), 26; *Riddle* 67 ('book'?), 126, 129n49, 136; *Riddle* 72 ('ox'), 5, 19, 27, 32–4, 116; *Riddle* 73 ('spear'), 26, 165; *Riddle* 74 (water bird?), 19, 37, 116, 136; *Riddle* 75 ('hunting dog'), 7, 19, 86, 98, 105–10; *Riddle* 76 (insoluble), 7, 19, 106–7, 110; *Riddle* 77 ('oyster'), 19; *Riddle* 78 (water animal?), 19; *Riddle* 80 ('horn'), 26, 123, 151, 166–8, 186; *Riddle* 81 ('weathercock'?), 101–2; *Riddle* 82 ('crab'?), 19; *Riddle* 84 ('water'), 26; *Riddle* 85 ('fish in the river'), 5, 16–19, 26, 55n63, 135, 154n5, 193; *Riddle* 86 ('one-eyed garlic-seller'), 6, 18, 69, 88n16; *Riddle* 87 ('bellows'), 26; *Riddle* 88 ('inkhorn'), 8–9, 19, 26, 136, 151–8, 161, 163–6, 168, 176, 186, 192; *Riddle* 90 (insoluble), 6, 19, 25, 74–9; *Riddle* 91 ('key'), 26, 84, 130–1; *Riddle* 92 ('spear'), 26; *Riddle* 93 ('inkhorn'), 8–9, 19, 26, 101, 136, 151–2, 156–66, 168, 176, 186, 192; *Riddle* 95 ('book'?), 136
Exodus, 97n46

Ferreolus, Saint, 187
Ferrucio, Saint, 187
formulas: concluding, 57–8, 88, 124–7; opening, 17, 75, 88n16, 90, 106, 110, 122, 192
Fulbert of Chartres, 53

Genesis A, 128n43
Gerald of Wales, 35n3
Gervase of Tilbury, 35n3
Gesta Romanorum, 15
glossaries, 39n13, 92–3
Gregory the Great, 22n29

Gregory of Nazianzus, 41–2
Guthlac B, 123n28, 164

Hadrian of Canterbury, 67
Harley Lyrics, 49
Hisperica Famina, 140
Historia Apollonii regis Tyri, 15, 137. See also *Apollonius of Tyre*
Homeric Hymns, 41
Hrabanus Maurus, 72; *De rerum naturis*, 42n23, 95n41, 142n19
Hugh of Fouilloy: *De bestiis et aliis rebus*, 95n41
Husband's Message, The, 84–6, 138n3, 163–4
Hwætberht. See Eusebius

Ioca monachorum, 58, 111–12
Isidore of Seville: *De natura rerum*, 64–6; *Differentiae*, 78n51, 114n1; *Etymologies*, 6, 22n29, 36, 42, 45–6, 51, 64n15, 93–5, 108–9, 114n1, 115, 141–2, 143n22, 156n9, 170–1, 183; *Synonyma*, 114n1; *Versus*, 149

Joco-seria Pseudo-Bedae, 4, 25, 78, 144n25
Jonson, Ben, 49n43
Judith, 97
Justus of Beauvais, Saint, 187

Lactantius: *De ave Phoenice*, 40–1
Leiden Riddle, 25n38
Letter of Alexander to Aristotle, 71
Liber monstrorum, 71n30
Lindisfarne Gospels, 119
logographs, 4–5, 7, 25, 71–4, 76–8, 87–92, 97–8, 104–7, 114–15, 119, 121–2, 126. See also runes
Lorsch Riddles, 4, 24; *Lorsch Riddle* 1

Index   217

('man'), 36n6; *Lorsch Riddle 2*
('soul'), 36n6; *Lorsch Riddle 3*
('water'), 36n6; *Lorsch Riddle 8*
('chick'), 118; *Lorsch Riddle 9* ('quill pen'), 139, 141; *Lorsch Riddle 11* ('ox'), 27–8, 32n56; *Lorsch Riddle 12* ('ink'), 139, 161

manuscripts: Antwerp, Plantin-Moretus Museum 47, 93n36; Bern, Bugerbibliothek, Bernensis 611, 22; Cambridge, Trinity College, MS R.17.1, 148n34; Cambridge, University Library Gg.5.35, 24n33, 25, 73, 78, 144n25; Karlsruhe, Badische Landesbibliothek, Codex Augiensis 205, 57, 73; Leiden University Library, Cod. Vossinus Lat. 4° 106, 25n38; Leiden University Library, Cod. Vossinus Lat. 8° 15, 57n2; London, British Library, Add. 32246, 93n36; London, British Library, Add. 47967 (Lauderdale manuscript), 84; London, British Library, Royal 12.C.xxiii, 25n37; Paris, Bibliothèque Nationale, MS lat. 2339, 143n23; Paris, Bibliothèque Nationale, MS lat. 8440, 52; Rome (Vatican City), Biblioteca Apostolica Vaticana, Barb. lat. 721, 72; Rome (Vatican City), Biblioteca Apostolica Vaticana, Pal. lat. 1753, 24n35; Rome (Vatican City), Biblioteca Apostolica Vaticana, Reg. lat. 1553, 24. St Gallen, Stiftsbibliothek, 196, 117–18, 141. See also *Beowulf* manuscript; Exeter Book; Vercelli Book
Martial: *Epigrams*, 94–5
Martyrology, Old English, 178–80, 187–8

Marvels of the East, 71
Maxims I, 127
Monasteriales Indicia, 147, 161

Neckam, Alexander: *De naturis rerum*, 35n3; *De nominibus utensilium*, 170n1

Order of the World, 18n15, 127
Orosius, Old English, 84
Oswald of Northumbria, King, 189
Ovid: *Metamorphoses*, 95–6, 137n2
Owl and the Nightingale, The, 49–50

Paulinus of Nola, 51
Pecham, John, 53
Phoenix, The, 37, 40–1, 43n24, 123n28
Physiologus, 155
Pliny the Elder: *Natural History*, 50–1, 54, 93–4, 108, 124, 143, 156, 171n3
Plutarch, *De sollertia animalium*, 94n40
Precepts, 127
Prudentius: *Peristephanon*, 179n20, 188
pseudo-Bede. See *Collectanea Pseudo-Bedae*; *Joco-seria Pseudo-Bedae*

Reichenau Riddles, 4, 57, 73
riddle collections. See Alcuin; Aldhelm; *Berne Riddles*; Boniface; *Collectanea Pseudo-Bedae*; Eusebius; Exeter Book; *Ioca monachorum*; *Joco-seria Pseudo-Bedae*; *Lorsch Riddles*; *Reichenau Riddles*; *St Gallen Riddles*; Symphosius; Tatwine
Riddles, Old English. See Exeter Book
Rufinus of Aquileia, 42
Ruin, 84, 163
runes, 5–7, 47, 83–92, 97–9, 104–7, 112, 120–2, 126–8, 130–1, 135

Solinus: *Collectanea rerum memorabilium*, 108
Solomon and Saturn, 112–13
St Gallen Riddles 117–18, 141
Symphosius: *Aenigmata*, 4, 14, 19–25, 52, 57, 72, 78, 110–11, 117, 129–30; *Aenigma* 1 ('stylus'), 36n5, 137, 140; *Aenigma* 2 ('reed'), 8, 18n16, 36, 137–9; *Aenigma* 4 ('key'), 131n53; *Aenigma* 12 ('river and fish'), 5, 15–18, 110n33; *Aenigma* 13 ('ship'), 89; *Aenigma* 14 ('embryo chick'), 110n33; *Aenigma* 16 ('bookworm'), 9, 18n16, 145, 191–2; *Aenigma* 30 ('lice'), 110n33; *Aenigma* 56 ('boot'), 32, 185; *Aenigma* 61 ('anchor'), 18n16; *Aenigma* 65 ('arrow'), 110n33; *Aenigma* 71 ('well'), 103–4; *Aenigma* 73 ('bellows'), 18n16; *Aenigma* 76 ('flint'), 110n33; *Aenigma* 93 ('woman pregnant with twins'), 70; *Aenigma* 95 ('one-eyed garlic-seller'), 18n16, 68–9; *Aenigma* 98 ('echo'), 110n33; *Aenigma* 99 ('sleep'), 110n33

Tatwine: *Enigmata*, 4, 14, 23, 25, 36, 75, 78, 126; *Enigma* 1 ('philosophy'), 36; *Enigma* 2 ('faith, hope, and charity'), 36; *Enigma* 3 ('four scriptural senses'), 36; *Enigma* 4 ('letters'), 36, 114; *Enigma* 5 ('parchment'), 36, 139–40, 173–4, 182–3; *Enigma* 6 ('quill pen'), 36, 139, 144–7; *Enigma* 8 ('altar'), 79n56; *Enigma* 10 ('lectern'), 101n9; *Enigma* 12 ('paten'), 101n9; *Enigma* 28 ('anvil'), 101n9; *Enigma* 29 ('table'), 79n56
Tertullian, 77
Theodore, archbishop of Canterbury, 67
Theophilus Presbyter: *De diversis artibus*, 161n23
Tullius. See *Berne Riddles*

Vainglory, 123n28, 127
Venantius Fortunatus, 51
Vercelli Book (Vercelli, Biblioteca capitolare CXVII), 84, 163n30
Victor, Saint, 179–80
Vincent, Saint, 180

Waldere, 84
Wanderer, 100, 123n28, 163
Widsið, 128n43
William of Malmesbury: *Gesta pontificium Anglorum*, 20n20
Wulf and Eadwacer, 163–4

Toronto Anglo-Saxon Series

General Editor
ANDY ORCHARD

Editorial Board
ROBERTA FRANK
THOMAS N. HALL
ANTONETTE DIPAOLO HEALEY
MICHAEL LAPIDGE

1 *Preaching the Converted: The Style and Rhetoric of the Vercelli Book Homilies*, Samantha Zacher
2 *Say What I am Called: The Old English Riddles of the Exeter Book and the Anglo-Latin Riddle Tradition*, Dieter Bitterli